TRANSCULTURAL LEADERSHIP

Empowering the Diverse Workforce

THE MCD SERIES
MANAGING CULTURAL DIFFERENCES

Series Editors: Philip R. Harris, Ph.D., and Robert T. Moran, Ph.D.

Managing Cultural Differences, 3rd Edition
Philip R. Harris and Robert T. Moran

Dynamics of Successful International Business Negotiations
William G. Stripp and Robert T. Moran

Transcultural Leadership: Empowering the Diverse Workforce
George F. Simons, Carmen Vázquez, and Philip R. Harris

Multicultural Management: New Skills for Global Success
Farid Elashmawi and Philip R. Harris

Forthcoming

Developing Global Organizations: Strategies for Human Resource Professionals
Robert T. Moran, Philip R. Harris, and William G. Stripp

Case Studies in Managing Cultural Differences
Robert T. Moran, David O. Braaten, and John E. Walsh

International Directory of Multicultural Resources
Peter Hayward, Editor

TRANSCULTURAL LEADERSHIP

Empowering the Diverse Workforce

George F. Simons
Carmen Vázquez
Philip R. Harris

Gulf Publishing Company
Houston, London, Paris, Zurich, Tokyo

THE **MSERIES**
MANAGING CULTURAL DIFFERENCES

Transcultural Leadership
Empowering the Diverse Workforce

Gulf Publishing Company
Book Division
P.O. Box 2608 □ Houston, Texas 77252-2608

10 9 8 7 6 5 4 3 2 1

Library of Congress Cataloging-in-Publication Data
Simons, George F.
    Transcultural leadership: empowering the diverse workforce/
George F. Simons, Carmen Vázquez, Philip R. Harris.
        p.   cm.—(Managing cultural differences series)
    Includes bibliographical references and index.
    ISBN 0-87201-299-9
    1. Communication in management—North America—Case studies.
2. Communication in personnel management—North America—Case
studies. 3. Intercultural communication—North America—Case studies.
I. Vázquez, Carmen. II. Harris, Philip R. (Philip Robert), 1926—   . III. Title.
IV. Series.
HD30.3.S555 1993   92-21508
658.3′041—dc20   CIP

To you, the women and men who form every level of today's workforce, as you build our common tomorrow out of the richness of your diversity today.

CONTENTS

ACKNOWLEDGMENTS

The authors are grateful to many people. Cathy Puccinelli, who pitched in wherever help was needed and provided encouragement and emotional support when the end was not in sight. Dick Colin provided leg work (research) and lightened the load with his humor. Linda Abbott, Cathie Olson, and Kei Miake played a major role in producing finished copy to meet the deadlines, and Graham and Susan Payne, Heather Skomsvold, and Kelly Patrick assisted with typing and other technical help. Zenie Barnett, Donna Ginn, Irene Campbell, and Honnay Malloy were generous with advice and perspective. John McPherson told us stories and Yusnita Ramdah shared her mother's proverbs with us. Lavina Weissman, Sondra Theiderman, and Janice Hepworth read the book in its draft stages and provided encouragement and advice. We are particularly grateful to LMA, Inc., of Milford, New Hampshire, and its president, LeRoy Malouf, for the support this organization provided in the preparation of this book. Furthermore, we appreciate the unique contributions rendered to us by Gulf Publishing Company's Book Division through the efforts of its editor-in-chief, William J. Lowe, and our editor, Elizabeth Raven McQuinn. Finally, we are grateful to Bob Abramms, president of ODT Associates, who played matchmaker to get us started and who in addition provided the insightful foreword.

FOREWORD

Here is a book that values the American experience of diversity in a global context. Throughout its history, the United States has had more ongoing, day-by-day experience in integrating greater numbers of people of diverse backgrounds into its workforce and society than has any other nation in the world. There are, of course, glaring failures and moments of history for which the piper has yet to be paid. Nonetheless, a great deal of the philosophy and technology for managing differences has had its origin on these shores.

Despite the stresses, conflicts, and aggravation of building bridges across cultural chasms at work and life, old and new Americans have continued to call upon their deepest values of equality, neighborliness, and love to make it better. Today, in this moment of opportunity, Americans are mobilizing to meet the global challenge of diversity with more resources and on a scale greater than that found in any other part of the world. As a result, *Transcultural Leadership* provides a case study utilizing the North American experience to better understand global development, as the workforce throughout the world, from England to Australia, from the former USSR to France, becomes more diverse and more multicultural.

The task before us is to apply what we do know, and learn what we do not, to make ourselves an even better nation and a more global citizenry. There could be no better starting point than the workplace, where difference must daily be molded into collaboration. The road will not be easy, but it takes us in the right direction. We are fortunate to have this book to guide us with its simple, practical, and timely wisdom.

This book appears at a critical time, when diversity and multiculturalism are encountering a powerful backlash. Since 1980, we have seen a sore lack of response from our national political leadership in the areas of intergroup relations and civil justice (with the singular exception of the Americans with Disabilities Act). It is a time when the nation and its enterprises feel betrayed by its educational institutions, and resent paying for the destruction of cultural values and the disillusionment of aspiring African-Americans, Hispanics, women, and other newcomers to the workforce, to say nothing of the members of its traditional workforce. There has been a significant rise in the number of racial and ethnic hate crimes. Rape, spouse beating, and child abuse are also on the increase. More than ever, therefore, it is incumbent upon business and industry leaders to take the lead. Many now recognize that their involvement in this area today, besides being an ethical priority, is essential to doing successful business. They will find the authors of this book, who have taken a position of commitment to fairness, practicality, and collaboration, to be their strong allies.

Bob Abramms, Ph.D.
President, ODT Associates
Amherst, Massachusetts

SERIES PREFACE

To thrive and, in many cases, to survive in the 1990s, it is necessary for organizations to globalize in strategy, structure, and people. Companies have realized that developing strategies or managing people as if the internal and external environments of the organization had not changed is a major mistake. "Bashing" others rather than taking the inward journey and becoming a revolutionary learning organization is dysfunctional and counterproductive to corporate survival. As expected, many organizations in various countries have taken the inward journey and are effectively managing this challenge. Some are not.

The books in the *Managing Cultural Differences Series,* including the first edition of the first book, *Managing Cultural Differences* (1979, 1987, 1991), through *Dynamics of Successful International Business Negotiations* (1991), *Transcultural Leadership* (1993), *Multicultural Management* (1993), and the forthcoming *Developing Global Organizations* (1993), have as their main purpose the making of a significant contribution to the effort of globalization in all of its dimensions. The books in the series have been widely accepted in academic circles and by practicing internationalists.

As series editors, we are pleased that Gulf Publishing Company has risen to the challenge of addressing questions of people, culture, organization, and strategy in a rapidly changing, highly interdependent community.

Philip R. Harris, Ph.D.
Robert T. Moran, Ph.D.

INTRODUCTION

Transcultural Leadership addresses a new global reality. Today productivity must come from the collaboration of culturally diverse women and men. It insists that leaders change organizational culture to empower and develop people. This demands that employees be selected, evaluated, and promoted on the basis of *performance and competency,* regardless of sex, race, religion, or place of origin. Beyond that, leaders must learn the skills that enable men and women of all backgrounds to work together effectively. This volume, the third in the *Managing Cultural Differences Series,* elaborates on the insights of the parent text by Drs. Harris and Moran (1991).

The book's primary audience is the manager as leader, whether supervisor, project manager, or CEO. Implementing the insights and suggestions in these pages belongs to contemporary leaders, whether in operations, marketing, or human resource development. The global marketplace daily grows more culturally integrated and diverse in terms of customers, suppliers, and workers. Although we write primarily from a North American viewpoint, we realize as international consultants that these phenomena are worldwide and what we say will be modified for use abroad. For example, *empowerment,* integral to the current thinking of American management, is likely to be adopted overseas in time. Becoming an Information Society requires knowledge and workers who are better educated and encouraged toward self-management wherever they are.

Our words confirm what readers see for themselves—women are entering professions, occupations, and industries formerly denied them. Their numbers in the global workforce not only have increased, but in many vocations, exceeds that of men. Other barriers that excluded people from our workforce are being eliminated, be they national frontiers, ideologies, unwritten taboos, or discriminating regulations. In the pursuit of a better life, a transcultural migration of labor from Asia, Eastern Europe, and Africa is in full swing. Workers flow freely from south to north, and from east to west, and vice versa, whether as illegal aliens, refugees, emigrés, expatriates on assignment, or simply volunteers. Business opportunities attract marketers abroad. The shortage of experienced personnel or economic circumstances prompts the return of older workers. How international joint ventures, acquisitions, and mergers further the process are described in another volume of this series, *Multicultural Management.*

Urban areas like Los Angeles and Toronto now contain millions of workers who, among them, speak scores of languages as their native tongue and struggle with English as a second or third means of communication. If variety is the spice of life, then today's workforce is one of the most highly flavored in history. It is the context in which we must manage, motivate, and collaborate for the common good, to achieve economic survival, no less prosperity.

Transcultural Leadership fills a gap in management development. It is about how diversity affects your everyday activities. It deals with conversations, meetings, interviews, making decisions, as well as with obtaining agreement, resolving disputes, providing appropriate training and performance reviews. It tells how to handle people from diverse backgrounds whether planning, working, or eating lunch together.

The book has a glossary of key terms used in the field of diversity. Other aids include instruments and checklists for data gathering, minicases and critical incidents for analysis and application, illustrations and graphics for nonverbal communication, references and other resources pertinent to each chapter, and a special appendix.

Chapter One is the key to understanding what follows. It focuses on the changes in the environment of business and in the workforce that make "Transcultural Leadership" a necessity. Chapter Two deals with managing intercultural breakdowns in communications and relationships when people have different mental maps. Chapter Three examines cross-cultural communication, and shows how to facilitate it within a diverse workforce. Chapter Four suggests ways to listen to others and hear the unspoken language contained in nonverbal messages, as well as to establish rapport with people who perceive things differently. Chapter Five offers leadership and motivation insights for those who would become truly transcultural managers. Chapter Six addresses management issues and stresses that occur with diverse staffs. Chapter Seven takes up the delicate issue of feedback and performance appraisal with diverse employees, especially those with differing cultural inclinations about work assessment. Chapter Eight looks at collaboration among workers with those who differ in gender sexual preference. Chapter Nine explores the tasks involved in organizational culture change and mentoring. Chapter Ten concludes with observations on how to empower the diverse workforce.

George F. Simons
Santa Cruz, CA

Carmen Vázquez
Washington, DC

Philip R. Harris
La Jolla, CA

CHAPTER 1

"WE ARE ALL IMMIGRANTS" AND OTHER HEADLINES FOR THE 21ST CENTURY

Portions of this book were written:

In the rain forests of Puerto Rico.
On Wall Street.
In the gas fields of Sumatra.
At the Midwest corporate headquarters of two Fortune 100 companies.
On the docks in Rotterdam.
At the United Nations.
During management seminars in Brussels, Havana, and Brisbane, and many points in between.
In a space project laboratory.
In a headhunter's longhouse in Borneo.
While recruiting in the Canadian Rockies.
In a New Jersey clothing warehouse.
On a chemical tanker in the North Pacific.
Aboard countless delayed flights, and waiting for connections at Atlanta, Heathrow, Changi, and most of all O'Hare.
And, occasionally, at home.

Five different kinds of computer systems processed the text, which was then conveyed by mail, courier, telephone, telefax, modem, satellite, and electronic mail. The manuscript has been stored on legal pads, ram cards, floppy disks, audio cassettes, and videotape.

During this period we three writers went through two promotions, two corporate job changes, the start of a new business, a marriage, umpteen software upgrades, and two hospital stays. To our embarrassment we must admit to (mal)nourishing ourselves to global pro-

1

portions on snack foods, empanadas, manioc chips, keropok, goldfisch, cumi-cumi, nachos, and Texas toast.

More amazingly, we considered all of the above quite normal, in the new global workplace to which we as consultants and trainers to business and industry, not without considerable stress, are becoming acculturated. In the new global and domestic workplace we are all immigrants, experiencing culture shock on a daily basis. Pick up a newspaper and you will see why. Changes in the workforce and the workplace are among the hottest news items of the 1990s. Here is a summary of the headline stories:

Workplace Headlines

Headline: *Worker Numbers Falling.* The workforce is shrinking. Without the large number of recent entrants, largely women and immigrants, this decline would be even more severe. Traditional sectors of employment are also diminishing as new sectors open. As Joel Dreyfuss observed in *The Atlantic Monthly,* "The shrinking workforce gives the diversity issue a level of urgency that affirmative action never had." Veteran commentators such as George Ordiorne talk about "Beating the 1990s Labor Shortage," by urging recruiters not only to hire women, immigrants, and older and handicapped workers, but to aggressively pursue undertapped resources such as temporary workers, part-timers, and even ex-convicts.

Headline: *Workers' Average Age Rising.* Baby boomers, once described as the "pig in the python" of the demographics of the American workforce, are aging, pushing the average age of all workers higher. Increasingly, people of retirement age are staying on the job, and recruiters are competing for their skills. America is not alone in this. Aging and a decline in the number of workers are also affecting the workforce of the European Community.

Headline: *White Male Worker a Numerical Minority.* While women will continue to increase as a proportion of the workforce (to a predicted whopping 47% by the end of the 1990s), the Bureau of Labor Statistics points out that white males, the traditional source of labor in the U.S., will drop to 39.4% of the labor force by the end of the decade.

Headline: *Former "Minorities" a Third of New Workers.* In the next ten years, as white male workers become harder to find, those who take their place will not only be white women, but, increasingly, minorities.

The number of Asians in the workforce will be up 80.6% and Hispanics up 75.3%, while African-Americans will show the smallest increase, 28%. Accounting for more than 80% of the net increase to the workforce between now and the year 2000, these microcultures will constitute 26% of the total workforce by the end of the decade.

Headline: *Immigration Unabated.* New U.S. immigration policies encourage many different kinds of newcomers, while the flow of illegal immigrants continues. By the year 2000, at least 10% of the U.S. workforce will be foreign born. They will account for more than 20% of the workforce's net growth. By the end of the next century, a full 50% of workers will likely be immigrants, or descendants of immigrants who arrived after 1980.

Headline: *Immigrant Patterns Changing.* In 1969, 78% of immigrants came from Europe and Canada alone; in the last two decades, 84% of newcomers came from Latin America and Asia, radically altering the cultural flavor of the workforce.

Headline: *America is doing it again!* Today's American-born citizens easily forget that the physical infrastructure of the United States was built by a mix of nationalities and cultures. Many immigrants fled wars or persecution of some kind, but all shared the dream of a better life. We still benefit from what they built: the Erie Canal dug by Germans and Swedes, the transcontinental railroad built by thousands of Chinese and Irish, and many other lasting (though sometimes now decaying) structures.

The American Advantage

"In the global economic competition of the information economy, the quality and innovativeness of human resources will spell the difference."

"In this regard, no country in the world is better positioned than the United States. It certainly has it all over Japan. Japan is a society that has one culture, one history, one race. Superb as the Japanese are, that is limiting. The United States, on the other hand, has the richest mix—including Japanese—of ethnic groups, racial

(continued)

(continued from previous page)

groups, and global experience that the world has ever known, and it is the richness of this mix that yields America's incredible creativity and innovation. Since 1970, the United States has allowed more legal immigration than the rest of the world combined. They are the most aggressive, most entrepreneurial, most assertive people, who fight fiercely to get to the United States."

"It is the habit of Americans to brag about previous immigrants and to complain about the current ones."

"In the 1990s the United States will have a younger population than either of its major competitors—Europe and Japan."

"America's great import is its people. Yet Americans have not even begun to experience the real potential of their fantastic human resource mix, which will be their competitive edge in the global economy as we move toward the next millennium."

—Excerpted from *Megatrends 2000,* by Naisbitt and Aburdene. Copyright © 1990 by John Naisbitt and Patricia Aburdene. Used by permision of William Morrow & Co., Inc.

The contribution of the world's peoples to the economic welfare of North America continues. The U.S. and Canada benefit from a brain drain of the Third World, as the most capable and ambitious flock here to work at our hospitals, laboratories, and universities. Where would U.S. service industries be without the refugees, migrants, and new immigrants from Mexico and other countries? What would happen to the U.S. gross national product without the investment of Japanese funds and management? Would we have developed a space frontier without the help of German and British rocket scientists? Today this tradition continues as international cooperation and multicultural teams lay the foundations of a new infrastructure in space.

Headline: *Service and Information Sectors Grow; Manufacturing Declines.* As Peter Drucker recently observed, "Now we are managing people paid for their knowledge. We have never done that, and we don't know how to do it." Managers and executives, technical and professional workers, are, as a group in the workforce, presently growing faster than average. It is not easy to shift workers from the declining sectors (see the next headline).

Headline: *New Workers Require Higher Skill Levels.* At a time when reading, writing, and making change for a dollar are no longer adequate skills for most occupations, fewer people are able to perform such simple tasks. Corporations, citing massive failure on the part of the educational system, now provide basic education for their employees, and at the same time raid other nations to recruit the brightest and the best. Poverty is on the increase as many Americans remain jobless and lack the education, resources, and motivation to start again. An aging personnel manager recently sardonically remarked, "I used to be worried about facing retirement. Now I know I'll never be out of a job—I can read and write."

Headline: *Job Mobility Upswing.* The shift from manufacturing to service economy is not the only factor unsettling job holders. Rapid obsolescence is quickly flattening old organizations and new ones are springing up in their debris. Workers in high-tech industries learn to keep their bags packed. The result is a workforce more dedicated to its own profession and personal interests than loyal to employers or companies.

Recruiting in the '90s

You are hiring for a large corporation, seeking the best entry-level candidates you can find. Today you have ten positions to fill. Eight of the jobs require more than a high-school education. When you walk into the waiting room there are only eight candidates. A close look at them reveals:

- 3 of the candidates are immigrants
- 4 are women
- 3 are young men under 25; 1 is older.
- 2 of the three young men are white.

When you examine their capabilities, you discover that:

- 6 have finished high school; 4 have not
- 2 cannot fill out a job application without help
- 1 cannot read

(continued)

(continued from previous page)

To make matters worse you will later learn that:

- 1 is on drugs
- 4 of those you hire will leave in the next two years.

Does this group surprise you? These are the new entrants to the workforce. Today you happened to get a close-to-average cross section of them. Who is actually waiting in the employment office of your organization? What diverse challenges do they bring to you as a manager, and to your organization?

Headline: *The Melting Pot No Longer Boils.* Changes in the North American workplace are so sweeping that it is no longer possible, necessary, or desirable (if ever it was) to try to eliminate cultural differences of individuals and groups entering the "mainstream." Melting-pot thinking assumes that cultural diversity is a temporary nuisance that will go away if we just put enough different people to work, give them fair wages and promotions, and, in general, blind ourselves to their differences.

North America will have a new culture, but not an assimilationist one. Janice Hepworth in her paper "When the Melting Stops," points out that ". . . we can begin to plan for new and emerging diversity traits which may become permanent changes in a culture, and . . . lend support to those traits which appear to be emerging and conversely, mitigate against negative traits which threaten a culture's balance." Assimilation is a dead end. Acculturation, learning how to survive and thrive in this new environment, is the waystation to power in the new workforce (see Figure 1.1).

Will the violent fragmentation that plagues Europe and Africa become the norm in North America as well? Today's diversity is a fresh challenge to transform the culture of work in ways that will guarantee our own survival and enjoyment and that of future generations. But this will happen only if we right the economy and find the means to value differences in such a way that everyone can share in the common good. As Zenie Barnett, our colleague, observed, "Equity is not the main problem of diversity. However, the lack of equity is a manifestation of the inability to properly manage diversity."

Diversity is the right issue, but it needs to be clarified and managed. The sharp focus of previous efforts like Affirmative Action and Equal Opportunity made a difference for many disenfranchised people. Now a different effort is required. "Empowerment" gives that focus. It is the revolutionary twenty-first century alternative to the melting-pot mentality.

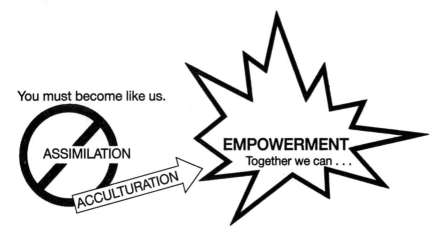

Figure 1.1 Acculturation, not assimilation, is the road to empowerment.

Headline: *Work Isn't What it Used to Be.* The New Workplace is anywhere and everywhere, and it is largely electronic. Francis Kinsman's book title, *The Telecommuters,* is very telling. Not only are individuals working from home, automobiles, planes, and other locations remote from the traditional work site, but entire electronic operations have followed manufacturing out of the country to become more competitive. Today you can ship your data halfway around the world, have it processed more cheaply during someone else's daylight hours, and have it back by opening time the next morning. The office itself is changing (see Figure 1.2). Robert Heller, author of *Culture Shock: The Office Revolution,* observes another mindshift: the office of the future is a tool, not a white-collar factory.

Headline: *All Business Is Global Business.* When Thomas Wolfe titled his 1939 novel *You Can't Go Home Again,* his principal character reflected a nation that, on the eve of its entry into World War II, would never again be peacefully aloof from the cares of the world. Yet the dream lingers. The behavior and assumptions of modern-day U.S.

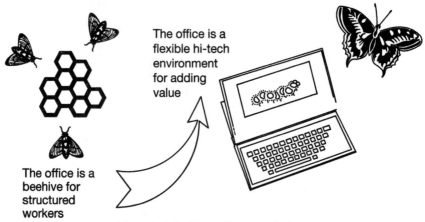

The office is a flexible hi-tech environment for adding value

The office is a beehive for structured workers

Figure 1.2. The office revolution.

businesspeople are still surprisingly reminiscent of the 1930s, even though we now live in a global marketplace where the exchange of money and labor are no longer dictated by national governments and domestic enterprise. Management is reluctant to replan its domestic operations and prepare its employees for the world as it is. As *The Atlantic Monthly* put it, companies continue to do international business as "innocents abroad."

"Think globally, act locally" must become more than an ecological bumper sticker. Bankers and brokers, who move information and money electronically and instantly around the globe, and haulers whose freight crosses more and more borders, are starting to understand the implications and possibilities of a global market. Many others are not. A comment made by Lynn Fritz about some motor carriers might be said of far too many of our enterprises: "The minds of some truckers may be overseas, but their hearts are in the U.S." It is incumbent on every manager to realize his or her interdependence on the global economy even while going about the most ordinary tasks at home. Our parent book in this series, *Managing Cultural Differences*, forcefully conveyed the message that global managers must be more cosmopolitan, and less provincial in both thought and action. Diversity and globalism are two sides of the same coin because they involve similar kinds of people differences, can be addressed by many of the same strategies, and require many of the same managerial attitudes. Throughout this book, we will connect the big picture with the little picture, to show how global change relates to your office or shop floor.

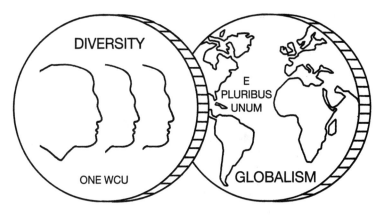

Figure 1.3. Diversity and globalism are two sides of the same coin—the new world currency unit of thinking.

Immigrants to Tomorrow

As was observed in *Managing Cultural Differences*, "Managers themselves are in transition to the new work culture." Both executives and workers are experiencing a new kind of culture shock similar to what Alvin Toffler more than a decade ago dubbed "future shock." We all land as immigrants on the doorstep of the 21st century. We are living in that future today and affected by its culture, but we are hardly acculturated to it. Few of us speak its language well, and while we are eager to make good in this new land, we are ill-equipped to take advantage of the full range of benefits it offers. Being immigrants, our old identity and roles are under assault. We look for something to hold on to, even when we are filled with enthusiasm for new frontiers.

Cultural Stress

Virtually everyone today experiences some degree of *culture shock.* Rapid change causes *stress* and *cultural fatigue,* whether we understand how it works or not. Three responses to culture shock are possible: *Resistance*—the rejection of the new culture and the tendency toward *fundamentalist* defense of one's own traditional values; *assimilation*—the wholesale rejection of ones own values in order to embrace those of another culture; and *acculturation*—learning to talk the language of another culture, while remaining rooted in the values and language of one's own. When it comes to the future, both individuals and organizations must go through a journey of acculturation.

All three responses to culture shock imply some change to one's own culture. Those who *resist* the new culture inevitably harden their values and beliefs. These people become brittle and lack the flexibility that their culture, like a living organism, requires to survive in a changing environment. They either drop out of the mainstream and become marginal, or in the few cases where they wield great power, attempt to impose their values on everyone else. Those who *assimilate* forfeit their own culture and with it, often, self-esteem. To *acculturate* one must live in two worlds, often simultaneously, and attempt to divide life into separate compartments, creating considerable cognitive dissonance, e.g., having one view of authority at work, another at home, and sometimes not feeling good or confident or competent at either. Of these three choices, acculturation will be, for most people in the workforce, the most practical and realistic choice. For most managers, this means a shift from assimilationist, melting-pot thinking to acculturating themselves to the new workforce and helping others to do so as well.

Assimilation—the one-way dead end	$\longrightarrow$	*Acculturation—a shared street*

In assimilation one culture is swallowed up by another. The values, customs, language, and ideas of one group are exchanged for those of the mainstream. This never happens totally. First, because the devouring culture gets "indigestion"—there are things that simply can't or won't be assimilated—and, second, since "you are what you eat," the dominating culture winds up being changed by the people it tried to swallow up.

The impossibility of assimilation matters less than its melting-pot premises. Those already established in the culture say, "Why learn about the newcomers? They should learn about us and speak our language correctly if they want to work here." "If *they* would just . . ., all *their* problems would disappear." This mindset puts others down, and labels and judges *them*, e.g., "They're all lazy, arrogant, secretive, just not right, etc." It tells the newcomers, "Out with your strange behavior, your funny languages, your smelly food." The newcomer can also buy into the melting-pot mentality: "I have to be just like them." "Where I came from is bad, here is good." "No matter what it costs, I have to fit in." "Don't teach the children about the old country, let them be Americans."

Even managers who try to manage diversity can easily fall back into melting-pot thinking:

"I don't have time to figure out how these people think."
"I've tried to learn a few words of their language, but I feel dumb saying those things."
"There are just too many kinds of people in this organization to make exceptions. They just have to learn to toe the line."
"If I don't manage in a perfectly American style, I won't be accepted."

The tendency toward assimilation is persistent and global. An Australian artist used a meat grinder rather than a melting-pot to lampoon "white Australia," thinking that still makes Foster-drinking mincemeat of that country's newcomers (see Figure 1.4).

Aussie Assimilation

Figure 1.4. Assimilation "Aussie" style. Reprinted with permission from *Cross Culture* magazine. Copyright © Richard Lewis Communications.

Women, people of color, white males, new immigrants—none of us actually belongs in a meat grinder or a melting pot. Many cannot and, today, would not if they could, disappear into a cultural or organizational mainstream. More people than ever are demanding that organizations adapt to cultural differences that they find important. As a manager either you will make it mentally and emotionally clear how everyone can win collaboratively, or else no one will win. If you allow differences to turn political, they can be irreconcilable for a long time.

Our objective is *acculturation,* not assimilation. Acculturation means learning enough to not only survive but to thrive in a new culture. It is a shared street. Certainly, newcomers to a workplace must learn enough to do their job, become comfortable, and collaborate well within the organization they join. It's their job to do this, and management's job to help them. But in the new workplace everyone is a newcomer. The changes are so great and happen so quickly that everyone, from the lifetime employee to the new hire, can be suffering from culture shock and need acculturation. The transcultural leader helps the whole organization acculturate to the new workplace culture and become collaborative and productive in it.

The Journey of Acculturation

In becoming acculturated, we pass through several stages. Let's look at them one at a time:

1. We enter the new situation with some level of emotional *excitement,* often surprise, caution, or even enthusiasm:

   - *"What's going on here?"*
   - *"I suppose we can get along with these newcomers."*
   - *"Here I am, in the land of opportunity."*
   - *"I'll show everyone how easy it is to work for a woman boss."*

2. When things turn out to be much more difficult or different than we expected, *frustration, anger,* or even *depression* sets in. We have an intercultural breakdown. It is easy to get stuck in Stage 2:

- *"I don't think I'll ever get across to these people."*
- *"These people are barbarians, worse than I could have ever imagined."*
- *"I can't believe she would say a thing like that!"*
- *"Working with them is hopeless; I'll never figure it out."*
- *"I'll never master this new corporate culture/technology."*

3. We emerge from this breakdown when we begin to take a more sober and objective view and start *acknowledging real differences* on a practical everyday level:

- *"We really are different."*
- *"I need to learn more to make things work."*
- *"She and I speak different languages. I'm beginning to see where the misunderstandings occur."*
- *"It's going to take me more effort than I thought."*

4. Finally, we negotiate *workable agreements in order to collaborate and produce new results.*

- *"I'll try it that way if you'll explain it to me."*
- *"You can take that time off, if we can find another way to meet the deadline."*
- *"We agree to speak English on the job, but we prefer our own language when chatting with each other."*
- *"We both need to listen very carefully to each other and ask more questions."*

Acculturation is not a onetime journey. We and our organizations will march through it again and again, when new people arrive, when working environments change, when we start new tasks and share new ideas. Once we know the four stages and recognize the one we are in, it becomes easier to make the journey more quickly. With acceptance and practice, cultural conflicts become easier to resolve and our differences become interesting and useful. We are on our way to valuing differences, empowerment, and the payoffs of multicultural synergy.

In *High Performance Leadership,* Harris detailed the demands put on leaders by the trends of the new work culture. Let's revisit the trends that, though they cause culture shock today, will be standard practice in the multicultural organization of the future.

- *Autonomy and Control over Work Space.* People seek more freedom of choice, as well as more authority and ownership, both psychological and literal, over their enterprises.
- *Participation and Involvement in the Enterprise.* Workers seek more democracy in their work organizations, sharing in management problem solving, planning, and decisions. Managers strive for more consensus and delegation.
- *Communication and Information Orientation.* People are looking for more open, authentic, and circular communications at work—input must be balanced by output and feedback. New communications technology makes this possible for both small and large organizations.
- *Informal and Synergistic Relationships.* People pursue work relationships that are more cooperative, less hierarchical, and more interdependent, even when the relationships are temporary.
- *Enhanced Quality of Work Life.* What is more self-fulfilling, meaningful, and mentally and emotionally rewarding is paramount. Healthy and pleasant environments, as well as entitlements to wellness and sabbatical programs, are highly valued.
- *Creative Organizational Norms.* Work standards will value competence, high performance, entrepreneurship, risk taking, venturesomeness, and creativity. Norms must encourage flexibility and management by exception.
- *High Performance and Productivity.* Professionalism and working smarter will become the norms as people see themselves having careers, not just jobs. High achievers will become the behavior models.
- *Entrepreneurial Orientation.* Focusing on where the opportunities are going to be, people will create the concepts, processes, products, or structures to capitalize upon them. People and resources will be matched with opportunities for greater choice, self-expression, and profit.
- *Technological Orientation.* A computer-literate population will use electronic devices to conduct both business and personal activities.
- *Research and Development Orientation.* More people will have greater R & D orientation. This will be largely market oriented to identify peo-

ple, products, and processes, both for the long term and for short-term payoffs.

Though these phenomena reflect American cultural standards, they are truly part of the worldwide change in management environment. Citing international competition and new and faster technologies, processes, products, and services, the new European workforce is more educated, more female, and less blue collar, but short in numbers because of a lack of skilled labor. There is more diversity and less solidarity. Western Europe will increasingly look to Eastern Europe for new workers. Europeans must recognize the natural cultural differences and use their expertise to manage culture shock in their organizations. A Hays International Business Culture Survey of more than 200 North American and European companies indicated that European management leads Americans in the venturesomeness and usefullness of organizational goals, innovativeness of decision making, responsiveness to changes in the business environment, and appropriateness of decisions.

Coates, Jarratt, and Mahaffie, taking a different cut at this in their book *Future Work*, cite seven critical forces that are reshaping work itself and, as a consequence, the workforce of North America, contributing to our culture shock. Each of these forces requires management decisions and efforts to not only meet the challenge, but to capitalize on these forces in a creative, productive, and socially responsible way.

Table 1.1
Seven Forces Reshaping the Way America Does Business

Challenges	Responses
1. Diversity in the workforce	1. Manage flexibly
2. Integrating home and work life	2. Reverse the hundred-year-old trend
3. Globalism	3. Compete in a world economy
4. More human resources planning	4. Improve business-unit planning
5. The changing nature of work	5. Reeducate for a knowledge-based workforce
6. Rising employee expectations	6. Balance demands and costs
7. Renewed social agenda	7. Corporate social responsibility

What Is Culture?

If we are all immigrants suffering from culture shock, what indeed is culture? Noted anthropologist Edward Hall describes culture as primarily a "system for creative sending, sorting, and processing of information . . . research reveals that anywhere from 80–90% of that information is communicated in other means than language." Culture, according to another, more detailed definition is:

> *A way of life.* It is developed and communicated by a group of people, consciously or unconsciously, to subsequent generations. It consists of ideas, habits, attitudes, customs, and traditions that help to create standards for people to coexist. It makes a group of people unique.

This definition gives a good picture of culture as we encounter it in the values, behavioral traits, and priorities as well as the organizations, work habits, etc., of a specific group of people. Our next definition focuses on how culture works within each of us and empowers us to deal with it in ourselves and others.

> *Culture is a set of mental formulae for survival and success that a particular group of people has developed. These formulae are stored as a set of instructions in the unconscious mind and are sometimes heard as "conversations with oneself" in the conscious mind.*

The best key to understanding culture is inside of us, not around us. Its essence is how we, as members of a group, talk to ourselves and among ourselves about what is right and wrong, good and bad, useful and useless, beautiful or ugly, true or false. It tells us what things are for, how to make them and how to use them. For example, depending on my background, inviting me to get comfortable, or to be at ease, could elicit internal instructions that tell me to

- Find a chair and sit down
- Squat on my haunches
- Sit cross-legged on the carpet
- Stand at parade rest

To get comfortable, some people build chairs and couches. Others weave rugs and stuff pillows. These are the external artifacts of culture, what we see and touch in others' homes and, eventually, visit in museums. How do we, though our minds are physically more or less the same, come up with such different maps of reality?

Transcendental Questions

No matter who we are, where we are from, or what language we speak, our human minds are structured to automatically ask certain questions. Though endless in variety, these can be boiled down to four questions, intimately related to each other, that our minds automatically pose when we perceive something. We ask ourselves these questions constantly to identify and to accept or reject things because of how well they fit the cultural definition of our needs or provide solutions that our culture says will work.

The Four Transcendental Questions

1. Is this ONE or MANY? Is what I am encountering one phenomenon or several?
2. Is this TRUE or FALSE, real or unreal—can I rely on what my senses tell me about it? In what order of reality does it exist?
3. Is this GOOD or BAD, moral or immoral, healthy or unhealthy, useful or useless?
4. Is this BEAUTIFUL or UGLY—does it please my aesthetic standards and feelings, or not? How does it measure up to my likes or dislikes?

By automatically asking such questions, our minds try to tell us what fits or works and what doesn't—including people! We not only decide who is "us" and who are "they," but set criteria to determine the grounds on which we are alike and how we are different.

We like to say that we judge situations and people on the basis of experience, but except for the moment of our conception, there is no such thing as pure experience: as embryos we are already affected by culture mediated by our mothers. Being human means being shaped by others. Our every experience is automatically filtered in or out, organized, and interpreted by the culture in us and around us, including the

organizational culture in which we work. Here are some examples of
how the four questions show up regularly in our work life:

1. Is this ONE or MANY?

- Should we consider complaints about parking as part of the larger
  employee morale problem, or should we address it separately by
  setting up a carpooling system?
- All these new workers look alike to me; why shouldn't I treat them
  the same?
- Should our group be taking direction from headquarters or are
  we autonomous enough to set our own standards?
- How much individuality must I give up to work in this multicultural team?

2. Is this TRUE or FALSE?

- Is this research finding valid?
- Is she reporting the facts?
- Is his perception of the problem skewed?
- Will a nylon part wear better than a metal one?
- Is this unit defective?

3. Is this GOOD or BAD?

- Will this marketing strategy work?
- Is the quality of her work acceptable?
- Will this packaging be durable enough during shipping?
- How risky is it to date someone from my department?
- Should these people speak English?

4. Is this BEAUTIFUL or UGLY?

- Shall we use green and blue on the wrapper?
- Do salesmen with long hair and beards hurt our image?
- How does the interior designer recommend we decorate this
  office?
- Is her hairdo too bizarre for a receptionist?
- Is this proposal elegant, or not?

To answer each question, our mind's culturally formed database automatically talks to us. We have opinions about anything and everything, and, most of the time, they come to us spontaneously and unbidden. We don't even have to try. Like a computer, our mind searches until it is satisfied that it has found the formula to understand the present reality, "What is this?" or "What does this mean?," and cope with "What, if anything, should I or we do about it?" Our minds conduct a running commentary on everything. Even while we sleep our mind makes a storyboard of dreams, and we may wake up in the middle of the night with the solution to a problem we racked our brains on during the day.

Cultural Paradoxes

Culture lives in us, and thus in our organizations, as memories, images, myths, procedures, rules, and algorithms that we use to understand, make distinctions, and act. Managing culture is therefore one of the keys to running an organization productively. Culture helps us filter and sort out the massive amounts of data that our senses plop into our mental in-basket at every moment. It tells us what to keep and throw away when the mail carrier or the electronic mail arrives. Culture is paradoxical.

- If we processed everything, we would process nothing. On one hand, we need culture to interpret our world; on the other hand, because we are not able to stop, think, and consciously analyze everything that happens to us each day, we are likely to miss changes and new developments.
- We depend on culture to understand and operate in our world, yet culture, by its very nature, filters our perceptions and skews our judgment so that we see and function with a narrow range of possibilities.
- Culture contains the solutions for the problems of surviving and succeeding in the world as we understand it, yet as our environment changes—and this is happening rapidly today—many solutions no longer work.
- Culture is ethnocentric by nature. It presents itself as a set of absolute beliefs. It does not normally equip us for living in a polycentric world full of relativities.

- Because of the availability of modern media, a common worldwide business culture is developing; however, the accessibility of these media allows them to be used to intensify individual cultures.
- Each culture provides models of the world and a sense of identity for those who participate in it. This gives the group power and cohesion and provides it with a strong identity. This is particularly true for more tightly woven groups. When culture is in flux, common purpose and individual identity tend to be weakened. This tends to occur in more loosely knit situations.

Because of these paradoxes and the rapidly changing environment in which most of us live and work, managing culture is a high priority not only for national and ethnic groups, but especially for organizations who must compete successfully in these volatile times.

Points to Remember from This Chapter

A new worldwide business environment is evolving as a result of factors that are now forcing organizations to assess their culture:

- The mixture of peoples of a variety of cultures and backgrounds in the workplace.
- The discovery and importation of new technologies and the pervasiveness of electronic media.
- Strong competitive market forces that demand the reevaluation of the ways in which people are employed and how and at what speed work is being done.
- Rapid change and new forms of instant communication.

Culture in its most basic sense is a set of internal understandings and rules developed by a group or organization for its survival and success. It determines how people think, what they value, and how they behave and communicate with each other.

CHAPTER 2

WHEN SYSTEMS CRASH

"An Hipong Tulog Ay Natatangay Ng Agos.
The shrimp that sleeps is carried away by the current."

—Filipino Proverb

Breakdowns—A Manager's Prime Concern

Breakdowns in work flow, schedules, communications, and relationships are the normal business of every manager. According to Fernando Flores, good managers become experts at troubleshooting, preventing, and handling breakdowns. As diversity increases, breakdowns tend to become more frequent and complicated. Let's look at a breakdown caused primarily by cultural differences (see box), in this case the most common form of diversity, that between women and men.

The Senior Women Who Didn't Fit In

A medium-sized advertising firm found it difficult to attract and retain senior women. The organization's heart seemed to be in the right place. They kept recruiting well-qualified candidates, but the women didn't stay long. Each of the women hired developed "personality problems" with the male managers and conflicts with their women subordinates, even though new hires had the right cre-

(continued)

21

(continued from previous page)

dentials, skills, and experience. They made special demands on the organization and had lifestyle needs that were not being met. They wanted more ownership of their work, special hours, and so forth. They felt that the company was insensitive and unrealistic in its expectations of them. The men and the lower-level women viewed them as prima donnas who didn't work or keep the same schedule as everyone else. Eventually each would leave, or in some cases be dismissed.

Before reading our analysis, you might want to reflect on or discuss these questions:

1. What cultural differences between the women and the men might be at stake here?
2. What kind of negative interactions do you imagine taking place between the men and the women? Between the senior women and the other women?

Learning from Breakdowns

To advance to its next stage of development, the organization featured in the boxed example had to learn from its breakdown. Let's revisit the case to see how. The clash between the women's and the men's expectations was a cultural one. What the senior women saw as legitimate ways to work was at odds with an organizational culture structured to meeting the work needs of a different group (men). The organization needed to understand how this anachronistic culture sabotaged the women managers who tried to succeed in it, and how it needed to be managed to keep the breakdown from recurring. To manage breakdowns, we generally go through four stages:

Stage 1—The Interruption or Break Stage

When a disruption occurs in the normal flow of our work, we begin to pay attention to things we took for granted earlier. The break may take the form of a slowdown in production, a personal conflict, a walkout, the appearance of new technology, language, or terminology that only one group understands, a supplier that fails to deliver on time, or a shift of buying habits in the marketplace. When is it an intercultural breakdown? In some situations, the cultural clues are close to the surface, e.g., someone complains of sexual harassment, or instructions are misunderstood or not carried out by someone whose English is imperfect. Prejudices or racial slurs are heard. Someone dislikes another group's attitudes, looks, or behavior. Cross-cultural breakdowns occur between personnel, work units, and organizations. Marketing and production, or engineering and sales, are at each others' throats. Whatever the cause, the smoothly running system crashes. What was seamless becomes disjointed. We are suddenly aware of our emotional discomfort.

In this case, the attrition among senior women was so consistent that some managers began to see a pattern and declared, "We agree that there's a problem here. Maybe it's not the kind of problem we thought it was." When a breakdown happens over and over again, it is usually a clue that it has cultural causes. The normal remedies, such as advice giving, blame, demands that others behave differently, and reaffirming old policies prove to be Band-Aid solutions that rarely interrupt the pattern for long. The cultural differences have to be seen and addressed directly.

Stage 2—Fallout

As soon as an interruption takes place we experience *negative and emotional* fallout. The advertising firm had already experienced this kind of fallout. Reaction to the women's behavior and their demands and, ultimately, to each decision to leave, or the company's decision to terminate, was highly emotional. The women blamed the men for being insensitive and not listening. The men accused the women of breaking the rules and expecting unfair privileges. Lower-level women labeled the senior women haughty and unapproachable. Among themselves, both the women and men used sarcastic names for each other.

From either side, the breakdown looked like a problem "our" group was having with "them." Neither side really knew how the other experienced and felt about the interruptions in their work, or whether it was even a breakdown for them. The fallout also revealed diverse values in the organization. Some rushed to help; others lashed out. Some feared what their boss would say and kept a low profile; others feared loss of face with their peers if they took the other side seriously. A few turned on themselves—"I should have known better." The organization was stuck and becoming nasty. It took a third party, outside consultants, to create a safe environment in which the cultural factors could be viewed and discussed calmly by both sides.

Stage 3—Recommitment

Recommitment involves meeting with those involved to come to a common understanding of the problem and what is to be done, then agreeing to do it. It means asking and telling each other about what we know, and then deciding on which steps will produce the right results. In this case, after considerable internal discussion and work with outside consultants, the organization was able to understand its own cultural development and commit itself to modify its structure and transform its culture so that everyone could work better. Needs for flextime and child- and eldercare were identified and acted upon. Communication skills were upgraded for both sexes. The women learned to become more visible and make themselves heard; the men discovered how listening to women was different from listening to men. They uncovered their assumptions and habits as a dominant group and began to manage better.

Stage 4—Synergy

Carrying out these commitments created a new synergy that enabled the organization not only to find and retain their senior women, but to produce better results than before the breakdown. The breakdown was a friend in disguise. Within a year, for example, a new service strategy was developed by a female-male team, which increased client loyalty substantially. Figure 2-1 shows an overview of the process.

The dynamics that occur at various stages of a breakdown teach us how to work across cultures and become better transcultural leaders. Let's examine some of these dynamics.

Unmanaged Fallout Contaminates the Working Environment

Not managing the fallout stage can badly damage an organization. Factions form and resentments flourish. People who seemed like "pretty good human beings" when things were working, start to look

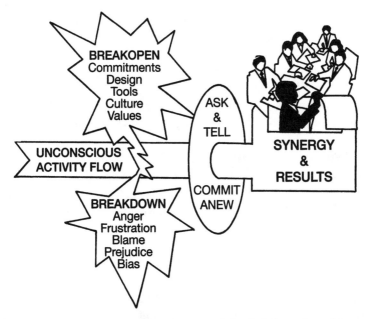

FIGURE 2.1. Intercultural breakdown model. Models such as this and others used in this book are characteristic of the more loosely knit Western culture, which is discussed extensively. Other cultures develop different models or metaphors to communicate what takes place when cultures clash.

like enemies to each other under stress. Breakdowns become blow-ups as people attack each other instead of the problem.

Some cultural breakdowns are silent. Unlike mechanical problems, which yield an answer once enough effort is put into understanding the problem, no one is willing to open the cultural can of worms. Lacking the transcultural skills to isolate the problem, both men and women, in our boxed example, were looking for a quick fix, but deep down they despaired of resolving the situation. No one, it seemed, could make a right move. Well-meant proposals were suspect, attacked because of their authorship even before people finished presenting them.

This organization had to turn its breakdowns from emotionally charged mysteries into everyday challenges and meet them with analytic tools and improved skills. In order to understand what the organization needed, these men and women needed to learn about and accept the differences of each other's culture, its language, definitions, and values.

Fallout Helps Us Understand Cultural Differences

Culture is a collection of mindsets, standards, or models that tell us who we are and how we should behave. For each area of our lives our culture provides "a set of rules and regulations that: 1) defines boundaries; and, 2) says what we must do to succeed within those boundaries." As Joel Barker observes in *Discovering the Future: The Business of Paradigms,* "Success is measured by the problems you solve using these rules and regulations." What a culture makes and does, its products, financial structure, work habits, language, art, and literature, and so forth, all those things we call culture in everyday speech are shaped by these mindsets. In turn, our internal culture is reinforced when we see and use its products. Our culture shapes our world and our world shapes our culture. Practically speaking, culture makes the world in which we live and work our reality.

Being *ethnocentric,* deeply invested in our own culture and its way of doing things, is normal. With rare exceptions, we all grow up thinking our culture is the only game in town, or, at least, the best one. Culture acts as a filter. As Barker notes, "What may be perfectly obvious to persons with one paradigm may be *quite literally invisible* to persons with a different paradigm." Inside a corporation, marketing may behave quite differently from manufacturing. They may not see each others' problems even when careful explanations have been made. Our ethnocentrism naively assumes that others are just like us, or should be, or at least that they should understand our position. If not, *they* have a problem, *they* are to be blamed. Both women and men in our case did these things.

A New 80/20 Rule

Most managers are familiar with the 80/20 rule. When we recognize, for example, 20% of our customers account for 80% of the sales, or 20% of our employees account for 80% of the absenteeism, we know where to put our energy. When a breakdown occurs with people who are different, especially when it recurs, applying the 80/20 rule in reverse can help us emerge from negative fallout. We make a working assumption that at least 80% of a breakdown has cultural roots, while 20% or less is personal. This frees us from blaming groups or individuals and helps us find the tools to resolve the issue. When someone is accused of having a personality problem, it is usually a red flag indicating that the issues of diversity have been overlooked.

Using the 80/20 rule frees us from needing to be right and to make others wrong. In our case, the consultants encouraged both women and men to invoke the 80/20 rule the moment their discomfort surfaced with each other. Provisionally accepting each other on a person-to-person basis, they could look at their differences together, and uncover how the system or culture of the organization created problems for both of them.

Distinguish Systemic Problems from Personal Issues

From their ethnocentric focus, the men accused the women of "female adjustment problems," while the women complained of a "male conspiracy" against them. Like freshwater fish thrown into a salt-water aquarium, the women were choking in the new environment and didn't know why. The saltwater fish (in this case the men) couldn't understand why the freshwater fish (the senior women) were acting strange and dying. The environment seemed normal to the men, and, after all, hadn't they invited the freshwater fish and generously shared the tank with them? What was *their* problem, anyway?

This calls for a second application of the 80/20 rule. When a workplace breakdown involves diversity, you can safely assume that 20% or less of the problem is *personal,* the result of what individuals consciously intend to do or say to each other in the situation, while at least 80% of the breakdown is *systemic,* rooted in the structure, values, and rules of the organization itself. This makes it hard to change. The system is reality for most people in it—*often including those who find it difficult to survive there.* Outsiders often spot this immediately—this is why outside consultants can be so effective. This is the 80% on which we need to focus in order to create the most productive changes in the environment. When our advertising firm changed its system, allowing the senior women the choice of flextime and keeping track of their own hours, for example, it was soon obvious that not only did the women not slough off work, but they put in longer hours than anyone, including themselves, had imagined.

What We Don't Know

Once they began to explore the situation from each others' point of view, the women and men recognized that they didn't even know what they didn't know about each other. When it comes to culture, few people know enough about themselves, other people, or the system they are in to spot potential trouble, or to even know if there is any. Ignorance about the culture of the other sex is legendary. Especially in the fallout stage, "We don't know what we don't know."

As a result of this ignorance, cross-cultural learning on the job comes the hard way. We are lucky if we see our mistakes or have someone point them out to us. Our own cultural values keep us from recognizing gaffes, and others' cultural filters may keep them from giving us feedback. Some mistakes are so disastrous that we never get a second chance. The deal is off or the relationship is dead. The boxed anecdote was related to one of the authors by Frank Davidson, MIT professor of macroeconomics, and illustrates the pitfalls of cross-cultural attempts at humor.

A Cultural Faux Pas: Why the Tunnel Took So Long

The tunnel between France and England might have been built much sooner if there had not previously been misunderstanding over cultural differences in humor. Decades before the actual start of the project, the French had come to a conference prepared to approve the plans to link the Isles with the Continent by tunneling under the Channel. De Gaulle asked the British prime minister at a cocktail party opening the event if the tunnel was to be on their agenda. MacMillan bantered, "Oh no, my wife is claustrophobic." The French delegates took the joke seriously and postponed all discussion and, as a result, all binational construction, until recently.

Assuming We Know

There is a further complication. Because we don't know what we don't know, the mind scrambles to make sense out of the unknown by automatically filling in the blanks with what we already know or think we know. Since the mind does this without consulting us, we begin to think we know what we don't know. Confronting culturally different workers, the mind reasons, "Well, they're human, aren't they, therefore they must ..." Making ones own cultural programming the criterion for what it means to be human, the manager fails to distinguish a reality that is different. Assuming that others think like us, our efforts to communicate no longer transmit what we intend to say.

In our advertising firm case, both the men and women interpreted each other's motives and behavior as if they were their own, and judged the other side negatively. Their unconscious conversations went like this: "If I (as a woman/man) behaved this way, it would be wrong." Because the premise was unconscious, no one could see its illogic. What people's minds did say was, "You are wrong." Cultural awareness training in organizations starts by helping people recognize their own biases, the premises behind what they automatically think about others. There can be great resistance to this. Opening ourselves to alien perspectives feels dangerous and wrong, even in cultures where people are not reluctant to talk about personal thoughts and feelings.

Confirmation Bias

Overlooking the uniqueness of an event or person in order to make new information fit into old categories is called "confirmation bias." Our work culture has a strong inclination to make things and people fit preconceived notions. It's quick. It's economical. Meeting deadlines may depend on it. But it also works against us. If our bias says that a certain group is lazy, we are likely to overlook when they work hard, but take special note of it (and confirm our bias) when someone from that group is late one morning or takes a nap after lunch. Bob Abramms, President of ODT, Inc., and nationally known diversity expert, lists more ways in which our mind's natural workings can cause trouble when cultures are mixed, in the boxed material that follows.

Perception Pitfalls

- **The Halo Effect.** Your general impression of someone leads you to an inaccurate judgment of unrelated traits and characteristics. For example, you work with a group of engineers from a different

(continued)

(continued from previous page)

ethnic background who are extremely conscientious and technically competent. You assume therefore that they will make excellent project managers.

Solution: Make sure your judgments are grounded in factual observations of individuals rather than on hunches or impressions of groups, which may conspire with biased thinking to give wrong information and create unnecessary breakdowns.

- **Projection of Emotions and Traits.** You assume that other people, whose values and needs might be quite different from yours, feel the same way you do. For instance, you feel upset about an industrial accident and assume that your associates share that feeling and will back your safety plan. Later you discover that they have a resigned, "What will be, will be" attitude. Or you have a bothersome trait like being disorganized, and so you constantly nag your employees who come from a polychronic culture (one in which many things tend to be managed simultaneously) about cleaning up their desks and interrupting you with frequent phone calls.

Solution: Monitor your own feelings and take a careful look at what others are actually doing or saying in order to compensate for your tendency to project. If you sense someone projecting their feelings on you, empathize with their feelings but be clear about what is true for you. ("I can understand how you might feel/see things this way, but . . .")

- **Closure.** Because we are uncomfortable with having incomplete information, we sometimes fill in the blanks and imagine something happened because it seems the most likely explanation. For example, John gives a report to his manager. Later he learns that his report has been shelved. Without knowing what happened, John assumes his manager didn't support his recommendations because John is the only person in the section who is not white.

Solution: Talk to people and get the facts. Try to imagine explanations other than what you have assumed.

- **Perceived Relationships.** In every organization there is speculation about how colleagues are related—as friends, conspirators, lovers, etc. Often your speculation, fueled by colleagues' speculation, causes a remote possibility to snowball into a certainty. For example, several people who speak the same language (not English) tend to have lunch together almost every day. Their English-speaking colleagues look upon them as a clique that is somehow trying to divide the organization. As a result, those using the foreign language in a social situation are made into outsiders and enter into a power struggle to get the information they need. The luncheon group was more comfortable speaking together in their native language. The observers were uncomfortable when they did not use the national language even off the job.

  Solution: Make sure your assumptions about relationships are explicit and can be confirmed by objective data. If you are on the receiving end of this phenomenon, make a special effort to keep lines and channels of communication open with those who are suspicious of you.

  —Excerpted from the audiotape training module *How to Avoid Stereotyping and Nine Other Pitfalls of Perception,* available from ODT, Inc., Box 134, Amherst, MA 01004 (800-736-1293)

The Rushdie Dilemma

On February 14, 1989, the Ayatollah Khomeni called for the execution of author Salman Rushdie on the grounds that Rushdie's book, *The Satanic Verses,* contained material heretical to Islam. Though Rushdie himself was Islamic in background, he was also a British citizen protected by the Crown. Cultural values held as absolutes by parties on both sides clashed. Such a "Rushdie Dilemma" will occur when two non-negotiable, absolute, or diametrically opposed cultural values are brought to bear on the same issue. The resulting breakdown creates a deadlock, putting both sides in a double bind. If they act true to their values, they transgress the sacred principles of another group; if not, they betray their group and dishonor themselves.

Rushdie Dilemmas occur in business and in the workplace as well:

- A salesperson from one culture is absolutely forbidden to give gifts to clients; the purchaser comes from a culture in which such gifts are seen as a sign of the friendship and good will necessary to do business.
- A hospital, for its own legal protection, insists on the absolute necessity of a medical procedure that violates the ethical or religious principles of patients or staff.
- Workers insist on wearing culturally or religiously prescribed clothing or ornaments that run counter to safety laws with which the company must legally comply.

Escalation in an unresolved clash of values may create a breakdown in which compromise no longer seems possible. The transcultural leader has to act proactively to avoid such situations. First she or he must make every effort to become knowledgeable about the principal cultural values of the different people in the workforce or group. In today's complex multicultural working environments, this can be a big order.

Then the transcultural leader must keep an ear to the ground to pick up tremors of approaching problems before they get too large, too emotional, and too polarized to handle. This means paying attention to even small discomforts in the workforce, keeping the lines of communication open, and handling what look like petty complaints without dismissing them as trivial. She or he respectfully and regularly enquires about what is or is not working for people both in their job and in their relationship with others in the workplace.

All of us carry the potential for acting out the prejudice inside of us when we feel threatened. We are like a bomb waiting to go off. Events around us or how others act may pull the trigger. Table 2.1 shows some of the dynamics that you should watch out for in yourself and your workforce.

Close Neighbors Have Real Differences

Male-female communication is so frustrating because we assume that we should understand each other. We live in the same houses, eat the same food, use the same words, yet, as the title of Deborah Tannen's best-seller proclaims, *You Just Don't Understand Me*. Somehow we don't speak the same language. Culturally or geographically close neighbors have similar problems. Australians and Britons, Canadians and Americans, Germans and Swiss-Germans, apparently alike in so many ways, feel they *should* understand each other. Invoking the 80/20 rule is especially useful when such close neighbors must work with each other.

Table 2.1
Triggers for Cultural Disruption in the Workforce

The Bomb Inside	External Triggers That Can Set It Off
Our own historical, cultural, or mythological memory. ■ "Remember what they did to us when . . ." For example, Pearl Harbor can be reflected in our thinking about U.S.-Japan trade relations.	**Physical characteristics of newcomers to the workforce.** ■ "They look strange, different." ■ "They're not like us."
Heightened stress levels urge us to enforce our own cultural standards. ■ "We've got to stay in control of this situation." ■ "They've got to do it our way."	**Behavioral traits.** ■ "They talk, dress or act *funny* on the job, or bring strange food to the cafeteria."
Ignorance leading to fear. ■ "What if they . . .?"	**Increased numbers of workers from a different culture.** ■ "There are more and more of them."
Our own ethnocentricity and absolutism. ■ "This is the absolute truth . . ." ■ "There is only one . . ." ■ "We've always done it this way . . ."	**"Eccentric" beliefs based on limited information about others.** ■ "They have strange ideas; don't think like us." ■ "For them, life is cheap." ■ "They work for nothing."

Look for the Context

Remember your first few days in a new organization? How often were you bewildered because you didn't understand the context out of which people spoke and acted? When we don't understand something we say, "Give me some background," or, "Put that in context for me." When an American and a Japanese speak with each other, or even when someone from research walks into a marketing meeting, lack of this context can cause a breakdown in communications. Until we understand the context out of which the other person speaks, he or she will not make sense to us. In our previous example, the failure of the men and women in the advertising firm to understand each other's context undermined their best intentions of collaborating. Once we know how contexts differ, given some time and attention, we can usually adjust.

Not only might another group's or individual's context be different from ours, but *the amount or intensity of the context,* the structure they regularly need or use when they think, speak, and act may be different. Looking at *how people within different cultures communicate with and behave toward each other,* we discover that the amount of context they employ ranges widely. On one hand there are cultures in which everything must be made explicit or spelled out to make sure others understand. At the other extreme are cultures in which vast amounts of information can be taken for granted, assumed to be known, and left unsaid without hindering communication. Such cultures speak with a kind of shorthand that is bewildering to the observer. Walt Hopkins, an American expatriate and president of Castle Consultants in the U.K., told us about a pattern of communication between conductors and passengers on the London buses that consisted of repeating the word, "K'yew." After a few rides he puzzled it out:

Conductor: "K'yew" ["Ticket please, thank you."]
Passenger: "K'yew" ["Here you are, thank you."]
Conductor: "K'yew" [Punches it and hands it back, saying "Thank you."]
Passenger: "K'yew" [Taking the ticket back says, "Thank you."]

Once one is familiar with the context, verbal shorthand makes sense.

A Cultural Continuum

Using the idea of context enables us to describe cultures and subcultures along a continuum, in which some groups are "high" or "more tightly woven" on one hand and others are "low" or "more loosely knit" on the other. More tightly woven cultures share a large amount of common background information when dealing with people of their own kind. Their words and actions, we could say, are loaded. Like the conductor and passenger on the London bus, they are able to communicate a lot with very little. While one of the authors and his wife, a consultant, were conducting human relations training in the Philippines, the woman consultant sensed that the local women had devised a complete communication system among themselves that was very hard for outsiders to detect. It was based upon the movement of their fans. How many invisible communications systems are at work in your organization?

As Marshall McLuhan discovered several decades ago, the *medium,* how we speak or act, carries its own *message* above and beyond what we actually say. What is said may not make sense by itself or could even mean its opposite taken out of context. In more tightly woven contexts, people automatically read between the lines to understand what is meant or expected of them. Those in more loosely knit cultures are just the opposite. They take little or nothing for granted. Because more needs to be specified, described, and explained each time people interact, questions and answers must be more direct. Many breakdowns can be managed once we understand the different cultural contexts from which our employees come. A model describing these differences is found in Appendix A.

We prefer the terms "more tightly woven" and "more loosely knit" because they are descriptive and avoid the implication that "higher" is better than "lower." When you read authors like Edward T. Hall who speak of "high" and "low" context, remember, no more value judgment is intended than when we speak about "high" or "low" tide.

White American women tend to belong to a somewhat higher or more tightly knit culture than white American males; if you consider how this difference played a part in our sample case, the reasons for misunderstanding and for the loss of the senior women employees becomes far more apparent. The women attempted to preserve harmony longer and were reluctant to bring their grievances to the men. Their earliest attempts to air their issues failed. Women spoke in what they thought were clear terms, but the men couldn't read between the lines. In order to surface the real issues, the women had speak with a force and directness that they found uncomfortable, but which fit the men's context better. Although the men spoke this way to each other, it still took them a while to hear the women's message because they, too, were uncomfortable by the women's unaccustomed directness. At first the men felt that the women were overreacting, blowing the issues out of proportion. Eventually more of the men learned to read between the lines and were able to fathom women's concerns even when they were not put forth so explicitly.

The effects of differences in context are even more apparent when dealing with different ethnic cultures. The older, more uniform, stable, isolated, and uninterrupted a culture or subculture is, the more likely it is to have developed more tightly woven values, rules, and ways in which things are done that are understood by all participants in the culture. In a very tightly woven culture—a Japanese workplace for example—simple things like the choice of a pronoun and the depth of a bow can contain a whole wealth of information about the rank and status of two people and their expectations of and duties toward each other. In Western Europe and particularly in the United States, cultures are far more loosely knit. Much less is commonly understood and much more needs to be specified, explained, or spelled out as people communicate across cultural lines. The mixture can be volatile. Polite deference may look like a commitment or a promise to Westerners, as has frequently occurred in Japanese-American trade negotiations, when, in fact, it is not.

As another example, Arabs and Latin Americans are reluctant to do business or negotiate until a relationship is established. They must put the stranger or foreigner in context, and determine if any action can take place with the other person. Working with such people is much more productive if attention is paid to what Filipinos describe as the SIR factor (Smooth Interpersonal Relationships).

Context is also imbedded in language itself. In loosely knit Western languages, there are elaborate grammar and punctuation rules to enable one to correctly bring out the nuances in meaning, particularly when the written word is separated from tone of voice and inflection. On the other hand, words in many Asian languages, especially those based on pictographs or ideograms, are like holograms. They tightly weave several concepts together so that the word is very rich in meaning and nuances and can be viewed from many sides. In English it takes four words to say "listen with undivided attention." The Chinese combine all this in the simple pictograph for "listen." (see Figure 2.2)

Listening is when you use . . .

EARS

EYES

HEART

to give *undivided attention*.

Figure 2.2. "Undivided attention."

One of the reasons the work culture of North America may be so loosely knit is because its people continue to come from so many different places and, as a result, North Americans have to maintain a "lowest common denominator" way of speaking to each other.

Today, diversity, globalism, and the rapidity of technological change makes organizations prefer more loosely knit cultural values and practices. The self-reliance that the immigrant needed to survive in very mixed company on a new frontier added individualism to North American culture and flavored its businesses with the spirit of entrepreneurship. On the other hand, ethnically unmixed peoples, or groups isolated from outside influences, such as the Japanese were for a significant part of their history, may develop a much more tightly woven culture. However, groups that developed tightly woven cultures but that are small or lack cohesive political structure often risk being overrun and destroyed by larger more powerful cultures.

In order to build a common context, managers and workers from a more loosely knit culture who want to collaborate with people from a more tightly woven one must do their homework and ask a lot of questions, often privately and beforehand, as the questions they ask could appear foolish or insulting to their listeners. Those from more tightly woven groups must make a different but equally taxing effort to work with individuals from more loosely knit backgrounds. Those from the more tightly woven groups can take little or nothing for granted regarding what others understand and must become exceedingly direct and explicit, which they may find painful and embarrassing. It was hard for the men in our case to admit that they really did not know much about the women's needs; it seemed even harder for the women to accept that the men were actually telling the truth about this. Use the information in Appendix A to help you analyze the impact of your own culture on yourself and steer you to ask the right questions about the culture of those you work with.

Mixing Contexts Creates a More Loosely Knit Environment

A multicultural organization, though it is made up of people from many contexts, tends to function as a loosely knit culture as a result of the mixture. Not realizing this causes breakdowns. Put Japanese, Chinese, American, and French engineers in the same room and they may do quite well dealing with a technical problem—as electronic engineers, they share a tightly woven context. But, how they run the meeting and take turns speaking may cause a breakdown. Ask them to discuss "how to motivate a work team," and the common context could fall apart entirely. Learning how to speak across contexts, to behave in another's context, is a formidable task. Fortunately in the workplace, we can limit our efforts to what people need to know to collaborate effectively.

Creating Common Contexts

Common contexts can be created in two ways. We can buy into someone else's culture lock, stock, and barrel (assimilation) or we can create a new context together (acculturation). Where many cultures and contexts exist side by side in a workforce, acculturation is the preferred path. Our breakdowns help us become acculturated to each other. The fallout stage tells us things we don't know about each other. Then, as we agree on distinctions and make new commitments, we build a common context in which we work together until the next breakdown forces us to a further stage of context development.

When participants do not automatically understand each other's backgrounds in a meeting, speech must become more explicit, questions more detailed, and language simpler until we share in each other's contexts. Listening skills are critical. By paying attention to context, Japanese management techniques have been adapted to American workers and Americans have become effective negotiators in Asia.

As sharing of contexts takes place, organizations of diverse people start weaving a new context. They develop their own jargon, definitions, visions, and understandings. They develop an overlapping set of distinctions in which people from different contexts can meet. Committing ourselves to understanding each other is a first step. It can be all that is needed to resolve some breakdowns.

Multiple Contexts

Every organization is a subculture of the larger culture in which it operates. An immigrant does not just come to work in the United States. He or she comes to work more specifically in the East, say Massachusetts, or in the West, perhaps California, and in a specific industry like computers or construction. It will also make a difference whether this person enters the workforce at a corporation called Digital, or IBM, or Hewlett-Packard. Understanding both the macro- and the microcultures that the worker is leaving, as well as the one the worker is entering, can help us facilitate her or his acculturation and performance.

When newcomers arrive slowly and in small numbers, their influence on the host culture may only be slight. They are likely to be assimilated rather than acculturated. But when a workplace is inundated by newcomers, as is often the case today, organizational culture begins to shift or even break down. Not everybody understands or obeys the old rules anymore. For awhile, traditional values and assumptions are used consciously or unconsciously to keep the newcomers in their place, but as their numbers and strength increase, the old culture begins to cave in. What may have been a very tightly woven organization now becomes a place where people must communicate the most basic things to each other. Communication breakdowns are common. This situation requires more powerful communication skills. We will learn more about these in the next chapters.

Now that you understand how cross-cultural breakdowns occur, the steps shown in the following section will help you explore, discuss, and manage such breakdowns. Think of a real incident you have recently had or are now having. Then follow the instructions in the next section.

Managing a Cross-Cultural Breakdown

1. The Interruption
   What happened? Briefly describe the breakdown in your own words.

   a. What actually took place? This time avoid any personal judgments—make this a step-by-step behavioral description. Who did and/or said what?
   b. With whom?
   c. When? What time factors were involved?
   d. Where? What was the environment?

2. The Fallout

   a. What automatic judgments did you make about the situation? what alternative interpretations are possible? (Later you will learn to use the "Mindshifter," on page 124, for this.)
   b. What different contexts are involved? (Consult Appendix A) What cultural differences and values (both your own and the other person's) surfaced as a result of the breakdown?

3. Recommitment

    a. What result are you committed to creating in this situation?
    b. Who can you involve or what resources might you employ to produce this result?
    c. How would you design a strategy for handling this situation face-to-face, using both listening and transcultural communication skills?

An example of how one person used this process to resolve a breakdown is shown in the following boxed example.

Managing a Cross-Cultural Breakdown: An Example

1. The Interruption
My manager speaks to me and orders me around rudely.

a. What actually took place?
I did not notice that the copy machine had broken down at the end of a job. My manager tried to make some copies and the machine failed. He started complaining loudly about the machine and then he signaled me to come and look at it by crooking and wiggling his index finger at me.

b. With whom?
My manager is an American who has been working in the Manila office for about one month.

c. When?
It was toward the end of the day and we were rushing to meet a deadline.

d. Where?
This took place in the office in front of all my co-workers and friends. They pretended not to see it, but I know that they were ashamed for me.

(continued)

(continued from previous page)

2. The Fallout

I think he must be a caveman. He is always shouting and yelling. He must think I am a dog by the way he calls me.

Possible alternative interpretations:
Though I find it hard to believe that people can treat each other that way and still work together, it is possible that our cultural differences have a lot to do with how we see and judge each other. Also he may have had something else unpleasant happen that day.

What differences in context are involved in this situation?
My manager belongs to a far more loosely knit group than I do.

What cultural differences and values surfaced as a result of this breakdown?
Westerners tend to speak louder than Filipinos. They also use gestures that must have a different meaning to them than they do to us, because I see them speaking to each other this way without being embarrassed. Some of my friends told me that this was true when I told them what happened.

3. Recommitment

a. To what result are you committed?
I want to respect my manager and be respected by him so that we can we can work harmoniously together.

b. Who or what resources might you involve?
I could tell one of his American associates to mention the matter to him. I could also learn more about American culture and why Americans behave as they do.

c. How would you design a strategy?
I could meet face-to-face with his associate, explain my Filipino sensitivities, and ask questions to understand the American point of view. I must be careful not to assume that when people from other countries do unpleasant things that they mean to attack me personally.

Points to Remember from This Chapter

- Breakdowns are the normal work of the manager. They go through predictable stages. They provide opportunities for us to learn and to perform better.
- Intercultural breakdowns on the job can be dealt with like other breakdowns.
- The fallout stage of a breakdown is critical. We can manage it if we
  —Pay attention to the cultural information it yields.
  —Apply the 80/20 rule.
  —Avoid perception pitfalls.
  —Prevent the Rushdie Dilemma.
- Context is a key concept in understanding how people from other cultures work and behave.
- Learn about differences in context and develop a common context in your organization where necessary.

CHAPTER 3

YOUR MOUTH, YOUR TIGER

"Mulut Kamu, Harimau Kamu.
Your mouth, your tiger."

—Indonesian Proverb

As we were writing this book and exchanging individual chapters with each other to read, differences arose due to diversity in perspectives, education, experience, and gender. As often happens, we sometimes responded to feedback from our colleague by saying, "Well, that's not what I meant." Then the writer would go on to explain what he or she had in mind. Invariably the answer came back, "Well, if that's what you meant, why didn't you say it that way?"

Saying It Right

Why don't we say things right in the first place? There are two reasons. First, when we communicate—it's especially evident when writing—we talk to ourselves much faster and say much more than we put down on paper or say aloud to the other person. It's as though we give them only the headlines or the leading sentence of each paragraph we say to ourselves. Secondly, we have no control over the listener's mind, which is also speaking to itself (faster than we speak aloud), trying to interpret what we say.

Researchers have estimated the speeds at which we speak and at which we listen or talk to ourselves. When we are under stress we think so fast that we may multiply that speed many times over.

44

How Fast We Speak and Listen in Words Per Minute

- 250 wpm—Ordinary conversation
- 125 wpm—Speeches and lectures
- 500 wpm—The average listener listening

Mindsets for Communicating

In the loosely knit context created by diversity, a transcultural leader must be able to shift back and forth from the mindset that says that communicating means saying something to someone else, to one that sees communication as a collaborative effort between people to create meaning and action. The first mindset is more representative of a more tightly woven culture where the participants share more of a larger context. But, since an environment with many cultures *de facto* becomes more loosely knit, the transcultural leader, whatever her or his background, must know how to operate out of both mindsets. She or he must also know how to help others make similar mindshifts, to move back and forth between the perspectives in the columns in the box that follows.

(text continued on page 47)

More Tightly Woven Mindset MEANING IS CONTAINED IN AND COMMUNICATED BY WORDS (SYMBOLS, ACTIONS, ETC.)	↔	More Loosely Knit Mindset MEANING IS CREATED HERE AND NOW BY PEOPLE
If the words (symbols, actions, etc.) are the same, then the message is the same for both the speaker and the hearer.	↔ **M**	Words and listening are conditioned by each person's cultural background and experience. Even within the same culture, no two people are exactly the same; thus, they don't listen the same way and perceive the same things.
It's the work of the hearer to listen correctly to the speaker's message and understand its nuances.	↔ **I**	Two people must cooperate by exchanging what they listen to, in order to create understanding and commitments that are as congruent as possible.
Hearers misunderstand or speakers choose the wrong way to express what they mean—this is usually how communication fails.	↔ **N**	Misunderstanding occurs when the speaker and hearer do not work effectively toward congruent listening.
Feedback is of little importance. Assent, or at least harmony, is.	↔ **D**	Congruence, understanding, and agreement cannot occur without feedback.
One-way communication is normally all that's needed.	↔ **S**	Two-way exchanges are required for all but perhaps the simplest messages.
The speaker concentrates time and effort mostly on creating the correct message.	↔ **H**	Time and effort are divided into preparing and choosing the initial message, obtaining feedback, and forming further messages.
Differences usually imply that someone, either speaker or hearer, has made a mistake.	↔ **I**	The same issue will be formulated in different ways by each according to their culture and background.
People can be blamed for failing to speak or hear correctly. Not getting the message can bring shame on both speakers and listener.	↔ **F**	People can create meaning only when they disclose what they listen to and when they listen actively to each other.
Credibility comes from the authority of the speaker.	↔ **T**	Credibility and reliability come from the quality of collaboration between the communicators.

Mismatched Contexts

How do we pass between these mindsets? Two imaginary pictures might help. First, imagine a computer. If you type in the right commands and press the return key, you invariably get the result you are seeking, except in the rare situation where there has been a malfunction. When you don't get the results you expect, when people behave out of context, you assume that *something is wrong with them*. This is how it feels when a communicator from a more tightly woven (MTW) culture encounters someone from a more loosely knit (MLK) one.

Next, imagine playing paddleball on the beach. The fun comes from seeing how long you can keep the ball in the air by hitting it back and forth. The game is frustrating and you soon quit if one partner rarely hits the ball back. This happens when a communicator from a more loosely knit background encounters someone from a more tightly woven context.

Following are some examples of what happens when people with mismatched contexts communicate:

- A Japanese (MTW) manager gives an order to American workers (MLK) and is annoyed to find it disputed and resented. The manager begins to distrust the subordinates and their motivation.
- A Swedish (MLK) manager gives/makes a request of her Turkish (MTW) subordinates and finds that they carry it out so literally, "without thinking," that the desired results are not achieved. The manager accuses them of malicious obedience.
- A Filipino seaman (MTW) is being disciplined by his Norwegian first officer (MLK). The seaman remains silent as the first officer pushes for an explanation or apology. The first officer thinks the seaman does not get the message, doesn't care about the situation, or is guilty of even more than originally suspected.

To make matters worse, the Norwegian first officer belabors the point and raises his voice with the Filipino seaman, who doesn't appear to get the message, admit fault, or apologize. Resentment builds in the subordinate. He stops communicating and becomes ineffective at his job for the rest of the voyage.

- A Canadian consultant (MLK), while being gently criticized by her Indonesian client (MTW), argues in her own defense. The client sees the consultant as rude and unteachable and, therefore, incompetent.
- A young British data processing trainer (MLK) is working with a group of Sri Lankan trainees (MTW). Because the trainees ask no questions, the trainer assumes they have grasped all that she has said.
- A newly arrived Swiss manufacturing manager (MLK) consults his Pakistani assembly-line workers (MTW) about the steps he should take to install a quality inspection system. They are embarrassed for him because it seems that he does not know how to do his job. They are reluctant to make suggestions. He sees them as unthinking and uncooperative.

The transcultural leader may have to employ both MTW and MLK context communication skills to create congruent messages and objectives. Congruence not only means that two people settle on the same meaning or direction, but that they are confident that this has actually taken place. This shows up as a certain degree of comfort with themselves and each other, some assurance that they are on the same wavelength.

Though there are many levels of context in the world, and many languages and dialects, what people do with language is relatively simple: we all ask questions, we all tell stories, we all make proposals and suggestions, and we all make agreements, though we may do each of these things in different ways and at different times. Some people are more direct than others. Even in mainline American culture, one person may say outright, "I want us to design a nylon part," while another might make exactly the same suggestion much less forcefully, "Does anyone here think that a change of material, to nylon, for example, might give us some of the qualities we are looking for?" Someone else might ask even more indirectly, "Are other materials available?"

A Linguistic Model of Workplace Communication

One of the most useful analyses of workplace communication that we have found comes from Fernando Flores, who based his work on research by the British linguists Austin and Searle. Flores saw four basic communication activities, or "speech acts," that people use in order to get or produce results:

1. We *ask* others to do things; for example:

   - *I ask you to complete the report by Wednesday noon.*
   - *Please give us a hand with this project.*
   - *I insist that you hear us out on this matter.*
   - *This is an order . . .*

2. We *promise* others that we will do things, or refuse (i.e., promise not) to do them; for example:

   - *I'll meet you on Thursday morning at ten.*
   - *I'll have the job put out for bids before the end of the month.*
   - *I refuse to work overtime this weekend.*

Sometimes requests and promises are combined in conditional offers (negotiation is usually based on such offers); for example:

   - *Give me a week and I'll have it on your desk.*
   - *If you'll do the phone calls, I'll handle the mail.*
   - *If you can't improve your offer, we won't do business.*
   - *I won't do this job without safety goggles.*

3. We *assert* that certain things are true or false; for example:

   - *There are three critical factors in making this decision.*
   - *The return on investment this quarter was down 3%.*
   - *The rumor of my promotion is totally unfounded.*

4. We use our authority to *declare* things to be valid or invalid for our-selves and for others. This speech act occurs whenever we say to

ourselves or others, "This is the way it is from now on (because I said so)." Each culture bestows a range of authority within which its members are entitled to make declarations about themselves, to commit themselves to having certain attitudes:

- *I will become an engineer.*
- *Thanks for the suggestion.*
- *I apologize for the delay.*
- *That project is not a priority for me.*

As leaders we are empowered to make declarations based on the authority we have been given to direct the activity of others. Our declarations are valid to the degree that they fall within our range of authority. For example, a personnel manager can say, "You're hired!" to a prospective employee, but the interviewee would sound ridiculous or would be joking if he or she said the same words to the manager. The executive committee might declare a bonus for the year, but the shop steward cannot. Unions call strikes, not management. It may be up to the CEO to define the strategic vision or declare, "Here's how we're going to do business around here . . ." and up to the sales manager to say, "I nominate you as salesperson of the year!"

To communicate transculturally, we must first observe how we talk to ourselves in our own minds. We must be clear about the commitments we are making and want others to make. Often this means disentangling what we want to communicate from the ongoing cultural chatter in our heads. Once we know what we want, we must translate it into words and gestures that are culturally appropriate for the listener and grasp the commitment we have made or are asking them to make.

Four Critical Questions

The manager's basic job, according to Flores, is to preside over a living network of commitments, most of them requests and promises, by which breakdowns are handled and the organization produces results. His or her role is to be a creator and communicator of commitments, one who listens and speaks in such a way that she or he knows at the end of an interaction the answer to four basic questions, found in the accompanying box.

> √ *Did one of us ask or demand something of the other?*
> √ *Did one of us promise (or refuse) something to the other?*
> √ *What did either of us assert to be true or false?*
> √ *Did either of us declare or define something, i.e., did we commit ourselves to a new direction, definition, attitude, or state of affairs regarding our work together?*

These four basic questions enable us to measure how successfully we communicate and delegate work to others. The questions are not always easy to answer. Workers from more tightly woven cultures may ask for things indirectly. Some seem to never say "no" or are reluctant to deliver bad news. Some tell stories as evidence that something is true, or to explain what they feel or how they behave toward someone or something. If we are from a more loosely knit background, other ways of speaking, especially the more subtle ways of reaching agreement or consensus, leave us wondering about the facts. If we are from more tightly knit groups, people from loosely knit backgrounds may seem harsh, insensitive, rude, or hard to deal with because they seem obsessed, like the hard-boiled movie detective bent on getting ". . . the facts, Ma'am, nothing but the facts."

With these four questions as keys to what counts in workplace communication, we next need to learn how people from different contexts do, in fact, tend to express themselves and make commitments. Here our continuum model (Appendix A) can help us ask the right questions. Do they ask for things, demand them, or infer them? When they say "yes" do they mean "yes" or "yes, but . . ." Is their response an acknowledgement of what they have heard, a good intention, or a hard-and-fast determination to meet a deadline?

Referring to the four questions and using the continuum model provide shortcuts to knowing what to look for in a multicultural conversation. There is no substitute, however for specifically learning how other groups and individuals actually ask, promise, declare, define things, and assert and test facts and evidence. When you have problems with this, search out people with more experience to advise you about a culture and teach you what to look for.

Negotiating Across Cultures

When negotiating, we need to know what degree of positioning or preliminary getting-to-know-and-trust-you exchanges must take place both before and while we talk business. The Dutch don't talk business before coffee. Many North American negotiators unconsciously think of themselves as card players. Each negotiation is a new game. They open quickly and lay their cards on the table. Getting the right numbers wins the game. In Latin America, entering a negotiation is like being invited to a dance. Negotiators want to like and trust people before they risk business with them, so they spend far more time on social amenities and getting to know each other. Traditionally the Japanese used long preliminaries and entertainment to bring potential business partners into the family, and they expect to do business together for a long time.

If we understand bargaining as haggling over price or as a situation in which only a single currency, usually money, is required to strike a deal, and negotiating as a situation in which multiple currencies are exchanged (SMS 1987), we can make a number of distinctions along the continuum from more tightly woven to more loosely knit cultures (see Appendix A). More information about negotiating across cultures can be found in *The Dynamics of Successful International Business Negotiations* by Moran and Stripp, a companion book in this series.

Communication could be simplified, some of us think, if all people talked directly about their requests, promises, etc., but the truth is that even in more loosely knit culture situations people often don't speak directly enough. Flores and his associates at Logonet have made a bold attempt to train people to think this way, and also designed the Coordinator™ software, which coaches its users in how to make clear commitments while carrying on everyday business on an electronic network. This "Pidgin English" of commitments and results, which they have embedded in software, deserves to be used much more widely as a learning model for oral and written communications, especially when we find ourselves in more loosely knit multicultural enterprises.

Creating common context requires the effort of all groups. Most people, whatever their culture, have some reluctance to make commitments. When we throw different cultures together it is hard to sort out what people are saying from how they say it. Often we resist the effort to create a new common context because we fear that we are giving up something by learning to play by the other person's rules. The truth is that we gain something, *the capacity to communicate transculturally,* and, if diverse people within an organization acquire this capacity, the organization becomes more agile, productive, and competitive.

Small Talk and Harmonious Relationships

Dr. Adele Scheele, writing in *Working Women,* reminds us that "small talk isn't just trivial chatter. It's a way to build trust and loyalty among colleagues." If we are "all business," we may function successfully with people for whom tasks are primary, and get nowhere with those who require harmonious relationships to act. Small talk with people from different cultures is hard when we don't know what to talk about. Asking questions or talking about each other's families, quite appropriate in some cultures, can be totally taboo in others, or simply convey different intentions. An American businessman told us how he tried to make small talk by asking a Singapore businesswoman over dinner if she were married. He was intending to talk about family, children, and the like with her. The woman heard this not as casual chitchat but as an expression of his amorous interest in her. Following are a few tips which can help you make successful small talk in a diverse work environment:

1. Do your homework. What do the members of this group like to talk about? What do they avoid? Who talks to whom about what? When and in what context is it appropriate to raise certain topics and when is it not? How does male conversation differ from female conversation? Read about the other group's cultural background. Observe what they do and how they do it. Listen in. Ask advice of others from their culture or from your own who have had more cross-cultural experience.

2. Get out of yourself and get a feel for them. When you start talking with someone who is quite different from you, especially if you are using another language, much of your energy can easily be taken up by your own preoccupation with how you look and sound, and worrying about if you're doing it right. Focus on them. Listen carefully. Put yourself in their shoes and ask what might they be feeling and thinking differently from you. What are their concerns and issues? Learn what they have recently experienced and how it affected them. Observe their rhythm and how fast they speak, and the order in which people speak to and interrupt each other. Realize that any discomfort or distaste you may experience is your problem, not theirs.

3. Start very small. Ask broad, open-ended questions rather than specific, pointed ones. Get others to talk about what they like to talk about. With some people, asking for stories rather than opinions may give you more information.

4. Do not be embarrassed either by silence or talkativeness on the part of the other person. Accept it and be patient with it for a while. See what develops.

5. Be persistent. Cultivate curiosity and wonder. At first you may find that what the other person talks about is not to your interest. Of course not! That's precisely the point. Valuing differences means paying attention to what might seem trite and insignificant but is of importance to others. When sampling a new and different cuisine, the unfamiliar can show up not just in the form of strange ingredients, but in the subtle seasoning of things quite familiar as well.

Reading this book will not automatically make you a transcultural communicator, but you will improve your communication skills significantly by practicing these five tips.

Managing a Breakdown by Listening and Communicating

Communication styles can confuse both people in a conversation because they have culturally different ways of communicating and because of the dynamics set in motion by speaking across cultures. Here are some examples:

1. Serving in the Philippines as consultants, and working with Filipinos in the U.S., two of the authors learned how uncomfortable most Filipinos were with American-style "telling it like it is." They avoid confrontation, cover their emotions, and bury their feelings or resentments until something happens to trigger their anger or hostility. In the context of their heritage, these normally gentle people do not wish to offend, and consider the "saving of face" to be very important. Thus, they smile often, but that facial expression may have varied meanings, as it does in other parts of Asia. Filipino immigrants will often find it painful to learn different communication skills in the U.S. They tend to be embarrassed and uncomfortable around

Americans, who seem overly direct, brash, and harsh in their interactions with one another.

2. Many African-Americans speak two kinds of English, "Black-English" and mainstream American-English, and will switch from one to the other at work, depending on to whom they are talking. Much emphasis is placed on body language and gestures. When communicating with their white co-workers, especially those in authority positions, some African-Americans will speak with contrived deference and exaggerated agreeableness, and hide their true feelings.

3. Many non-U.S.-born Hispanics also communicate differently, as a result of their Latin American cultural context, when they immigrate to the U.S. When they master English, their expressions are influenced by their native Spanish or Portuguese. Hispanics tend to express less emotion and colorfulness in English than in their native language. They often speak more slowly, quietly, tentatively, and perhaps more hesitantly in English, especially when dialoguing with "Anglos." Like the Filipinos, they favor indirectness, saying what they think the receiver wants to hear. Becoming bilingual gives people very real language advantages in business, as discussed in the next section.

Language Barriers

New workforce demographics and the rapidly changing nature of today's work are causing managers to take a second look at bilingualism. When immigrants were fewer and huddled together on the shop floor, and when work was routine, an occasional interpretation was all that was needed to get a point across and a job done. Today basic language-skill requirements are much higher. Machinists and even maintenance people need to regularly interact with computers and participate in staff meetings. Some companies like Motorola have met this challenge with massive English-language training programs. Others have chosen the course of bilingualism, making sure that managers and supervisors are appointed who understand reports written by non-English-speaking workers, and by providing translations of all communications into the languages of the receivers.

Language differences can cause discomfort and misunderstanding. When groups cluster and speak a different language, it is not uncommon for those who can't speak that language to think, "They are talking about me," or "They are hiding something," or even, "They are laughing at us or making fun of us." Because of this discomfort, some U.S. organizations have even tried to ban the use of languages other than English in the workplace, contrary to EEO rulings on the matter.

International English

English is becoming the first language of a new international work culture. Some industries, such as airlines and travel, have standardized forms of English to link them together so that, for instance, airline pilots and travel agents can speak and write to each other with minimum misunderstanding. International English creates a context that enables the Germans to do business with the Saudis, and the Scandinavians to work side by side with Taiwanese.

When communicating in such an environment, in another culture, or with foreign-born employees, remember that some, perhaps most, of your listeners (if not you yourself) will use English as a second language (ESL) or a dialect of English quite different from yours. British, Irish, East Indian, Caribbean, and African-American forms of English are first languages to most speakers, but differences of vocabulary and pronunciation can confound other English speakers. For example, many people born in India speak English as a second, or "link," language, but it is a British-derived English to which they have added intonations, pace, and vocabulary that sound strange to other English speakers. Though Americans and British often excuse themselves from learning other languages by citing the fact that English is becoming the universal business language, they are in fact at a disadvantage. *Most speakers of English as a first language do not know how to speak ESL!* Those speaking ESL frequently complain that native English speakers are more difficult to understand than other ESL speakers. Native speakers use a larger vocabulary often laced with slang expressions, speak too fast, and assume others have caught and even agree to ideas that have been missed entirely. The tragic 1990 crash of a Venezuelan airliner on approach to New York may have been due to differing nuances in the use of English phrases. Misunderstandings like this can also occur across functions within an organization. Though people may share the same ethnic background and macroculture, some speak advertising while others talk engineering.

How to Speak Transcultural English

Here are ten useful tips when working with people whose English is quite different from yours:

1. Slow down! If you're a native of New Orleans and have worked in Boston, or vice versa, you may already know how hard it is to comprehend what someone else is saying. People from a different ethnic group or from another country can find it doubly difficult to understand you.

2. Use basic vocabulary and keep it simple. Stick to the commonest and easiest words in the language. Don't say, "I need to have a conversation with you at your earliest possible convenience," when, "I want to talk to you this morning," will do! When studying a foreign language, many people plateau at a vocabulary of 2,500 to 3,500 words. They learn the basics in the first couple of years of language training or foreign experience and expand their repertoire very slowly after that. When writing, use computer programs that check the level of difficulty of your English, as well as correct your grammar for simplicity and directness. Many popular word processors include dictionaries for both the United States and other spelling variants. Use them if you wish to put your written communication in the form most familiar to the recipient.

3. Listen actively. From time to time, ask people what they understood you to have said, and paraphrase what they have said to you. One of the authors of this book tried to talk about "influencing" as a communication skill to a group of Asian managers. When he asked them to paraphrase what he said, he discovered that they thought he was encouraging bribery!

4. Repeat, rephrase, and illustrate messages and instructions. Repetition is *still* the mother of learning, and a picture can *still* be worth a thousand words, maybe more. Say what you have to say in several ways unless your audience's English is so basic that this will confuse them. Giving your audience the same message in a variety of words and images and appealing to several senses will help them understand you.

5. Avoid slang, jargon, and colloquial expressions. If you ask, "Where are you coming from?" others may tell you the name of their hometown or their last travel destination instead of explaining why they said what they just said. "Are you into movies?" may get a puzzled look, not an answer. A post office clerk who greeted a recent immigrant with, "How's it going?" got the answer, "Airmail." Many slang expressions, besides being hard to understand, may have damaging (sometimes forgotten) ethnic or racial connotations, e.g. "to *gyp* someone," to "go *dutch* treat," etc. As organizations weave their own context they tend to create their own jargon, which should be carefully explained to newcomers and used sparingly until they are acculturated.

6. Go easy on the acronyms. Using initials, acronyms, and made-up product names may be a convenient shortcut in your own culture where OPEC, EPA, and IRS are household words and have a potential for reducing your ROI. Realize that many acronyms change in foreign languages (for example, where romance languages are spoken AIDS is SIDA). The initials you create in your own company for groups, products, and functions may not make any sense at all to listeners from another culture or, even worse, may spell out something unpleasant or even obscene in another language.

7. Pre-test humor. Humor and jokes frequently depend on intricate nuances of language. The same joke can be funny for an entirely different reason. Try them out beforehand with someone who knows the culture and sensitivities of the audience to make sure they do not offend before using the jokes in public.

8. Expect delayed reactions. Reactions from people not speaking their native language may be longer in coming than you are used to. This is especially true when speaking publicly to a group or through an interpreter. Participants take more time to understand a joke, and laugh at it only when they feel that it is safe and polite to laugh—usually when the non-native speaker thinks she or he has bombed and is embarrassedly moving on to the next topic. However, some compassionate interpreters, when doing simultaneous interpretation, will say something like, "The speaker is telling a joke. Please laugh . . . NOW!" This could give you a false sense of security. (Incidentally, interpreters resent your calling them "translators." Translators work with written text, interpreters with the spoken word.)

9. Don't assume congruence. Your experiences are yours, not theirs, and their metaphors may be different—a male woman-chaser in Sumatra is a "crocodile," not a "wolf." Tell about your experiences, feelings, and reactions as your own and as a member of your own cultural group. Then ask others if what they experience is different and how it may be different. When creating a metaphor, test it with the listeners, e.g., "Here's how I would picture that . . . , how would you see it?" or, "We would compare that to. . . . What pictures or images would you have for it?" Believe others when they tell you about perceptions, images, values, and feelings that are not the same as yours. Listening to the images and metaphors of people from a different culture, besides being very interesting, tells you a lot about how to communicate and work with them. For example, a Japanese negotiator observed, "American businesspeople are like hunters. They go on expeditions and expect to fire a couple of shots and come home with a trophy. My people, on the other hand, do business like we farm. We carefully plow, plant, and water and hope for many harvests from the same field."

10. Use visual aids. Keep pictures, models, and diagrams simple, just enough to help the listener to see what you are seeing. Make sure that the images or training materials you use are not so culture-bound as to cause misunderstandings or offense, or nonverbally send the message that your culture has the only right way to see or do things. Monica Armour and Friere Armour have produced an excellent handbook, *Human Resource Development Programs for Multicultural Multiracial Contexts,* for checking your presentation and training materials for cultural bias.

Make these tips work for you, and you will not only communicate more successfully with people different from you, but you'll also learn much more about how you and your culture are unique.

Insights for ESL Speakers

If you speak English as a second language, these tips are useful in a different way. They show how difficult dealing with native English speakers can be and help you avoid some of the traps. These tips will help you talk to people who have not had the experience of trying to speak another language. The authors of this book have all worked in languages other than their native ones. We know how tiring it is to try to capture everything others say. We can't identify the important highlights as a native speaker would. We have struggled to find the right words, wondered when and how to break into a conversation, and been confused by trying to listen to several people at once.

When learning a language, give yourself permission to make mistakes and rely on the good will of others. Let your enthusiasm and your interest in people and the topic override your worries about getting every word right. This is usually easier for those from more loosely knit cultures, but not always. Most native speakers, alas not all, are delighted when you try to speak their language. Unfortunately, just when you start to get good at a language, native speakers begin to assume that you are much better at it than you actually are—flattering to you, but not always practical. Reminding them of your limitations may be unpleasant but safer in the long run.

Language Concerns

Here are some common concerns that people have had about speaking English as a second language, or in speaking English with an accent, when communicating in a U.S. business environment. How many of these concerns do you and the people you work with share? How can you alert others to them? What can be done to overcome these worries? Use this list as a discussion starter.

- I don't want to sound foolish because of my accent.
- I am afraid that people won't understand what I say, or perhaps they won't understand the way I think.
- They must think of me as incompetent or slow because it takes me longer to absorb information in English.
- I worry about making an embarrassing error by choosing the wrong English words.
- I don't want my compatriots to think I am boasting or believe I am better than they are by speaking up or calling attention to myself.
- If I ask for help, others might think me unprofessional.
- Saying "I do not understand" makes me lose face.
- If I ask questions of my boss, I may make him or her look bad or feel ineffective. Or, it may look like I am challenging authority and being disrespectful.
- If I look like I am being aggressive on the job, will it turn into an aggressive confrontation afterwards?
- I fear I cannot do my job well because I cannot read fast enough.
- It makes me uncomfortable to speak up when I have not had time to think through the consequences of everything I have to say, so I avoid activities like brainstorming.

Points to Remember from This Chapter

Breakdowns in multicultural communication recur, not because individuals are ignorant and malicious, but because we make false assumptions about the context of each other's speech.

When differences in background thrust us into a more loosely knit situation, we fail to communicate when we:

- Are not specific in what we ask or promise;
- Do not know whether we have made or received a commitment;
- Do not get or give enough feedback to make sure that the other person has heard us;
- Do not renegotiate when conditions change.

Simple communication, adapted wherever possible to the listener's context, is the best choice when we ourselves speak, or when we must speak with those to whom English is a second language.

CHAPTER 4

MASTERING THE UNSPOKEN LANGUAGE OF CULTURE

*"What you are speaks so loudly,
I can't hear what you say."*

—Ralph Waldo Emerson

Communicating with a computer or a fax, one can push a button and get an identical printout halfway around the world, or even half the way to Mars. Two factors—let's call them "economy" and "diversity"—make communicating with people in the workplace a challenge of a different order.

Economy in Human Communication

Humans communicate so well (and so poorly) because we don't blurt out everything that we think, and we don't listen to everything that others say. We filter out what biology and culture have decided are unimportant for our survival and success. Our bodies are constructed to receive a certain range of sound, see a certain spectrum of light, and to perceive certain sensations and not others. The average person takes in only 25 percent of what is spoken to him or her and actually remembers only about 10 percent. Amazingly, this is enough to function in normal circumstances, but when cultures are mixed this mental economy works against us. So we try to listen better, to take in and sort through more information. What is important to the speaker may be different from what is important to us, or the process is impaired by the unfamiliarity of the words, or contradicted by other information we receive. To discover the meaning of what is coming in we must ask our minds to suggest alternative interpretations, and get and compare more information before drawing conclusions.

Imagine that human beings had a volume knob, and we could actually turn up our listening to the level where we could hear it all. Because we listen, or talk to ourselves, two to three times as fast as we actually speak out loud, we would sound like recordings played at high speed. So we don't say everything we think. We select from a much larger reservoir of inner talk what we will actually say. As we transmit our message in words, gestures, etc., the hearer selects from a like reservoir of possible ways to listen, a meaning that he or she, using the rules of culture and personal experience, finds most likely or useful.

Such mental economy helps us survive. If we did not or could not do this, the opportunity knocking at our door would in many cases have long disappeared, or what threatens us would have done us in before we got the message and acted on it.

Diversity in Human Communication

Diversity is the normal state of human beings. It is the reason we communicate in the first place. If we all sensed and understood the same things, we would have nothing to talk about. We communicate to create unanimity, agreement, and action when there is richness and difference of perception and behavior. Because cultures and experiences differ, speakers and hearers not only may, but almost inevitably will, listen differently even when they say the same word. From the same

VACATION

Figure 4.1. We "listen" different things.

stimulus, we remember or create different sensations and images as we listen.

Let's assume that the couple pictured in Figure 4.1 are middle-class white North Americans.

When this couple talk about taking a vacation, they don't get the same picture nor attach the same value to it. They probably wouldn't get the same picture even if both were men—one might visualize a fishing trip, the other a theater binge in Manhattan. When people come from different genders and cultures, the range of how they listen makes the task of creating understanding much greater. Let them speak in different accents or languages and making sense is even more challenging. Whenever two people talk to each other, three conversations are actually going on, one each in how each of them listens, and a third in what they actually say with words, gestures, tone, body language, etc. It looks like Figure 4.2.

"Of course," you might say, "sometimes people hide their true feelings and say only nice or polite things." The point is that, whether or not we consciously choose to alter what we say, our whole message is never sent, nor is the part of the message that we send likely to be interpreted in exactly the same way as we meant it. What is remarkable is not that the process is so sloppy, but that it is so economical and works so well so often.

Figure 4.2. Whenever two people talk, three different conversations are actually taking place.

When communicating transculturally remember that *the message that ultimately counts is the one that the other person gets or creates in their mind,* not the one we send. Conversely, the message we get when the other person speaks is created by us, and may or may not bear a strong resemblance to what they attempted to convey to us. In the broadest sense, then, *listening* is *our human system's best guess about what is being said and done or is happening in, to, or around us, and its best guess about what we should do about it.* Listening is a basic human function even in one whose hearing or other senses are impaired. Listening is culture at work, helping us survive and be successful in our world and in our work.

Listening and Nonverbal Communication

Listening and nonverbal communication are intimately linked. When communicating, we listen to nonverbals; in other words, we find a meaning for another's inflection, tone, speed and pace, gesture, posture, and so forth, just as we create a meaning for the words they speak. Although we tend to regard language as the main channel of communication, research reveals that anywhere from 80 to 90 percent of information is communicated by other means.

When people from different contexts work together, one individual (MTW) can place more importance on the nonverbal and environmental factors and perhaps even devalue the words, while in another (MLK), the opposite is likely to occur. He or she may be ill-equipped to perceive and listen effectively to the richer context of nonverbal signals and behaviors common to a more tightly knit group. Focusing on the spoken or written words alone, he or she may miss or misinterpret the message the other has in mind.

How to Listen Better

When working within our own culture, we can be incredibly perceptive. We can feel acceptance or rejection of an idea. We can sense when others are listening and when they are not. Across cultures we may read other people wrong and they may read us wrong. The trouble starts when we don't pay close enough attention to what people are trying to say. At work, focusing on getting the job done is important. Under the stress of meeting deadlines and performing tasks, we run great risks by ignoring others, pretending to listen, or only listening selectively to them. Today, when individuals from all over the world, as well as of different ages, gender, and work values fill our workplaces, inattention to people can be fatal to business. Companies who now strive to recoup the "L" (loyalty) word from their employees cannot succeed if managers focus on tasks alone; this is why it is important that you pay attention at three levels:

1. *Pay attention* to both the person and the message—unless you do so, understanding nonverbal and even verbal communication and behaviors across cultures is impossible.
2. *Empathize and create rapport.* Empathy can go a long way, especially with people isolated by visible differences or accents. Feeling that my boss has been or is in my shoes builds a bond of trust and loyalty. Being on the same wavelength is possible even when our cultures differ.
3. *Share meaning.* Share your understanding of what the other person is demonstrating or saying. Paraphrase for understanding and verify the message you're getting.

Pay Attention

Paying attention means focusing our senses and listening to a person to best hear the messages that he or she is sending. We may unconsciously ignore another's messages simply because we are not attuned to them, or because they occur at a level that our system does not recognize as significant. Sometimes we consciously decide to ignore what another has to say, or, driven by politeness or expediency, pretend to listen while we give our mind and sometimes our hands free reign to busy themselves with other things. Our "unh-hunhs," "yups," and nonverbal nods and eye contact may be used to suggest that we are paying attention when we are not. Often we select what we actually pay attention to when the other person is speaking to us. There can be a number of reasons for this. We may be bored, unable to understand, disagree, or even dislike the other person. We may also be preoccupied, pressed by business of our own, or just find it difficult to switch tracks. In cross-cultural situations, four factors may incline us to not pay attention.

1. Unfamiliar Thinking Patterns

An individual from a more loosely knit background may find himself or herself wishing that the speaker would quit talking in circles, come out and say it, or just get to the point. The speaker, from a more tightly woven context, is seen as circuitous, hard to follow, or simply (as has now become an inappropriate word for Asians) "inscrutable." Conversely, the speaker may find the listener naive, simple minded, rude, forward, aggressive, etc. Such unfamiliar thinking and speaking patterns incline us to turn off or pay less attention to a worker who has much to offer.

2. Disruptive Behaviors

One may also find the behavior of workers from different cultures disruptive. He or she may seem too emotional, cold, or excitable, use too many gestures, jump to conclusions, talk to third parties when being addressed, not get along with co-workers, not follow orders, and so forth. One kind of person, frustrated over not being able to communicate obstacles, might simply fall silent, while another will give way to anger, shout, and bang on the table. These behaviors may simply indicate another level of context or different cultural habits, but they make it harder for people to pay attention to each other. They tempt us to ignore others, pretend to listen, or listen very selectively to them.

3. The Need for Extra Help

Today's manager may be beset by colleagues or workers who, because of their weaker language skills or unfamiliarity with the dominant culture, regularly need extra help. This often means changing pace, switching gears, and assisting another with something that feels elementary or unnecessary. Resentment and irritation build. The stressed manager may withhold attention or give as little attention as possible. Unfortunately, this is often done to the people who most need attention. This is one reason many new hires from different backgrounds make less progress and have more difficulty getting ahead in organizations.

4. Strange Accents and Grammar

Getting the message can also be impeded by our unfamiliarity with the speaker's accent. We struggle to get the words and work to put them in understandable order. It is easy to turn off and not listen. While accent reduction courses are available for those whose accent is so different as to be barely understandable, a mindshift about people who speak differently can enable us to listen more carefully.

Those people are a nuisance to talk to because of their accent and grammar.	→	Differences in speech are not only manageable but interesting and add color and personality to individuals.

We may also have to deal with our own stereotypes about accents. When training, the authors play recordings of men and women with different accents saying the same sentence, "Ladies and Gentlemen this is your Captain speaking . . .," or, "I want this report finished and delivered to my office no later than noon on Friday." We ask our listeners to tell us what they hear, e.g., who is more intelligent? Friendly? Aggressive? Competent? This simple exercise shows how differences of accent and gender change how we perceive, feel about, and judge others. If we have a negative prejudice about an accent, or find it too difficult to hear and understand easily, we are inclined to give the speaker less attention than she or he deserves. Accents have also been the stock in trade of comics since long before the ancient Greeks mocked their neighbors by calling them βαρβαροι (mushmouth), the origin of the word "barbarian." Your patient listening will prevent accents from becoming a source of embarrassment among your workers.

When someone speaks in an accent or with grammar different from your own, watch for these dynamics:

1. Stereotypes and even unconscious racial prejudices are immediately triggered: "This person is one of *them.*"
2. We suspect that people with accents speak the language less well or are just learning it. We are tempted to laugh at them, or to treat them as children.

3. We may judge them more or less intelligent or competent than people who speak as we do. Many Americans think a British accent indicates superiority or intelligence and sometimes affect it for that reason. It is not uncommon for a person with a Mexican, Chinese, or Pakistani accent to be judged inferior or less educated and competent than one with a Canadian or Australian one. Outsiders may tag a southern accent as more friendly or less intelligent. Brooklyn and New Jersey accents do not indicate Mafia connections, despite the Hollywood stereotypes. Some languages have fewer distinctions between different words than does English, others have more. For example, Indonesians, who have a single word *dia* for "he," "she," or "it," might accidentally say, "I saw Jane. He went to the store." A German, whose nouns are far more genderized, could slip into saying, "There is a big bowl. Bring her to me." Funny as they sound to native English speakers, such expressions are not signs of stupidity, just clues that the speaker has made the effort to acquire a new language and hasn't yet mastered all the fine points.

Accent and grammatical deviations are not sufficient evidence to confirm any such judgments. A New York waiter and a stockbroker from Glasgow may not understand a single word the other is saying, even though each is master of the English tongue at home. There are many ways of speaking English. Yours is only one of them. If you are uncertain about what is the ideal or dominant strain of speech in the language spoken where you happen to be, radio and television newscasters usually model the most widely accepted version.

Let's now distinguish those efforts that we make to *pay attention* to a message from the efforts we make to *create an appropriate meaning* for the message we receive. We will call the first set of skills "paying attention," and the second set, "listening skills."

Paying attention is thought of differently by different context cultures. Researchers describe some cultures as *monochronic* (Figure 4.3) and others as *polychronic* (Figure 4.4). People in monochronic cultures tend to do things in a linear fashion, one thing at a time. One person speaks, others listen, then speak in turn. Not to do so seems rude or chaotic. *Robert's Rules of Order* is a classic guide for managing meetings in a monochronic culture. Teachers with a monochronic background are often shocked to see how noisily learning takes place in Chinese, or even traditional French, grammar schools.

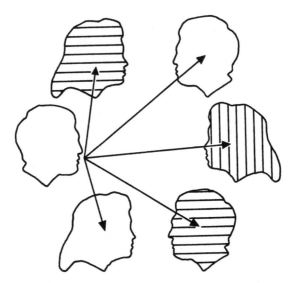

Figure 4.3. Monochronic behavior.

In polychronic cultures, several things take place at the same time. Gatherings in such cultures can look more like "holding court" than they do like meetings. People may arrive at different times and go in and out of the meeting. Many conversations can be going on at the same time. The agenda can change from moment to moment. The monochronic person in such an environment never seems to know when or if anything will be concluded, or if a decision has been made.

Monochronic behavior tends to occur in more loosely knit cultures, while polychronic behavior is more likely to appear in more tightly woven cultures. Managing your attention in another's context can require considerable personal adaptation. Since mixing cultures automatically creates a more loosely knit situation, we will focus on listening skills that work in such a situation. Such listening skills developed in the U.S. (though at times not practiced well by Americans), as well as in English as a second language courses, become integral components of international management culture. Not surprisingly, they can be experienced as acts of cultural imperialism by more tightly woven cultures. When we discuss how to listen more effectively, we will use the best developments of more loosely knit cultures and suggest how to use them in workplaces where diversity has created a looser kind of environment.

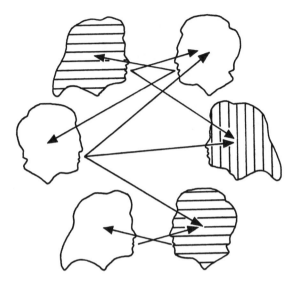

Figure 4-4. Polychronic behavior.

How Much "Distraction" to Allow?

Minimizing distractions can be a first step to paying attention—not always easy on a noisy shop floor, or in the engine room of a ship, or when your desk is cluttered. Putting things aside or inviting the person you are speaking with to a quieter space can help. If you are a more loosely knit group, external distractions may trouble you more than they do those who are used to polychronic contexts. Inviting someone to your office may take care of your own need for privacy or quiet more than it does theirs. You intend to be polite, helpful, and a good listener but in more tightly woven groups, taking an individual aside might be seen as divisive or viewed with suspicion. That person may suffer for it from his or her group. There is no single formula. Your cultural awareness and savvy must determine what works best.

Parroting

The most basic technique for paying attention is repeating back what another says word for word. Such "parroting" works best with very simple messages, or when messages contain important details that the hearer must assure the speaker that he or she has grasped correctly.

Repeating military orders or playing back the directions someone gives you when you are lost are examples of parroting. While most ships today are automated, most of us have movie memories of the captain shouting "Full ahead!" down the tube and the voice coming back from the engine room saying "Full ahead, aye aye, sir." Parroting can also be useful when talking to a person whose emotions run high. It can help establish the rapport you need to move the conversation to its next stage. We will talk more about rapport later in this chapter.

Paraphrasing

Paraphrasing is a second "active listening" skill often taught to managers. It means repeating back to the speaker what you have heard, but in your own different words. This not only establishes that the message has been received, but checks how well you understand what has been said. If you repeat back to me in your own words what I say and it sounds okay to me, we know our listening is at least somewhat congruent. If I object to your rephrasing, we know we have more work to do.

Paraphrasing, useful as it is, can cause problems in a multicultural environment. When one or more parties are unskilled in speaking a second language, searching for the words to paraphrase may be too hard, or the paraphrase itself may cause confusion. The speaker may suspect that she or he has said something wrong, or that the one paraphrasing is trying to change what was said the first time. More tightly woven cultures may see paraphrasing as disruptive or disrespectful, especially to an authority who is speaking. In most loosely knit situations, these skills of paying attention need to be taught and their use encouraged.

Empathize and Create Rapport

To influence people different from yourself, to move them in some direction, you must first establish solid contact. Imagine an engine connecting to a railroad car. The two must connect before one can push or pull the other. Solid linkage between people may not be easy if there is a large contextual gap. Fortunately, you do not have to know everything about another culture to link up successfully. If one establishes a linkage and moves slowly and cautiously, quite a bit can be accomplished. However, violating another culture's essential values is sure to break the link. Neuro-linguistic programming has shown us how to link or establish rapport with others, in ways that are not too culture bound. The verbal and nonverbal cues that people give when communicating reveal their thinking style. If you can read these cues and then match or mirror their speech or behavior patterns, their level of contact and comfort with you increases. The works of LaBorde, e.g., *Influencing With Integrity,* and others apply these findings in detail to workplace needs. Let's look at how to use these techniques to our advantage when communicating across cultures.

Sense Preference Cues

People prefer one sense over another when they think, remember, and when they give or get information. Some like to think in images and pictures, others prefer words and sounds, and even others think spatially, physically, and conceptualize things in terms of feeling and movement. For example, at the Camp David Peace Talks, Anwar Sadat asked to have the draft of the accords read aloud to him, while Menachem Begin preferred to see and read the written text himself. The famous physicist Einstein is said to have first conceived the theory of relativity as something he felt, something he described as almost muscular. If we know the person we are dealing with likes to see things or hear them or discover them in a hands-on way, then we can communicate with them more effectively using their preferred way rather than ours.

A speaker's sense-preference cues may be revealed by his or her choice of words. If the speaker uses lots of images and figures of speech, or says things like, "I *see* what you mean," or, "How do you *picture* that?," it suggests that this person will respond to graphic or visual language. People who focus on what they hear and like to get information that by listening often say things like "I *hear* you," "*Listen* to this," or, "Does this *sound* right to you?" In our work with women and men we found that many women preferred this hearing approach while their male partners were visually oriented. Many a domestic spat was based on each sex using the wrong approach to the other. She would *tell* him things, but he would forget. He would *write* her a note, but she would not notice it. Similarly, a person who says, "I don't have a *feel* for that," or, "Help me *grasp* it," may be telling you that they best deal with information hands-on or kinesthetically.

Without creating inflexible stereotypes, try to discern the preferred way of giving and receiving information of the groups and individuals with whom you work. Then try to match these when you interact with them. This creates a level of comfort and understanding, a linkage or connection that you can use to go deeper into their thinking or to motivate them in the direction that you want to go. Look for sense clues when you listen to others. It will give you the information you need to establish rapport.

Other Body Patterns

Other cross-cultural linkages can be made by patterning your behavior after that of another.

Desmond Morris, in *Manwatching,* observed that people naturally tend to mirror or imitate each other's behavior as a way of becoming comfortable. You may have noticed how two people sitting next to or across from each other in conversation act in tandem. One folds the arms, the other follows suit; one leans forward, the other moves back to maintain the balance; one crosses the legs, the other does the same a few seconds later. Working cross-cultural situations, we sometimes see less of this because we are preoccupied with the business at hand or too concerned about differences to be normal and relaxed. To make better contact with others, we can consciously shift and adjust our bodies to reflect the posture and behaviors of the other as they move, shift, and adjust. These adjustments can connect us to others, just as deliberately avoiding people's physical cues, as we may sometimes do out of strangeness or dislike, may actually prevent or destroy rapport. Lack of such rapport may be the reason we fail to do business with some people, or feel that we don't collaborate well. "The chemistry isn't right," we say, but have not identified why.

Get Out of My Face!

One of the most common and natural adjustments people make toward each other is that of finding the right physical distance. While white North Americans speak socially to each other at arm's length, other cultures may find their conversational comfort zone closer or further away. When a person who is comfortable speaking to their partner from about three feet away talks to a person who insists on being scant inches away from their face, problems arise. The first person feels invaded and may describe their partner as too pushy, and tends to move away. The other may think this retreat signals coldness or dislike. A normal cultural preference for space is misinterpreted as personal rejection, and their working relationship deteriorates. Learning to become comfortable with, or at least to tolerate, others' preferred distance without negative judgments can be a big help. When meeting a person for the first few times, we would recommend you stand at a bit of a distance and allow the other to adjust to you, at the same time observing what distances the other finds comfortable.

Other kinds of rapport can be created by matching another's breathing rhythm or speed. Though this sounds esoteric at first, it is actually quite simple to do if you let go of your own preoccupations and simply pay close attention to the other person for a few moments. This connection gives the individual who makes it some insight into the other's feelings. Once connected, one can more easily work with the other person, or even change the mood.

Speech Patterns

The timing and pacing of speech, as well as tone of voice, can affect how we feel about others and how others feel about us. Big city folk who find it stimulating to talk over the ends of each others' sentences may think people who pause between sentences have nothing to say. Rural folk may be equally judgmental about the glibness and rudeness of city slickers. Deborah Tannen has shown how such differences can annoy and destroy even the intimate relationships of men and women. Recognizing and adjusting to these differences reduces tension and lets us move in new directions once the connection has been made.

Applying These Techniques

At first the techniques for creating rapport may seem like juggling too many balls at once, especially when you have business to conduct as well. You can, however, begin with one behavior at a time, and perhaps experiment more in casual situations until creating rapport starts to become second nature and you can do it while paying attention to other things.

There are a few warnings. First, establish rapport slowly and not too obviously. Exaggeration or mimicry create a negative reaction instead of rapport. Don't imitate the accent or speech peculiarities of another. After moving to a new place or after sustained contact, you may pick up another group's accent, but affecting an accent on purpose can cause the other person to think you are making fun of him or her.

Matching another's tone or voice level can also enhance contact. This does not make it productive to sustain a shouting match with another, but the other's tone can be matched to make a quick connection so that we can move the conversation in another direction.

Avoid behaviors that are specific to the other sex or to a specific level of authority, if you don't belong to that level, in the culture of the person with whom you are trying to establish rapport. A male imitating a woman's behavior may give off confusing signals of effeminacy. A woman imitating men's behavior, as many women do in more loosely knit work situations, could raise eyebrows and cause problems in more tightly woven cultures. Observe and ask questions if you are uncertain. This can spare you serious embarrassment. Likewise, those one level up in a hierarchical culture may be allowed to posture themselves or touch others in ways that are not okay for their subordinates. If you choose to do these things as a political statement, realize that breaking others' rules about authority and gender may have a penalty.

What do you do once you establish rapport? You may test this by changing your pattern slightly and seeing if the other person naturally follows suit. They may not only imitate your behavior, but even agree with what you propose or consider important. Is doing this manipulative? No more so than learning to speak another's language or learning the art of effective presentation. Rapport is just another set of tools available to the good transcultural communicator.

Keeping in mind what you have read so far about the unspoken language of culture, what is your response to the boxed test case?

When Learning Styles are Different—A Test Case

Marie Therese Ridenour is the operations manager supervising the opening of a new luxury island resort hotel. Most of the new staff come from an African nation not far away. She has prepared very good written documentation with copious illustrations for each of the functions that the staff members will be required to perform, so that everyone may refer to them should they forget or become confused. When meeting with the staff, she goes over these instructions one at a time, often

(continued)

illustrating them with role plays. After the training, when the staff starts to work, she discovers that virtually none of the behaviors and habits that she has tried to inculcate are being used.

Here are some of the reasons that could be offered for the failure. Check the one you believe is the most likely. Compare your answer with our comments.

☐ 1. The African staff have compared their wages with those of the non-African staff and believe that they are being underpaid and exploited. This disobedience is their way of showing that they are dissatisfied.

☐ 2. The African culture is much more tightly woven than the manager's. She should identify the native group leader and ask him or her to straighten things out with the rest. This person could make up for the authority that she does not seem to be able to exercise.

☐ 3. The culture she is dealing with is much more oral and kinesthetic than the one she comes from. She should resume training sessions, so that the participants hear the same information repeated a number of times as well as each have a chance to role play several times what they are expected to do.

Here are our comments regarding each suggested answer. Compare your responses to ours.

1. Working for such an establishment, the staff are probably being paid well in comparison to the standard of living to which they are accustomed, otherwise they would not emigrate to take these jobs. Passive disobedience or slowdown could be a higher context tactic to express dissatisfaction, but no such dissatisfaction is apparent in what we know about the case.

2. Though Marie Therese does have authority, knowing and using the authority figures of a higher context group to communicate directions can always be useful, particularly when not doing so may step on someone's toes. However, there is no indication that this is the main problem here.

3. Probably the best answer. The staff's information processing skills and learning style are quite different from those that Marie Therese would find familiar. Repetition, practice, patience, encouragement, and a smile are likely to be her best strategies. When correcting errors, she should use the "sandwich method" described on page 144.

Share Meaning

Ask and Tell

When working with people who are different from you, being curious and open will help you to create common context. The skills that flow from these attitudes are particularly valuable when a breakdown has occurred, because they bring the information we need to move from the fallout stage to recommitment to the surface. These skills are:

1. ASKing useful questions about the thoughts, feelings, and values of others in the situation;
2. TELLing other(s) what we know, our thoughts, feelings, values, and considerations.

ASKing means repeatedly posing powerful, open-ended questions about what is at stake in the breakdown. There is a list of such questions in the left-hand column of the following boxed information. In the right-hand column, there is a corresponding list of leading lines that enable you to share or TELL your own thinking in a useful way to others.

The questions and leading lines in this list are not the only phrases that work this way, but they are good examples of the interest and openness that is helpful in such situations. Many more ways of asking and telling will occur to you. This list, adapted from a previous work (*Men and Women, Partners at Work* by Simons) should definitely be taught in communication courses to those studying English as a second language for use in the work environment. Language training, in its earlier stages, too often teaches people to ask closed questions, ones which suggest a one-word answer, often a "yes" or "no." Though useful for very basic information gathering, closed questions limit our ability to respond to breakdowns and to think collaboratively and creatively on the job. Whether or not you are working in your first language, learning these techniques will be especially useful if you work in a loosely knit environment.

The skills of ASK and TELL help you get the information you need to resolve breakdowns. When ASKing, use the skills of paraphrase that we described earlier to sum up the other person's responses.

Ask & Tell	
ASK ABOUT	TELL ABOUT
HIDDEN CONVERSATIONS *What each of you is thinking or feeling but not saying.*	
What (else) does . . . mean to you? What do you tell/ask yourself about . . . ? How do you feel about . . . ? How would you define/ picture . . . ? What evaluations are you making about . . . ?	I (also) hear myself saying . . . I ask/tell myself . . . I feel . . . I have a sense that . . . Here's how I imagine/ feel/define . . . I've been judging it as . . . I have a gut feeling that . . .
EVENTS *What's happening, going to happen?*	
Has something happened to bring this about? What's going on for you now? What do you foresee/hope/fear might happen? What occurs to you when . . . happens?	Here's what's happened that leads me to . . . What's taking place for me now is . . . What I foresee/hope/fear might happen is . . . When . . . happens, I usually . . .

You can use these *basic questions* and leading lines over and over again in the course of the same conversation to go deeper and understand more. In conflicts, or when you are trying to agree on ya course of action, it will be helpful to continue to ASK and TELL using the categories below.

(continued)

(continued from previous page)

ASK ABOUT	TELL ABOUT
WINDOWS OF OPPORTUNITY *What could come out of this?*	
What opportunities do you see in . . . ? What could come out of this? What (other) changes would you like to make? What do you see yourself doing about . . . ? What do you imagine would happen if . . . ?	I see the possibility of . . . There's a chance that . . . I would like it to be . . . I have a dream that . . . When it comes to . . . I imagine myself . . . It ran through my mind that if . . . then . . .
FAILURES & OBSTACLES *What's missing, or not working?*	
What problems are you experiencing now? In your view, what (else) is going wrong with . . . ? What do you believe is missing in order to . . . ? What do you see as standing in the way of . . . ?	Here's what I see myself faced with . . . What's going wrong or not working for me is . . . As I see it, I/we need to . . . I feel blocked by . . .
COMMITMENTS *What obligations are there?*	
What agreements or promises have you made? What plans or preparations do you have for . . . ? What are your deadlines/limits/debts/constraints? To whom are you answerable for . . . ? What are you working on now?	I promised . . . I agreed to . . . Right now I am involved in . . . I see myself ready to . . . Some of my constraints are . . . I have already asked for . . . I see myself responsible/required for . . . I've already started to . . .

ASK ABOUT	TELL ABOUT
ALTERNATIVES *How else could we look at it or do it?*	
What are the pros and cons/ (dis)advantages of ...?	On the other hand, I see these (dis)advantages ...
What other solutions do you see for ...?	It also occurs to me that ...
Is that absolutely the only way for ...?	Maybe we could ...
Let's/can you brainstorm a bit ...?	Some possible alternatives might be ...
Will you give it some thought?	Let me speculate a bit ...
	Let me sleep on it ...

ASK ABOUT	TELL ABOUT
BELIEFS & VALUES *What differences of perspective or perspectives are at stake here?*	
What is important for you here ...?	Here is what is important/critical for me ...
What do you believe is the right way to understand this situation?	Here is how I would interpret the situation ...
What different perspectives do you contribute to the situation that might be different from mine/ours?	Here are some perspectives that I have, which might add to how we understand or approach the problem ...
How do you usually go about understanding/resolving such issues?	Here's how I generally think/ approach these things ...

Talking About Feelings

Some more tightly woven cultures are quite reserved, so a direct, open expression of feelings may prove offensive. Presenting your request or feeling from a "help me understand" approach helps. Admit to the person who you are trying to communicate with that not belonging to the same culture group makes it harder on you to behave and communicate in the right way. Tell how you would behave in your own culture given the same circumstances, and ask what is appropriate now.

Nothing is more treacherous than nonverbal communication across cultures. More than 80 percent of feelings are shown nonverbally. Sensitivity can run high. Do your homework. Try to find out as much as you can about the culture and the individual with whom you are working. Never assume that your nonverbals are clear and simple. A raised voice or a misplaced touch, arriving at the wrong time, or in the wrong dress, can deeply offend without our even knowing it.

The best response to nonverbal and emotional behaviors is empathy and openness. The use of "ask" and "tell" skills is a good start. In addition, we would recommend that you:

- Don't judge what you don't understand. Ask questions first. When, where, how, with whom, and how often do people behave in this way?
- Don't try to "fix" anything unless it is clear that you have been asked to do so.
- Apologize if you misinterpret or send the wrong message. While mistakes can be costly, some recovery is usually possible.
- Advise those whom you see making such mistakes—its part of a transcultural leader's job.

Sincerity First

Build bridges when communicating with others. Fake or insincere behavior and mockery are extremely disruptive and destructive. They create suspicion and dislike. No one benefits and everybody loses.

It is important, however to distinguish "faking it" from your own or others sincere efforts to learn and participate in a culture different from one's own. When we try something unfamiliar, e.g., learning a new language or eating with chopsticks or a fork for the first time, we don't do it perfectly. Our words and behaviors look affected, not quite right, and may seem insincere. We need both the courage to imitate and learn, as well as the ability to suspend judgment when our own and others' attempts seem more like a caricature than real.

Points to Remember From This Chapter

In the context created by mixing cultures, communication and listening are best viewed as creative processes in which we try to shape a workable agreement that is congruent in the minds of both parties. This works best when we remember that there are always three conversations in every exchange and that the message is what the other person gets.

To manage such communication we need to:

- Pay attention to what is said and done, particularly when differences make that hard to do.
- Penetrate the meaning of the other person's communication with paraphrase and other listening skills.
- Establish and maintain verbal and nonverbal rapport throughout the process of listening and communicating.
- Use the skills of Ask and Tell to create congruent understanding.
- Be curious and open, alert for opportunities to learn and share about culturally specific differences in verbal and nonverbal behavior.

CHAPTER 5

LEADING AND MOTIVATING A MULTICULTURAL WORKFORCE

"Dreams are like the rudder
of a ship setting sail.
The rudder may be small and unseen,
but it controls the ship's course."

—Kim Woo-choong, Korean Businessman

At a seminar that one of the authors of this book conducted, a senior manager asked for advice:

"My youngest daughter is twenty-four. She has just finished school. Not only has she found a well-paying job in her field, but she has become engaged to a young man, who is both handsome and well-to-do. She told me that they intend to marry in September, only a few months from now. My daughter is very headstrong, and I know that while she wants my blessing, she will go ahead with the marriage no matter what.

"Her elder sister is very upset. She is twenty-seven and does not yet have a boyfriend. She worries about losing face, if her younger sister marries before she does. To make matters even more complicated for me, her mother takes her side.

"I would like to persuade my younger daughter to go slowly, to wait a bit. I also want my older daughter to realize that times are changing, and to allow her sister to marry first."

This father's dilemma so disturbed him that he chose it over management-related predicaments as his major case study for the week-long seminar.

A Strange But Familiar Story

This story took place in Indonesia, yet it has a familiar ring to it, a timeless human dimension that provides a powerful metaphor for how many managers experience workforce diversity today. The eldest daughter fears losing her honor and her place in the family. She can be loving, faithful, and hard working, but also bullheaded and petulant in her claims to being first. One part of our workforce is like her, frequently upset with newcomers who are different and want to do things differently. The established workforce feels threatened by change. As a manager you respect, cherish, and care about this elder workforce. It has been here for a long time, and has done and continues to do much good work.

Another part of today's workforce is like the younger daughter, different and hard to understand. While you care about her too, she is less predictable and growing strong enough to go in her own direction, even without your approval and help. You are also aware that you all have much to offer each other if you can preserve family unity and help each daughter to get her needs met. Mother, to extend the metaphor, is like the comfortable traditional institutional or corporate culture. She shows up to support the eldest daughter's position just when you think you are making headway in reconciling the daughters.

The father's dilemma remains your dilemma whether you side with one daughter or the other. You may have deep affinity and respect for the elder daughter, representing the more traditional workforce and its track record. It may be more predictable, more like you. Or, your kinship may be with the younger workforce, the powerful and impatient newcomer. You identify with its needs and are frustrated with the structures and traditions that hinder its progress. Like the father, you are torn in two directions.

Putting on your manager's hat, you realize that each needs to understand, respect, and collaborate with the other if your organization is to have the bottom-line productivity, creativity, and agility it needs to survive and thrive. You don't want to lose what either brings to your organization. You realize that without addressing the predicament of diversity it makes little sense to get on with business as usual. While this is a big part of your job, you also know that this effort must start at the top, and the higher the better. If you are not the CEO, at least you are at the top of what is below you, and can be a leverage point for others. To be effective, you must have a vision of a multicultural workforce.

A Global Cultural Vision

In his keynote speech to the 1990 Society for Intercultural Education Training and Research Conference in Kilkenny, Ireland, Pierre Casse, an international management development consultant, noted that most of us accept that the world is changing and that we have to adjust to the changes. While this helps us cope, the real challenge is to turn that process on its head, to think about what we want to be, and to let that vision or image drive us as we create a common future. Casse cited as an example the dream that Europeans have long had of a Common Market in 1992. 1992 was a vision, a myth—in reality, only a small part of it was to be actualized in 1992. However, the vision, first articulated by Jacques Delors and then spearheaded by him as president of the European Community, had already brought about momentous changes before 1992, because leaders made decisions and took action in the 1980s based on what they envisioned 1992 would be like. However, because of the divided voting results among European Community nations in 1992, the leaders failed to get the citizenry to fully share their vision.

Organizational Vision and Information Systems Must Interact

Casse pointed to the ultimate paradox of our changing environment: We simply cannot adjust our minds to the changes that are going on around us. They are happening too fast. The real challenge is to think about what we want to be, and to create a "global cultural vision" of what we can become. As Roosevelt Thomas, author of *Beyond Race and Gender,* insists, the future belongs to organizations that recognize that valuing people's differences and managing diversity is state-of-the-art managerial practice, and that are able to create a vision of how to make that happen.

Multicultural Synergy

In *Managing Cultural Differences,* Harris and Moran used the term "cultural synergy" to describe how diverse individuals and work units cooperating contribute more than the sum of their individual efforts.

Multicultural synergy may be something we don't know how to do yet, but by having a vision of it, we will create it a step at a time. It is the job of successful transcultural leaders to articulate and nurture such a vision. Organizations and the individuals who make them up must be driven by the hope of success or they will be haunted by fear of disaster. They will either dream dreams about diversity or live nightmares. To the degree that you are a leader, the choice is up to you.

Diversity and the Executive Vision

Let's look at what you as a leader must do (and get your leadership to do) to create a common vision that will not only support your organization's present diversity efforts, but lead it into a successful multicultural future.

We all know what it is like to have boredom, mistrust, or resentment demotivate a workplace, but few of us can picture what it would be like to have an organization where people are excited about and enjoy each other's differences. Imagine knowing that you can always count on finding someone whose experience fills in what's missing in your own. Imagine using the range of skills and perspectives found in our diverse workforce to lead the market in innovative products and productivity. If you were a leader in making this happen, what would you be doing? How would your part of the organization look if you were successful?

The boxed paragraph is visionary language. It offers listeners an image of the future and invites them to share in a picture and contribute to it. Read it once again. How would you create such a vision? How do you make it believable and compelling? How do you find in it not only the glue to bind your workforce together and the fuel to motivate them, but what you need to nourish yourself? How do you make a vision a habitual way of thinking for yourself and others? Effective leadership and charismatic, visionary influence is not an extra, it is the way an organization and its people move from today to tomorrow. While tending the corporate vision is the CEO's chief responsibility, the skills of visioning can help leaders at every level.

The EXEC Formula

Here are the four steps a leader can take to create a powerful vision. We call it the EXEC formula:

1. **E**nter into the needs and aspirations of the people in your organization. Know the important issues of each group.
2. e**X**press how these needs will be fulfilled through the success of the enterprise. Make the future present in the images and metaphors you use.
3. **E**nroll yourself personally in this vision. Make carrying it out your obsession.
4. **C**ommit the vision into the hands of others, and remind them of it constantly, consistently, and powerfully.

Let's look at these steps one at a time.

Enter Into the Needs of Others

Involve the people in your organization in developing the vision with you. A successful vision is based on the real needs of others as they perceive them. To discover these needs, in addition to using formal meetings and processes, make contact and small talk, rub elbows, and look and listen carefully. Then accept what you see and hear. Take people seriously when they tell you their needs and they will follow you wherever you need to go. Some years ago a group of Peace Corps volunteers arriving at a Latin American *pueblo* were appalled by the lack of sanitation. When they asked how they could help, they expected the townsfolk to ask them to fix the sewage problem. Instead the town leaders said they needed a statue of the patron saint for the town square. Wisely the volunteers helped make this happen. From that moment, they had the respect and confidence they needed to work hand-in-hand with the villagers not only to improve the sanitation, but to solve many other problems as well.

Your task may be more complicated than that of the volunteers. Competing and even contradictory needs of many different groups may demand attention at the same time. If you assume that everyone chooses to be a part of your organization because they have a real stake in it, no matter how small, you will ultimately be able to find and articulate the common ground upon which a vision can be built. With this fulcrum you can leverage everyone's stake and move it to the next step of synergy and growth.

How to Talk About Visions

Tavistock psychologist and author F. Emery clues us in on some common human values upon which to ground a vision. While some cultures may have other needs or different ways to express items he mentions, Emery's list shows us what many people look for in their work. In Table 5.1 we have taken his items and put next to them examples of how a leader can speak about them as the common ground upon which to build a vision.

Table 5.1
Common Human Values Upon Which to Build a Vision

What People Look For in Work	Articulating it as Common Ground
The opportunity for variety in work rather than pure endurance.	No one wants a job that is all monotony and drudgery.
The chance to be able to learn on the job.	Everyone would like to do his or her job better and more easily.
Having an area of decision-making that the employee can call his or her own.	We would all like a say in how our jobs are done.
The need for social support and recognition in the enterprise.	No matter where we came from, we all want to be treated with respect.
The employee's ability to associate what he or she does and produces with his or her social life.	We want to know and we want others to know that what we make (do) here makes our world a better place.
The job leads to a desired future.	We all have plans and hopes for the future.

In addition to these common values , the experiences and history we share, the events in which we have participated, both positive and negative, and the conditions that put us in the same boat provide the basis for visions of a better future:

- We all know how difficult it has been for us to work when we hardly speak the same language.
- We have had a painful history of dealing with discrimination problems.
- We were all sad to see how the old policy resulted in a loss of . . .

Glossing over people's differences and ignoring their real needs is disastrous. Highlighting differences, however, can be a compelling way to speak about what we have in common:

- Together we are facing a situation in which some have a lot more power and resources than others.
- Among us we have a great variety of cultures and backgrounds.
- Together we have a rich fund of differing ideas and approaches.
- In our differences we have the potential for using conflict creatively. It's an opportunity for all of us.

Express the Fulfillment of These Needs in a Picture

Jacques Delors's vision of a single-market Europe by the end of 1992, like all powerful strategic visions, was specific and had a time frame. Somewhere there is a picture that expresses what your organization can and will be at a future point in time. It may not start as a detailed picture of the whole organization, but as some small detail or symbol that speaks eloquently for the whole and represents the stake others and you have in the outcome. You must create that first picture, and in the course of time, many pictures. Paint them in words that others can understand. Ask yourself questions like:

- What is possible here?
- If we were succeeding at making it possible, what would it look like? What would be happening? (Get a vivid mental PICTURE!)
- What would your organization or your shop look like if this were happening?
- Who would be doing what? With whom? (Don't leave anyone out of the picture of success.)

- If I were to look at us a year from now, what would I see? Two years? Five?

A vision is not a full-blown strategic and operational plan. It shows people where to aim, not how to get there step by step. That comes later, when people who have bought into the vision are compelled by it to think and act. The specific details of the pictures you draw may change as time goes on, but this should not keep you from expressing them in vivid images that people can see, touch, taste, and smell. The drawing power of an image is its positive nature, its concreteness, and its detail. If you express your hopes for the future in abstract terms, you can be sure that others will fill in the blanks with pictures of their own, which may or may not be aligned with yours. If you start with a concrete vision of your own that taps into other's needs, you can then invite others to build on it. Here are a few examples of visionary statements that could be built into the kind of picture that would direct and motivate others:

- I see a sales staff as diverse as the customers in our area.
- When we walk down this hallway a year from now, we will catch snatches of conversations in five different languages.
- What it would be like if every newcomer to this organization was put under the wing of a manager who knew how to bring out his or her best?
- This will be a place where grandparents and grandchildren work side by side.

Time Factors in Creating a Vision

When addressing a multicultural workforce, the visionary leader should make sure to include images that appeal to the past- and present-oriented segments of the workforce, as well as to those who look to the future eagerly. By and large, the U.S. is a future-oriented society, although perhaps the West Coast, with its here-and-now attitude and concern with life-style, seems a bit less so. Such people value present activities by their future payoff rather than their immediate costs. In a diverse workforce not all people are so oriented. Those oriented toward the present will need to be given far more short-term goals and be motivated by the quality of life they experience while moving toward them. Those from more tightly knit cultures will look for continuity with the past. Knowing which orientation our employees have will help us position our company vision in the right time frame, whether that be a month from now, in a year or two, or in five. Far-reaching organizational visions need to be supplemented by lesser ones; in other words, by clear visions of the steps that lead to the end state itself.

Enroll Yourself

Empty rhetoric is worse than no vision at all. The leader who mouths platitudes about diversity comes empty-handed to the hungers of the workforce and menaces the organization's future; everyone will sense that there is no hope or help to be expected from above.

Leaders who formulate a vision of diversity must be aware that such a commitment extends, as Henri McClenney, Recruiting Coordinator for the City of Seattle, astutely observes, to sharing power. For example, placing diverse people in entry-level positions to avoid attack is not commitment. People respect commitment, not cheap sales tricks; they think highly of service, not self-aggrandizement. Your vision will always be tried in the fire of follow-through. You must place yourself on the firing line by committing the resources needed for carrying out the vision.

Commit the Vision to Others

Your efforts alone cannot change what people say and do out of habit, bias, fear, and small-minded thinking. If your organization is of any size at all, you must enlist others. Entrust the vision to them and invite them to build on it. Recognize and reward their efforts and support them with your influence. Reexpress it in new ways when they tire of it. Make it be your obsession. Then challenge and rely on others to turn it into action steps at every level, in strategic planning, recruitment, training, marketing, career pathing, assessment procedures, and so forth.

More information about the skills and uses of visioning can be found in Peter Block's book, *The Empowered Manager,* and in *The Positive Power and Influence Program* created by Berlew and Harrison.

This short questionnaire in the following box will tell you how well you perform as a visionary leader. You may wish to give it anonymously to several people in your organization and tabulate your score. Then use the feedback and examples that they give you to improve your performance.

Evaluation for EXEC Visionaries

Instructions: In the boxes at the left of the following comments, rank the leadership qualities of the person you are evaluating on a scale of 1 to 5, where he or she:

        1 = never does this
        2 = does it rarely
        3 = sometimes does this
        4 = does this frequently
        5 = does this regularly and habitually

Wherever possible, use the space below each item to give an example to illustrate why you chose the ranking you did.

☐ 1. Creates and uses a variety of pictures, images, metaphors, and stories to communicate the vision of a successful multicultural organization.

_____

_____

_____

☐ 2. Reflects the needs of his or her audience or collaborators when articulating the vision and goals of the organization in respect to diversity.

_____

_____

_____

☐ 3. Shows by commitment of resources as well as by public statements that he or she is committed to what he or she is or was saying about diversity.

_____

_____

_____

(continued)

(continued from previous page)

☐ 4. Personally practices what he or she preaches about diversity when dealing with those diverse individuals with whom he or she is working or speaking.

_____

_____

_____

☐ 5. Instructs, encourages, and supports subordinates to take the steps necessary to broadcast and actualize the vision of multicultural success throughout the organization.

_____

_____

_____

☐ Total Score

How to Interpret your Score

20 or above   *Black Belt—Master of visionary leadership*. You are on a roll, keep up the momentum.

12–20   *Brown Belt—Proficient*. You are on the Quest. Look for more opportunities to test your skills.

7–11   *White Belt—Apprentice*. Keep practicing the basics. Look for a mentor who is a master at this.

6 or below   *No belt—No Rank*. The trousers of your multicultural *gi* are falling down. Enroll in a course, hire a consultant, get help wherever you can find it.

Motivation—What Else is Needed?

Vision is the key that unlocks the door, but managers must regularly step over the transom to motivate their people. Motivation is easy to define: "Getting people to want to perform better." But both in the long term as well as in the short run, there is much to do. People must be motivated to:

1. Join the organization
2. Remain in the organization
3. Learn in the organization
4. Take initiative in their work
5. Generate and contribute ideas to the improvement of the organization and its product
6. Work efficiently and effectively
7. Trust, communicate with, and support others in the organization
8. Make temporary sacrifices for long-term gains

These are not objectives that can be met by one-shot programs. An across-the-board motivational plan based on dominant white-male cultural values alone will not move a diverse workforce. It could, in fact, be counterproductive.

Motivation Begins With Recruitment

Scattershot recruiting can actually demotivate a diverse workforce. As Esty and Wheatly, principals of the Ibis Consulting Group, point out:

> "Recruitment and manpower planning systems are the key. AT&T, in a recent study, learned that within the next 12 years, at least 80% of their new hires would be women, immigrants and minorities. This statistic is typical, yet most companies have not yet adapted their recruitment and sourcing programs to reach these new populations. A few pioneering companies such as Westinghouse, Dow, Xerox and Kodak have realized that tomorrow's scientists and managers are in schools today and have undertaken initiatives to improve the education of those far down in their pipeline."

Canadian organizational consultant Rebecca Chan Allen notes that recruitment needs to be part of an overall strategy in those places where the workplace is not ready to receive this mixed workforce. "They cannot make the kind of contribution they intended." Costly turnover is more likely than ever, because, as Allen notes, today's people "no longer want to put up with assimilationist corporate culture." High-quality employees will now vote with their feet.

Matching the recruit with the job, so critical to motivation, is no longer as easy as it used to be. Not only is there a shortage of skilled personnel for many positions, but there seems to be a great deal of uncertainty as to what, for a diverse workforce in a global economy, are the requirements of many jobs. Recruiters are an organization's first line of motivators and they need to have the diversity know-how for today's workforce. Our sourcebook, *The Questions of Diversity,* included a "Transcultural Competencies Survey" that tried to establish the diversity competencies personnel need to serve effectively at various levels in an organization. Such generic checklists can be customized to enable recruiters and career planners to ask themselves and their candidates hard questions about the diversity expertise needed to do their job.

Interviews and Credentials

Most of the people who will make up the new workforce in the U.S. and Canada will be coming from more tightly woven cultures. This makes it difficult for the recruiter, unless she or he shares a similar background, to create rapport and get the information she or he needs to understand and position a candidate correctly. Recruiters are faced with credentials from educational institutions that they have never heard of, and do not necessarily know how to value learnings and skills that were developed in unfamiliar circumstances. There is a tendency to undervalue what is foreign, so organizations may be losing out on much-needed expertise. People from other cultures will not necessarily know how to tailor their resumé for the job they are seeking, if, indeed, they even have a resumé. Consulting services that specialize in evaluating unfamiliar credentials and work experience can help.

Whereas young American job applicants, who are from the dominant culture, will see an opportunity for self-promotion in every question asked by a recruiter, applicants from some cultures will be prone to understatement and modesty. Jim Kennedy and his associate Anna Everest of MTC Consultants in San Rafael, California, specialize in teaching how to interview in a diverse workforce. They suggest several techniques that will improve the recruiter's efforts:

1. *Use team interviews.* By involving a culturally diverse group in the actual interviewing, the candidate gets a visual and functional answer to often-unasked questions about whether they will fit in and be accepted, find role models, and have a network of support.
2. *Rethink traditionally required behavioral qualities.* Must you have an assertive person, when a quiet, persistent one may be just as effective?
3. *Probe for unseen or missing skills.* If a candidate is uncertain or modest about accomplishments and skills, the interviewer may have to pose questions like, "Have you used this skill in the past?," "How often?," "In what circumstances and with what results?," and "When did you last use it?" to draw out the answers the recruiter needs.

Career Development and Employee Retention

Paying close attention to recruitment gets people in place in the workforce. Then the career development process must take over. This, too, as consultants Esty and Wheatly report, can be problematical in a diverse workforce:

> "Although many companies have developed systems for training and development, these frequently do not work equitably. Social similarity—the fact that we instinctively trust, feel comfortable with and take more risks with those who in some ways resemble us—can wreak havoc with career development. It is difficult for managers to give accurate feedback, or personalized coaching, or risky assignments to subordinates with whom they feel uncomfortable. Managers require a great deal of coaching in this area and the organization needs to have systems for monitoring the subtleties of successful career development, e.g., who's getting chosen for non-routine assignments, special projects, rotational opportunities, training, and conference participation.
>
> "At the formal level, clarifying career steps, providing lateral rotations, supporting mentoring and networking programs, and designing jobs that support skill development are all essential."

Gathering further valuable information about how an organization can attract, prepare, and keep the best of the new workforce is a research project of Ann Morrison at the Center for Creative Leadership in La Jolla, CA. Studying some of the most progressive U.S.-based organizations, she hopes to identify the best tools and methods for achieving diversity, and to recommend specific steps and practices for advancing women and people of color into senior levels of management. The research focuses on the barriers that presently constitute a glass ceiling for such groups, and the approaches that have been most effective in penetrating them. This search for "Guidelines on Leadership Diversity" (GOLD) has recently been published as *The New Leaders*.

Bias and the Perception of Bias

Hansen and Kinnich, in a study called "Changing Diverse Workforce Practices with Behavioral Feedback," identified as indicators of a diversity problem the extent to which each employee perceives bias, the extent to which each employee is contributing all that they have to offer in terms of their talent and expertise, and the extent to which each employee is contributing all that they have to offer in terms of energy and commitment. They went on to show how perceived bias creates "Barriers to Contribution." This bias is reflected when an employee of any background thinks:

- I am expected to fail rather than succeed.
- My opinions, expertise, or contribution is not respected, not valued, or not taken seriously.
- I am an outsider in my work group, department, or organization.
- There is a ceiling on how high I can advance that is not related to my qualifications or the number of openings.

When the Melting Pot Stopped Cooking

Today's manager must squarely face the persistence of differences. As Janice Hepworth, president of University Center, a Denver consulting firm, observes, "For two hundred years the assimilation process transformed selected forms of diversity in America into a culture whose glue was common purpose. Today the melting has stopped as the question of diversity and assimilation is reconsidered." Treating everybody the same used to be the maxim and the ideal when assimilation was either a conscious or unconscious goal in dealing with diversity. In a monocultural, assimilative society the Golden Rule reads "Do unto others as you would have them do unto you." In a multicultural environment the rule now reads, "Do unto others as they would have you do unto them," or you and your organization may be perceived as biased. Now we are required to treat people differently in order to treat them fairly—a much taller order.

This perception of bias more quickly and easily disappears and people become more motivated to perform when they see that their diverse needs are met by flexibility about when and where work is done. As Esty reports:

> "Different work arrangements, including part-time and consultant work, are a means to retain valued and skilled women who are new mothers. Job-sharing, contract labor work, condensed work week, and work-at-home options can support workers who have demanding family responsibilities (either young children or aging relatives). And support for child care is essential; many innovative approaches for support are now available, from consortium day-care centers and voucher systems to childcare referral services and centers for sick children. Unfortunately, according to Department of Labor statistics, only 11% of U.S. companies have actually implemented any of these options."

The Work Environment as Motivator

Changing the work environment to meet diversity needs goes far beyond providing special equipment to enable the differently abled to get a job done most efficiently. Most people spend their greatest number of waking hours at a work site where the environment is barely neutral to their efforts, if not actually demotivating and dysfunctional. While sexual and racial harassment are legally proscribed, there can be many subtle factors that make an organizational environment hostile.

Reward systems should not only address the values systems of the people being rewarded, but can be used by the organization as a tool to encourage managers to develop their diverse employees. For example, Mark Reuben, CEO of Colgate, made a part of each executive's bonus contingent on hiring or promoting at least one woman or minority member. His philosophy, reported in an interview in *The New York Times,* is that "Putting money on the line puts teeth into management's value statements." Where discretionary compensation exists, let it be used to support diversity efforts. In the more loosely knit new work culture, rewards go for high performance, regardless of who you are or what your background. The only bias the transcultural leader has is toward those who contribute best to an effective work team.

Motivational Speaking

Many of us grew up with the parental philosophy of "actions speak louder than words." This is particularly true when it comes to motivating our workforce. How we handle the critical moments of hiring, promotion, and termination will always determine whether the CEO is telling the truth when he or she proclaims the organizational vision or eulogizes at the awards banquet. But these and the hundreds of other occasions when managers are called upon to address their workforce do have their significance. While they are opportunities to motivate, what we say may or may not be moving to those who are listening, particularly if their cultural values differ from ours. As members of the National Speakers Association, two of the authors of this book were in a position to frequently hear professional motivational speakers. These speakers are often hired by organizations to make speeches at sales meetings, annual company meetings, or industry gatherings. Most are masters of motivation American style, and listening to them reveals the fundamental tenants of motivation in this culture:

- People are individuals first and foremost. They are ultimately answerable only to their own conscience.
- Individuals should be free to determine their own lives. They often do this by overcoming great odds alone, or by turning to the help of God.
- The best way to motivate individuals is to appeal to their ego and self interest. An individual should possess an enlightened self-interest; good customer services is a part of this self-interest.

These tenants form the traditional, more loosely knit American mindset harkening back to Horatio Alger, and are religiously echoed in each month's pages of *Reader's Digest*. There is no question that these values motivate powerfully in the right context, but that context is not the only one, and may not even be the dominant one in the workforce today. Those same values fall flat or are even seen as offensive when the values of an audience with a more tightly woven mindset might read:

- We are a people, a family first and foremost.
- Individuals exist to serve and benefit from the common good of the family. They undergo great sacrifices for the sake of the unity and harmony of the family.
- The best way to motivate people is to remind them of their responsibility and duties to each other.

When the audience has these or other, different sets of values, the high-priced motivational speaker or the CEO's annual address, to say nothing of the motivational words that managers use on a day-by-day basis, will fall on deaf ears. They remind the listeners once more that they are misunderstood outsiders. It is true that many immigrants come to this country because they believe in the American dream of opportunity, but even for many of these, the deeper cultural values they grew up with continue to operate. Nor does the myth of being self-made serve the great numbers of women and traditionally targeted minorities well, nor even, as we are now discovering, all white males. The great majority increasingly depend on networking and group solidarity or remedial services for their gains. So, when coaching and speaking, and also when choosing speakers, remember that the diverse needs and values of your listeners must be addressed if you are to motivate or influence them effectively.

Penalties vs. Participation

In too many organizations the positive side of motivating groups who are different has been overlooked, and pressures and penalties have been put in place to keep deviant or disruptive behavior under control. People are told what not to do, but not how to participate. This is particularly true of guest or migrant workers, the people a society feels it needs to use but doesn't want to have. Northern Europe has vast numbers of Southern Europeans, Turks, and North Africans, while Latin Americans populate the service sector of the coastal cities and penetrate the heartland farms of North America. Countless service workers from Asia surfaced as refugees during the recent Gulf War. In addition, the merchant marine exists worldwide, and expatriate individuals of all sorts—people who are willing to endure the hardships of heavy work in an unfriendly climate and in an unfamiliar environment in order to improve their own lot and that of their families back home—are found in almost every country.

Unless management and government understand the values and aspirations of these growing numbers of people, the people in charge will wake up suddenly to find themselves dependant on an alien and alienated workforce. The open-border Europe is both an acknowledgement and a symbol of the world in which, as we noted, globalism and diversity cannot be separated. Keeping people in line may be a temporary expediency, but it is not a long-term solution to motivation and participation. Whether at home or abroad, the transcultural leader promotes the democratic free enterprise system best by modeling desired behavior and by positively reenforcing appropriate behavior on the job.

One area of conspicuous failure in this regard has been the effort to eliminate sexual and racial harassment in the workforce. Civil law and company policy is rarely instructive beyond telling people what they may not do. Under stress, people fall back into old familiar behaviors. Now, more than ever, with what people say and do in training sessions becoming admissible in court as evidence of discrimination, it is necessary for organizations to develop effective educational programs. Training that gives people the skills to work better with each other is needed, instead of just admonitions about what they may not do, mere advice about how to file complaints about each other, and basic awareness of what the penalties are for misbehavior. One of this book's authors, Simons, and his partner made a foray into this approach in their book and training video about *Men and Women, Partners at Work.*

You Don't Have to Change

A new boundary issue has emerged in many workplaces. When people, often women and traditional minorities who are recruited for organizations, begin to say they are uncomfortable about what the organization is asking of them, they are told such things as, "You don't have to change to work here," "We accept you as you are," or "You don't have to give up anything to work with us."

Even though voiced as an ideal rather than as a promise, such a statement is nonsense. Cross-cultural collaboration always and everywhere means changes on everybody's part. Working side by side, pursuing the same processes, and producing the same product always demands that people create a common context, a new culture, which inevitably differs from that from which they came. What is remarkable is not that culture changes, but that it has so much staying power.

Subtle Discrimination and Intent vs. Impact

In corporate EEO and Affirmative Action training, describing people as victims and oppressors is giving way to a deeper understanding of the role culture plays in *subtle discrimination.* Our associate, Diane LaMountain, uses this term to describe the unintended but nonetheless real effects of unenlightened behavior that is likely to disadvantage women and minorities in the workplace. This is distinct from overt and intended discriminatory practices and behaviors. Though the intent to discriminate may not be there, the impact of certain things people do or say may be the same. Here are some examples:

- Someone humors a work group by telling a joke whose punch line puts down a particular ethnic or gender group.
- A manager "protects" members of a disadvantaged group by not giving them challenges at which they might fail, or by failing to give them negative feedback when they are doing their job poorly or incorrectly.
- A peer or superior warmly or affectionately touches the person they are recommending or introducing. This can communicate domination if done to a minority person, and imply sexual intimacy if the person is of the other sex.

From Victim to Actor

A mindshift is in order here as well, for the many members of traditionally targeted classes and their advocates.

I am the victim of a deliberate conspiracy of oppression on the part of the dominant culture. They will not change. They must be exposed and resisted.	→	Much, if not most, prejudicial behavior is unconscious and unintended. People will work to change if they know what they are doing is not working. I can alert them to what is not working for me.

The best person to manage subtle discrimination is the person to whom it occurs. LaMountain recommends approaching the perpetrator, and gently but firmly informing him or her that "When you do X behavior, the result for me is. . . ." If harassment is not intended and the person is approached calmly and privately, they will usually apologize and make efforts to change their behavior. This takes some patience and repetition, as many habits formerly ingrained as polite or friendly are now recognized as subtle discrimination. Instruct your people in the dynamics of subtle discrimination and encourage people to speak up to each other.

The "Ouch!" System, described in the next chapter, can alert us to these subtle breakdowns. Now that we are aware of the extent of diversity and globalism, mechanisms we have used in the past to prevent or correct sexual or racial harassment need to be broadened to cover everyone in the workplace. It is a powerful motivator for multicultural work groups when employees feel empowered to handle the little aches and pains of cultural friction before they get out of hand.

In summing up this section on leadership and motivation, we are reminded of the dentist who was emphasizing the importance of flossing to a teenager. The teen asked, "But do I have to floss all of them?" "No," replied the dentist, "Only the ones you want to keep." Likewise, we might be tempted to ask, "Do we have to pay attention to all of our employees and their differences?" The same answer comes back, "No, only the ones you want to keep!" The critical factor for the metaindustrial organization is to recruit people of competence, regardless of their backgrounds and origins; then to manage them so they may productively apply that competence to their job responsibilities; finally to evaluate them for career assessment and development on the basis of their performance. The corporation or agency or association's task is to capitalize on human assets by developing human potential.

The same may be said of nations who cannot afford to waste their human resources. This is evident in the growing "underclass" who lack adequate education and skills to earn and compete in the new work culture. To avoid greater social disruptions, political and social leaders might devise innovative programs that ensure that *all* citizens be afforded equal opportunity in a post-industrial society.

Points to Remember From this Chapter:

Motivation

- Motivation starts with vision from the top.
- Use the EXEC formula to create powerful visions based on common need, experience, and goals.
- Traditional motivators may be culture bound and ineffective in a multicultural environment.

Recruiting and Retaining Employees

- Matching the recruit with the job requires special diversity competencies on the part of personnel and employee relations staff.
- Today jobs may have to be reconfigured for people rather than the right people being found for the job.
- Identifying subtle discrimination and distinguishing between intent and impact will help you create a congenial workplace for diverse employees.

CHAPTER 6

MANAGING A DIVERSE STAFF

"A vision without a task is but a dream,
a task without a vision is drudgery,
a vision and a task
is the hope of the world."

—From a Church in Sussex, England, 18th Century

Monocultural Management

Most people tend to manage others and to work in ways that are comfortable for them. In other words, they behave in ways that agree with their culture, experiences, and background. What happens when another's comfort is our discomfort? Slowly read the list of behaviors below, one at a time. Pause after each to note how your mind automatically judges a person who would behave in the way described. Then move on to the next item.

What would you think and how would you react if someone you work with were to:

1. Come to your meeting fifteen minutes after the announced starting time?
2. Make an important presentation without preparing notes and visuals?
3. Interrupt you often while you are speaking?
4. Not shake your hand when seeing you each day?
5. Give you compliments and praise almost every time they speak to you?
6. Politely say "yes," but often fail to do what you ask or to do it by the requested deadline?
7. Normally speak at length without quickly getting to the point?
8. Put off making important decisions and then defer them to you as the boss?

9. Fail to respond to a memo or request?
10. Take a day off without notice, and give as an excuse a religious or ethnic holiday.

Chances are that whatever your background, you would find some of the above behaviors disturbing. Yet each item is a normal part of the behavior pattern of a major cultural group. Managers cannot immediately assume that the subordinate who behaves in one or more of these ways is lazy, careless, rude, obsequious, dishonest, incompetent, or irresponsible. That worker may simply not be acculturated to a new working environment. With some patient coaching, the same person may come to perform excellently to local standards.

Recently a group of executives was surveyed about what they found most irritating about others with whom they worked. The ten top irritants turned out to be:

1. Interruption
2. Inappropriate eye contact
3. Taking phone calls during appointments
4. Lack of feedback or acknowledgement
5. Side conversations
6. Completing others' sentences
7. Correcting grammar and word choices
8. Grooming behaviors (nails, makeup, hair)
9. Doodling
10. Sorting and reading mail while engaging in conversation

While the study focused on teaching people what to avoid, it failed to notice that most of the items on this list could be commonplace in a variety of cultures. They would not necessarily mean that the person engaged in these behaviors is busy, in a hurry, or otherwise disinterested in communicating. As we noted, in some polychronic cultures, it would be quite common and not disrespectful for several conversations to be going on simultaneously and to be frequently interrupted by phone calls or people walking in.

What the survey did, in fact, reveal was a set of more loosely woven cultural values common to the dominant white-male business culture of the U.S. Those who have assimilated to this group are linear and monochronic (they prefer to do one thing at a time) in their thinking and behavior. They have a strong need to control both people and situations. If you consider the list again, you may discover that it is this kind of manager who is most prone to act in most of the ways described, and who has to work hardest at controlling these tendencies in his own behavior. Only item 8 is less typically thought of as male, but therefore even more irritating to males.

This survey reveals how hidden and pervasive a set of cultural values can be, and how hard it is to admit that what bothers us is not very different from our own behavior. This has been cited as the biggest challenge in American culture today. It may be at the root both of family crises and poor work productivity. The days of monocultural management—managing by a single set of traditional values—are over. A mindshift is in order, as shown in the boxed figure.

Old Mindset	→	New Mindset
I/we/my kind are at the center of the universe.		We all live in a polycentric world.

A recent *Washington Post* headline read, "Kiss Number One Goodbye, Folks," warning about the economic competition that an isolationist and ethnocentric America can expect from a united Europe. Today ethnocentrism is an economic concern for any nation. The Japanese, as a single-culture society, may have been enormously successful in recent decades, but ethnocentrism hurts them both with the U.S. and with other trading partners. Today, even Japan is having to rethink its attitudes toward foreigners because of its need for workers.

Ted Turner helped CNN, his news organization, make the mindshift to being polycentric by declaring that the word "foreign" would never again be used in the company. "Foreign" employees became "international." "Foreign subsidiaries" would henceforth become part of "global operations." With this single stroke he created a vision of a larger entity to which everybody belonged. "We versus they," without anyone losing their individuality, became "us." What commonly used words in your organization perpetuate myopic thinking? Make a list of them and make special note of any that divide and estrange people from each other. What words can you find to replace them? Ask people who are different from you to help you come up with a full list. After all, each of you sees things differently in a polycentric world, and you can do a better job compiling it together. How else can you affect the way you and others see things so that you continue to value yourselves without valuing others any less?

This mindshift from ethnocentrism to a polycentric world view corresponds, in fact, to a shift in vision. We learn to see through many eyes, or from more points of view rather than through a single set. M. Maruyama, in the *Asia Pacific Journal of Management,* contrasts this as polyocular vs. monocular vision. Some consequences of this distinction in the workplace are presented in Table 6.1.

Table 6.1
Monocular Versus Polyocular Vision in the Workplace*

Monocular Vision	Polyocular Vision
Belief in "objective" truth. Differences are often attributed to error—monocular vision prevails; let us stick to where we agree and discard or avoid our disagreements; do not clutter thinking or problem-solving with too many viewpoints.	Objective truth is neither important nor useful; different individuals have different points of view and that "difference" enriches us with indispensable information; it is important to see same situation from varied views.
Consensus is reaching the same unanimous decision that satisfies all; no adjustment is needed.	Decision-making by consensus aims at agreement that allows opinion or conclusion so that future adjustment of benefits or inconveniences resulting from the choice can occur.
Job rotation on a team is to prepare human substitutes when a worker is absent, or to relieve fatigue and monotony associated with doing same job.	Job rotation's value is "being in one another's head" and to feel mentally connected; individuals in team or worker group are then able to see same situation from different viewpoints.

*Excerpted from *Asia Pacific Journal of Management.* Used by permission.

Installing an "Ouch!" System

The range of differences found in almost any organization today force us into more loosely knit situations where differences need to be noted and discussed to be understood and accepted. When it comes to diversity, according to Bob Abramms, "a critical skill is to be able to tell people when you're confused about their behavior, and then use that as a means to explore cultural differences without creating a confrontational mood." In *Working Together*, one of the authors suggested the regular use of an "Ouch! Technique" to help diverse groups become aware of each other's sensibilities and to talk about their sore spots. It's like having one's toe stepped on in a crowded elevator, not like being mugged. When we say "Ouch!" the other person realizes what has happened, lifts the offending foot, says "Oops," and apologizes, and we all get on with where we're going together.

Once people understand that a great deal of their discomfort in working together results from cultural differences, and not personal-

Figure 6-1. An "Ouch!" system

ity problems or conscious ill will on the part of others, an "Ouch!" system can continue to educate us about inappropriate words or humor, breaches of etiquette, etc., in working groups. We agree to say "Ouch!" and/or "Oops!" out loud when they happen. This brings the discomfort to everyone's attention. Then we can move on without piling up resentments, or if the incident is critical to what we are doing, we can stop to discuss it right away. We can also discuss our ouches later, if they are not critical, to learn more about the sensibilities and preferences of others. Groups without an ouch system can find their agenda being regularly disrupted by diversity issues. Or, minor clashes will go underground, be stored up in resentment, and later explode.

How to Say "Ouch!"

It is important to tailor an ouch system that works for your people and your operation. Some individuals and groups hesitate to say "Ouch!" out loud. Some will take to it once they have found that it reduces tensions and makes it easier to work with people who are different from them. Some will initially resist an ouch system because they see it as complaining or causing others to lose face. Others will be defensive, particularly when they have stepped on someone's toes. Help them make the mindshift to see this as an educational process designed to prevent people from losing face again and again. Less direct ouch systems can be devised for workers from more tightly woven cultures. An ouch box can sit side-by-side with the suggestion box, or be one of the suggestion box's functions. People can jot down ouches and report them at the end of a meeting or discuss them with their mentor. Occasionally part of a staff meeting can be set aside to review ouches. When you design your ouch system, remember that the more time between the event and the ouch, the harder it is to learn from it.

It is also a lighthearted, no-fault way of calling attention to discomfort without making someone responsible for other people's feelings. "The use of feelings [to penalize others] as a trump card, John Leo in his incisive editorial "The Politics of Feelings" in *U.S. News and World Report* points out, "is becoming pervasive. The codes and laws generated by the campus-based race and gender alliance are aimed at real problems, but almost all are disastrously rooted in the demand that negative feelings must not be felt. If they are felt, as is so often the case when the individual collides with the real world, then someone must be penalized for it."

The elegance of an ouch system lies in its ability to keep small gaffes from turning into systemic problems. It surfaces and changes the behaviors of subtle discrimination. It lowers stress, eliminates the feeling of walking on eggs, and lessens much of the culture clash associated with breakdowns. It can even prevent some.

Consultant David Tulin adds these "Do's and Don'ts for Preventing and Handling Intercultural Breakdowns"*:

- Do anticipate cultural differences in *any* new environment—corporate, social, or personal—and expect that breakdowns will occur.
- Don't be diverted or distracted by surface differences that you perceive in others, e.g., tone of voice, style, accent, grammar, physical differences, or personal appearance; rather, judge the merits of what people say and do. See differences for what they are, just differences, not good or bad.
- Don't buy into assumptions about others whom you don't understand. When assumptions do arise, be alert to catching yourself in the process and start looking for alternatives. Your best intentions can be sabotaged by old assumptions and prejudices that sneak in unannounced.
- Do have an open attitude toward what you can learn and enjoy about others' cultures, but don't lose pride in your own cultural identity.
- Do learn about the expectations, values, and communication styles of other cultures.
- Don't be afraid to ask yourself, "What's going on here?," as well as other questions that you may feel are "stupid." A lot of times these are the most valuable questions. They will signal your interest and concern to others and help you to discover, understand, and appreciate your differences.
- Do look for win-win situations, and ask, probe, listen, and consider other alternatives. Learn from these experiences.
- Do commit to learning about the cultures or culture around you. This will give you a broader global perspective and help you develop effective interactive skills in a global marketplace.

*Reprinted courtesy of Tulin DiversiTeam Associates.

- Don't stereotype "cultures" or individuals. Every culture has its ambiguities and inconsistencies, as well as individuals and groups within a culture who depart from the norm.
- Do make sure that an "Ouch!" system is in place and that you make use of it, especially to avoid hot buttons or blunders such as ethnic jokes, sexualized expressions, inappropriate touching, stereotyped job assignments, public scolding, etc.
- Do protect and cherish the diversity you already have. It may be the key to your organization's future survival and success.
- Do be yourself! Allow some personal interaction. "Business only" creates a distance that in itself can become a barrier.
- Do be kind to yourself. Maintain a high self esteem. Understand that acculturating is a stressful process for both the local culture and the newcomers, but also a rewarding and fascinating experience.

"E pluribus unum," The One and the Many

Writing for visitors to the U.S., Esther Wanning in *Culture Shock: USA* has described America's unique individualism with elegant simplicity: "The individual comes first. We do not consider this selfish. A person serves society by living up to his potential." This myth, which drove the frontier settlers and still drives the entrepreneur and the immigrant, is the jewel in the crown of American culture. It causes us to resist restrictions both of personal freedom and organizational activity. Americans may pride themselves on their ability to pull together when they need to, but it's usually for the short term. They give a lot together as long as the emergency lasts, then return to their own private business. This has a down side. Today, when we must respond to long-term pressures of global politics, international competition, and the deteriorating environment, our greatest strength can prove our Achilles heel. Americans have always been reluctant participants in overseas entanglements. Americans still act like there are no limits, though the physical planetary frontiers still resist global cooperation. How can the transcultural leader use the very loosely knit individualism of America in concert with the more tightly woven values of the newer people in the workforce?

First, let us compare these differences in context as Maruyama does in more detail as shown in the following box:

In more tightly woven *Collectivist Societies,* the individual is understood in the context of social relationships, e.g., the family, the organization, the community, etc., and is less differentiated as a self in contrast with others. "We" is usually more important than "I." Failure causes others to "lose face" and results in shame, so it should be covered up and not seen. This mindset predominates in Eastern cultures, and is held by a majority of the world's people.	In more loosely knit *Individualist Societies,* the individual is highly differentiated from others. Growing up means separating from others and becoming more of an individual. Failure is the "sin" of the individual and leads to guilt and reparation. In such a society the collective goals are often subordinated to the needs of individuals. This largely Western mindset is held by a minority of the world's people and is most strongly held among Americans. The mindset tends to be stronger in males than in females.

According to the research of French interculturalist Madeline Cohen-Emerique, this difference affects American workplace attitudes toward people from collectivist backgrounds in several ways:

- Thinking and acting as an individual is a condition of successful adaptation and promotion. The one who takes responsibility personally is rewarded. Proverbs, common cultural conversations that we repeat over and over, are often good indicators of these cultural values. Compare American and Japanese attitudes: "The squeaking wheel gets the grease"—standing up and sticking out are American virtues; "The nail that sticks up gets hit"—maintaining harmony is an essential Asian behavior.
- Individualism becomes a theory for excusing one's own behavior and labeling others and their motives, e.g., "I am exhausted because I have worked so hard; they are lazy."

Furthermore, according to Maruyama, many more tightly woven societies tend toward being "paternalistic" in the worker-employer/manager relationship, while more loosely knit cultures—particularly the trend in America—tend toward "contractualism" (see Table 6.2).

Table 6.2
Employer and Employee Relationships in Different Cultures

In a *Paternalistic Society,* the boss or owner is obliged to support and care for the worker, who in turn owes the boss total loyalty. The power distance between the boss and the worker will tend to be greater.	In *Contract Cultures,* the boss and the worker are independent of each other. They must negotiate and agree upon who owes what to whom. The power distance between the boss and the worker will tend to be smaller.

In comparing Asian and African (MTW) groups with European and North American (MLK) ones, Maruyama has also noted the consequences of these differing values in how groups work together (see Table 6.3).

These differences pose challenges for managing a multidimensional workforce or team that a leader must effectively manage.

Table 6.3
Group Relationships in Different Cultures

Asian and African	European and North American
Groups are networks of interpersonal relations, for the individual to use to his or her own advantage, as well as to the mutual benefit of the members; self-sacrifice for the group is ultimately for one's own benefit; shared responsibility.	Group is a supra-individual entity in which the person sacrifices for the good of the group or organization, for joint advantage, or in the interests of others; individual responsibility to group.
On the job, new employees must establish relational identity with fellow workers and mutually grow—multidimensional.	To be effective at work, each employee performs a specialized function that contributes to role identity—one dimensional.

- Individuals from more tightly woven groups may experience themselves being exploited or ripped off by individuals from more loosely knit groups when they make sacrifices for the group and for individuals in it but do not feel reciprocated.
- Workers from different contexts may expect different forms of teamwork, support, responsibility, helping, advice giving, initiative, etc.
- When dealing with individuals from more tightly woven groups, there may be other stakeholders besides the person with whom the manager from a more loosely knit background assumes she or he is directly dealing.
- There may be a conflicting sense about what is private and public behavior, about who should receive or who actually gets information, or who should be involved in meetings, and about how tools and other materials are used and shared.

Here are some situations that illustrate these differences. What would you do to handle them, respecting on one hand the needs of people from different contexts, while encouraging efficiency and productivity on the other?

1. Elsa, a Filipina, coordinates an international group of specialists in a chemical research and development organization located in northern Europe. She is constantly struggling to get information updates from the individuals to avoid duplication of expense and effort. She feels herself continually upset by how difficult it is both to get the people in her group to report information regularly and by what she describes as the lack of team spirit among the members of the group. Though Elsa's boss believes that her performance is flawless, Elsa herself complains that she is a failure and that her group is working very poorly.

2. The supervisor of a group of machinists is berating Tom, one of his charges, because of the "clutter" the supervisor sees around Tom's workplace. Ishaak, who works with Tom, comes and stands beside him and gets into the discussion. The supervisor dismisses Ishaak by saying to Tom, "Look, I'm not dealing with him, I'm dealing with you."

3. The owner and manager of a small but growing high-tech assembly operation employs a variety of workers from Latin, Arab, and Asian backgrounds. He feels himself continually under pressure from a number of employees to hire or find jobs for both near and distant

relatives of people already working in his plant. He feels frustrated, because despite his repeated explanations of the legal and professional requirements, the requests keep coming.

4. The captain of a merchant marine vessel does not know where to draw the line with what seem like endless requests on the part of some seamen for salary advances because of recurring family emergencies. When the captain asks why the last advance didn't resolve the situation, he is told that that money had to be used for another emergency that arose in the meantime. In most cases, the money is being sent to family members and not being squandered by the crewman. A number of the seamen are in debt beyond their ability to repay because their culture demands such workers support an extended family.

5. Irene has a challenging new position in marketing for an international publishing firm. Sometimes she feels that she is doing everything she can just to keep her head above water. Consequently, she has little time for socializing. She misses out on important information because she doesn't seem to be able to tap into the grapevine. Some people, particularly the group from which she was promoted, have started to speak of her as haughty and standoffish.

6. Luis, a Guatemalan worker, is terrified of Billy, his supervisor. When Luis brings problems to him, it seems like Billy bullies Luis, blames him, and pushes him around to change things right away. If Luis does not bring a problem to Billy and Billy finds out, it is even worse. Luis is not sure about how long he can work with Billy and does not know what to do because other workers tell him that American bosses are like this everywhere.

Using Values to Manage Those Who Are Different

Most managers would agree that they have a set of values by which they manage others. Sometimes these values are consciously and powerfully expressed in an organization's mission or values statement. At other times they are simply the unconscious driving force of an individual manager's decisions and actions, deriving from the culture and experience of the individual and the organization.

We have already seen how important it is for today's successful organization to be motivated by a common set of images and values, which includes diversity. Valuing diversity also means that we respect the values of others when they differ from ours. For example, if I am a manager from a more loosely knit background, I may not value family or group ties in the same way my co-worker from a more tightly woven group does, but I can accept that he or she values it in that way. Then I can consciously incorporate that value into how I communicate, motivate, and collaborate with him or her. There are several steps to this process.

First, *discover the other person's values*. Begin by watching how others behave. When someone chooses or behaves consistently in similar circumstances, it suggests a value at work. However, because culture and experience set us apart, the same value might not motivate me to behave in the same way, or, two people could behave the same way out of two entirely different values. To make a new worker comfortable, for example, co-workers from one culture may express curiosity and interest by asking personal questions, where others would find such behavior intrusive and would try to make the newcomer comfortable by not intruding on her or his privacy. The more you know about a culture, the easier it is to do this. When uncertain, the model in Appendix A will help you understand or ask the right questions.

Filipino management expert Tomas Andres insists that knowing another's values becomes most useful to us when we *identify precisely which value or values are at play in a given situation*. The technique of the Values Clarification movement, developed in the 1960s and '70s can be valuable here. It is one thing to know that an individual values family ties more than you do. It is quite another to recognize that that is the value at stake when that individual is absent from work for what would seem like an inconsequential family event to you. Your tendency is to judge the person negatively by your standards about consistent attendance at work rather than positively in line with his or her standards of family faithfulness.

Because other people's values appear negative when they conflict with ours, or we fail to see how they could be useful in our system, the next step to managing by values, Andres says, is to *look for the positive side of the other person's values*. This means not only seeing how the value functions beneficially in another's cultural system, but how that same value could be applied in ways that are consistent with your values or the objectives of the organization in which you both work. More tightly-woven-group-oriented values, for example, can be very functional, for example, when a manager needs teamwork to accomplish something previously done by individuals. Similarly, in a more tightly woven organization, an individual with more loosely knit background may be chosen for an assignment requiring more isolation and independence or personal confrontation than others in the group find comfortable.

Once this positive side of the value is clear, Andres tells us how to *apply the value to the issue at hand.* For example, when the authors of this book train individuals from more tightly knit cultures, they are often seen as authorities—not to be interrupted and not to be questioned. As instructors from more loosely knit backgrounds, we thrive on a high degree of participant involvement. Calling on our students' own values points out how serious our responsibility is to our own clients (usually their bosses), and how we will lose face if we cannot work with their personal questions and opinions. This creates a values conflict that is usually resolved by giving us more of what we want. Were we to insist on our own values of individualism, directness, and openness, we would simply build resistance and passivity in the group.

Andres says that when people begin to use their values in new ways, the cognitive dissonance can be turned into cognitive resonance, if you *reinforce the new behavior.* Choose reinforcers, recognition, and rewards that the recipients value as such. Culturally inappropriate rewards can actually be punishments.

The critical difference between managing by values and traditional motivation techniques lies in recognizing how differently values function from one cultural group to another. Once we get beyond our ethnocentric disbelief and disdain for how others actually think, we can explore how those values, different as they are, can be called upon to make relationships work and get the job done.

Cost/Benefit Analysis

Many managers are reluctant to approach the new workforce from the point of view of valuing and managing differences, because they fear that the cost in time and money will far outweigh the benefits they could hope to receive. This may show that they are still, usually unconsciously, locked into the old industrial manufacturing model, which prizes repetitive motion and economies of scale. In the new work and market environments that prize quick and flexible response, customization, and customer service, valuing diversity and investing in it are not just added costs of doing business, but the way successful business must be done.

Jamison and O'Mara, authors of *Managing Workforce 2000,* give a wealth of examples and stories of the ways and benefits of treating differences differently. Though most of the managers we deal with need less of the "how to" and more of the "why to," looking at these success stories provides good motivational reading for the hesitant.

Managing Prejudice with American Values

One of the authors of this book recently did an organizational culture survey in the midst of what seemed to be a powerful hate campaign against women and minorities promoted to first-line supervision in a federal government agency. The new supervisors were being harassed by having the air let out of their tires, having offensive phone calls made to their spouses, and other forms of direct and indirect intimidation. The survey revealed that less than 3% of the other employees were behind the hate campaign. From that point on, it was rather easy to challenge the majority with American pluralistic values of fair play and respect for the individual so that they could set organizational norms that would condemn and uproot the abusive behavior. It is a leadership failure when a small, bigoted group is able to subvert an organization by setting biased standards of behavior. Having 3% of a company's employees bigoted enough to create sabotage is still intolerable. Management by values ensures that such behavior becomes socially unacceptable by changing organizational norms, so that all employees are more tolerant and accepting of people's differences.

Guidelines for Dealing
With Culturally Diverse Employees

If you manage diverse groups of people, here is a set of do's and don'ts that should become second nature to you:

- Educate your worker: Some never faced the complexities of the U.S. corporate system before. Explain even the basics.
- Abstract and hypothetical thinking may not be familiar to some workers. Examples, stories, and hands-on experience may be necessary.

- Be patient. Answer all questions, even the ones whom you might feel should be common knowledge.
- Don't assume that all foreign or minority workers are impoverished or deprived.
- Don't take emotional outbursts personally; these may just be a natural way of speaking for people from other backgrounds.
- Accept compliments gracefully and without suspicion. Some cultures use compliments and flattery more often.
- Don't confuse race with ethnic identity. You may end up with a case of mistaken identity. There are plenty of Hispanics with Asian features and plenty of Blacks of Hispanic, Jamaican, and African ethnic orientation who strongly distinguish themselves from other groups, but who may seem similar or alike to you.
- Make time for conversation. The more you learn about your employee, the better you will be able to collaborate with him or her.
- Remind yourself that not understanding others may keep you from knowing what you need to do your own job right.

Diversity in Times of Stress

While the authors worked on this book, organizations around the world experienced three major stressors: the Gulf War, the global recession, and the destabilization of the Communist bloc. All three affected how people managed and worked with people who were different from themselves—immigrants, expatriates, soldiers, refugees, or owners abroad—and produced resentments.

Is animosity and aggression the natural result of difference? We think not. However, the mind is powerfully focused on managing breakdowns. A great deal of our ability to survive is the ability to perceive breakdowns when they occur, or to foresee them, and prevent threats to our survival and well being. So, whenever a difference of appearance or values shows itself, the mind worries about a breakdown in business as usual. Even though the difference could result in a breakthrough, a breakdown of the existing way of doing things must occur before we can take advantage of it. In other words, every breakthrough has a breakdown associated with it. You can't have one without the other.

The way others look and talk, their values, and their behaviors, can represent either threat or opportunity to us, depending on the kind of breakdown we associate with them and they with us. However, when stress is high, our survival or way of life seems threatened and we are prone to either flight or fight. It is hard to see positive possibilities when we are under stress.

The Effect of Global Stressors

The everyday stress of working with differences is intensified by stressors in the national world situation. Under stress, most of us become protective. When pushed, we instinctively resort to our earliest learned ethnic and gender behaviors. Our biases toward those who are different more quickly surface and get out of control.

Fresh from handing out compensation checks to Japanese Americans interned during World War II, the American government engaged in the Gulf War. Again, it showed concern about the potential danger of "foreigners" living within its borders and working in its organizations, this time Americans of Arab descent and Arab residents in the United States. In a cautious public statement, the FBI alerted the nation of its security concerns. First, some of these people could be involved in domestic sabotage or terrorism, or might be sources of information to others who were so involved. Secondly, Arab-Americans and Arab residents could become targets of ethnic hatred on the part of other Americans whose fears and resentments would mount during the conflict between Iraq and the U.S.

Managing security concerns without violating civil rights and harassing individuals is a major challenge both for government and private organizations involved with sensitive information or technology. This concern is not simply paranoia, since industrial sabotage and espionage can take place in even seemingly peaceful times and be perpetrated by other organizations even within the same cultural group. The cool-headed leadership of management is critical at such moments. If security needs to be beefed up, do it, but avoid creating stereotypes and profiles that create undue suspicion about those who are different. This results in paranoia and discrimination in the everyday behavior of employees to each other. Paradoxically, during times of stress, both long-term or old-family Americans, as well as more-recently arrived Americans, immigrants, and visitors from abroad try their best to be committed citizens, good workers, or well-behaved guests. Yet how they look and behave is even more likely to cause misunderstanding and conflict.

Economic downturn, in the nation and within specific industries also stresses our intergroup relations. When the economy is booming and when expertise and labor are in short supply, recruiting and employing minority and immigrant labor seems like a necessary and positive step. When a recession occurs, however, people who are different are seen as part of the problem and are accused of stealing jobs from "our own." Guest workers who are highly visible because they act like themselves, speak their own language to each other, cook or eat their own food in the workplace become irritants or even targets for bias. Managers who see this happening can diffuse some suspicion and resentment if they explain and interpret, to both sides, what is taking place.

Under stress microcultures can dig in and become reactive and hostile as well. Vulnerable, but wanting to avoid becoming targets, they try desperately to be less visible while at the same time working to succeed and to please. This adds more stress. Under such pressure they may give up, retreat to their own cultural patterns, and lose the flexibility to adapt. Their acculturation to the new society or workplace may slow down and even reverse itself.

How Stress Affects Us

Stress focuses us on survival. It readies us to fight or run. If we pay attention to our thinking—harder to do when we are stressed—we hear the more primitive levels of our mind talking to us. We are more inclined to make quick and simple distinctions. Everything becomes black or white. As the old saying goes, we are prone to shoot first and ask questions later when we encounter someone of the wrong color or background. We become more "ethnic," or more male or female, more of what we were brought up to be, and less of what we learned to be to get along with others. Different cultures can even interpret survival differently. Under stress some members of higher context groups may become desperately clannish while some individuals in lower context groups are wildly independent.

Stress can occur at any time. It doesn't require war or recession. A man who strongly supports the women he works with daily can become reactive, for example, when he loses a sale to a woman or is thrown into competition for promotion with his female colleague. Old negative judgments about women and their place, suspicions about how she got-what he failed to get, etc., start surfacing in his mind. Managing stress at times like this means managing the mind, making sure that old cultural messages are recognized for just that and do not turn into angry or unfair words or actions.

Being a newcomer itself is a major stressor. The newcomer to an alien culture functions closer to his or her survival level. He or she also behaves according to the survival norms of the culture she or he comes from, *not* those of the culture she or he is entering, and this may make things worse rather than better.

Since the transition from an old to a new work culture contributes to stress, preventing, reducing, or containing such tensions in the organizational environment is good business. California, for example, is experiencing an unprecedented rise in disability insurance claims related to stressed-out employees. While a percentage of these claims turn out to be scams by fraudulent legal firms, the majority are probably legitimate. To some degree, at least, these types of lawsuits may have been prevented by sensitive management, especially by proper personnel selection, orientation, and training. You may complain, "How am I going to find the time to do the things the authors are proposing?" We counter that if you set a behavior model, delegate properly, and encourage team management, you will have the time for people maintenance, which is at least as important as plant maintenance. Transcultural leaders make sure that enhancing human assets is a top priority!

Managing Stressors

Here are a few tips to follow when stress is high.

- Be aware, and make others aware, of how added stress affects people's thinking and behavior. People who are conscious of how they react to stress can often catch themselves before saying or doing something for which they will be sorry later.
- Coach newcomers about the best ways to manage stress in the culture in which they are working.
- When conflicts arise, and you are involved or must mediate, remember and remind others of the 80/20 rule.

- Above all, manage your thinking. When you hear yourself making negative thoughts and comments about others, say to yourself, "Stop!" Then ask, "What alternate ways can I think about this?" or "What other images, solutions, possibilities can I see here?" We call this technique "The Mindshifter." Some people imagine a big red stop sign to remind themselves to do this. They use stop signs along the road to remind them to think transculturally. One of our clients who wanted their workforce to be more aware of diversity issues put posters on the wall that looked like Figure 6.2.

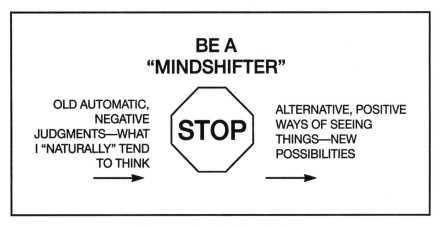

BE A "MINDSHIFTER"

OLD AUTOMATIC, NEGATIVE JUDGMENTS—WHAT I "NATURALLY" TEND TO THINK

STOP

ALTERNATIVE, POSITIVE WAYS OF SEEING THINGS—NEW POSSIBILITIES

Figure 6.2. The Mindshifter.

- Nip trouble in the bud. The damage done by whispering campaigns, wild rumors, and inappropriate ethnic humor may be seen as ways of dealing with tension or letting off steam, but the damage they do often cannot be repaired.
- Keep channels of communication open. Let everybody know what is happening. If you speak a different language, take the time to fill others in on what you discuss with your own group, or ask someone else to do it if you can't.

The organization that continues to tangibly value *all* its people when the chips are down is the organization that will have the morale and the teamwork to not only survive troubled times, but be ready for new opportunities when they arise.

Points to Remember From This Chapter

- Develop and sustain polyocular vision. Try to see the world from many perspectives.
- Managing diversity in the new work culture also means managing continuous change.
- Know what kinds of diversity exist in yourself and in your organization.
- Install an "Ouch!" System.
- Maintain fair standards for all workers.
- Remember that managing diversity is not easy, but it can be rewarding.
- Learn the values of others and use these values to manage differences.
- Be prepared to manage both stress and conflict—be a "Mindshifter."

CHAPTER 7

THE GIFTS OF FEEDBACK

"I am the mountain over which
The clouds of your life must pass.
Storms will spill on my head.
But at the stubborn mountain's center
There is ore you must mine . . ."

—Daniel Bukowski

Feedback—An American Peculiarity

Most of us who are 45 or older, even white middle-class Americans, can recall living and working in a different, far more tightly woven world. Telling it like it is, with openness and directness, especially subordinate to boss, is relatively new, a product of the last thirty years. The Free Speech and the Humanistic Psychology movements of the 1960s marked a change in how Americans relate to each other personally and at work. They have rapidly become part of the essence of American work culture and spread to the new international English-speaking workplace.

Those from more tightly woven cultures now coming to work in North America or for a transnational organization, find it a stretch to give and get feedback and reconcile this with what they have been taught about relating to others. Even quite loosely knit groups like the British are more subtle when communicating about performance, while many Asians and Middle Easterners never confront directly. Now that feedback is a standard part of performance assessment, and integral to our approach to management practice and creative collaboration, how can we maintain its benefits and yet enable other less direct cultures to participate? How can we marry it to the values of harmony and consensus that other cultures can bring to management practice?

127

This chapter is about how we and others have positioned and practiced feedback in such situations.

Feedback as Empowerment

Feedback enables people to know how they affect each other, and how well they perform their tasks and meet their objectives at work. As such, the skills of getting and giving feedback are critical in the new fast-moving, loosely knit work culture. Feedback ranges from the informal comments we make about our reaction to something others do or say, to the formal performance appraisals we give each other. Feedback rightly given and received *empowers* the individual by informing him or her about how to behave in more effective ways, and thus gives more choice and focus to his or her efforts.

Over the past decade, Drs. Walt Hopkins and George Simons have developed a system called *The Gifts of Feedback* that people from a variety of backgrounds can use.

How to Give Effective Feedback

Effective transcultural feedback results from *commitment to our objective and to each other* and *pays attention to the relationship as well as the task*. If the relationship is pragmatic and compartmentalized (more loosely knit), we can place most of our attention on the task at hand. If the relationship is highly defined by factors of authority and harmony (more tightly woven), it will be important to emphasize harmony, respect protocol, use intermediaries, and so forth (see Appendix A).

Learning to give and receive feedback directly will be more demanding for individuals from more tightly woven groups, and they will move more slowly. A good training program will create a context for feedback, so that people from both more tightly woven and more loosely knit backgrounds can attune themselves to it. Here are some principles for cross-cultural feedback that can inform such a program:

- Choose a culturally appropriate time and place for feedback. The sooner the better is the general rule. However, cultural factors may determine whether we give feedback to individuals or groups, to an individual in private or in front of others, in a formal session or informally, directly or using a third party. Likewise, decide if feedback should be oral only, oral and written, etc. Many Germans, for example, are most comfortable when a written message has been sent before a discussion takes place.

- Clarify and declare your commitment to the person receiving or giving feedback, stress the results you are working toward, and the importance of the process of asking for, giving, and getting feedback. *I want your help in dealing with . . . As your boss, I would like to give you some information that can help you do your job better . . . Is this a good time . . . ?*
- Use the *Gifts of Feedback* strategy discussed below and inform your listener of which particular gift you are offering. These categories of feedback are described in the following pages, along with suggested ways of saying them.
- Get feedback on how the other has listened to feedback you have given before you declare the session complete.

The *Gifts of Feedback* is a set of ten categories or ways of giving feedback that balances the concern with task that those from more loosely knit backgrounds have, with the emphasis on relationship, so important to more tightly woven groups. They are positioned as *gifts* because, although the meaning and practices of gift giving may differ from culture to culture, it normally involves respect, reciprocity, and a number of other relationship-building qualities that can be used to reframe feedback as a positive and respectful activity. Here are the ten gifts:

PERCEPTION AND UNDERSTANDING: Tell the other person what you have seen or understand them to have said or done. "Understanding" here means what you were aware of and comprehended in the other's words or actions. It does not refer to compassion, emotional acceptance, or empathy, though these may be present.

The gift of perception and understanding involves sharing what you see and are aware of, not your judgments of good or bad. When reviewing another's behavior or work, tell them in a factual, non-evaluative way what they did as you saw it done. Ask for details about what you do not see clearly and for information you might have missed. With new hires from different cultural backgrounds it will be important to outline what you expect of them relative to their job description, skill development, reporting relationships, and behavior.(See Gift #7, Clear Expectations.)

When you give feedback about another's written reports or communications, tell the speaker or writer what you understand the gist of his or her message to be. Summarize or paraphrase what you heard. Tell what you understand clearly and what you are confused about. This lets the sender know what got across, and helps her or him clarify the content or improve the style.

Starting a feedback session with the gift of understanding, the person will know exactly what specific behavior performance, action, or work is under discussion, and how it has been seen from your point of view.

Ways to Share Your Understanding

- In a sentence or two it seems to me that you are saying/what you have accomplished is . . .
- Your key accomplishments/concepts seem to be . . . [list or quote them]
- I understand that . . .
- You did/conducted/made/found . . . [summarize what you understood to have happened].
- This is my picture of what is taking place . . .
- When you did/said . . . here's what I heard/saw . . .
- What else are you saying/have you done?
- Would you add anything . . .?

 APPRECIATION OR EXCITEMENT: Tell what stands out for you or excites you about what the other person did or said. Tell what grabs your attention, what struck you as graceful, elegant, particularly well done or said, or what you perceived as effective or on target.

The aim of the gift of appreciation is not to make the receiver feel good, though it usually does. People need to know what they're doing right, what works or strikes a cord, or makes others take notice. Knowing this "keep" feedback encourages them to continue good work, do more, or do it even better. Many of us give feedback only when what others are doing is wrong or doesn't fit, is not working, not useful, or when it has turned out other than we expected, requested, or agreed upon together. Even when we must give such "change" feedback, it is advisable to give "keep" feedback first to create both a positive and understandable context for the rest that you want to say.

For most people, negative feedback demotivates and hinders learning and creativity. They become afraid of doing the task wrong. They become confused and uncertain about what is right or useful and hesitate or avoid acting. Pointing to only the swampland does not help a builder find solid ground on which to lay a foundation. Such negativity may entirely demotivate those from more tightly woven cultures. The positive climate created by the first two gifts of feedback conveys your good will, and makes it easier for the person to listen openly and nondefensively to suggestions or criticisms, whatever their cultural context.

Ways to Express Your Appreciation or Excitement

- I appreciate the fact that you . . .
- I was excited by . . .
- I thought you did well to . . .
- I found . . . particularly . . .
- I was moved by . . .

Do *not* follow these statements with a "but" and negative evaluation. Giving the gift of appreciation and excitement forces you to look carefully at others. Allow yourself to appreciate what you see in people and their work, however small it may seem. If you can't find something to appreciate, you have probably fallen into one of the pitfalls of perception described in Chapter 2. Look for evidence of confirmation bias or the halo effect in your thinking. Later gifts of feedback will help you express differing views and corrective comments.

 INFORMATION: Share information, data, or facts that you have that pertain to what the other person has done. In appraisals, contribute whatever data you have that could affect their work or behavior. Ask about the data on which the person based their thinking or performance. Explore whether your data collaborates or conflicts with theirs.

When assessing presentations, communications, written reports, etc., provide any *factual information* in your possession that could support, contradict, or add to what the speaker or writer is saying. Raise questions about the facts that he or she has presented. Cite your reasons for believing differently.

It cannot be said too strongly that the gift of information concerns the realm of *facts,* things that have happened or can be documented, pointed to, and corroborated by evidence you can show. It differs from the next gift of feedback, *Opinion,* in which you share what you think, surmise, prefer, or intuit about a situation.

Ways to Say It

- Here's what I know about the situation . . . How does that square with what you know?
- Do you know this (background) info . . .?
- Here are some facts that have come to my attention. . . .
- Are you aware of this information . . .?
- Here's the data I have . . .
- What are the sources of your information?

It is not your purpose here to bludgeon your listener with facts or make them wrong. If you do so, it is likely they will resist and defend at least interiorly. Offer facts just as you would share any other resource.

Many people in more loosely knit cultures don't give or receive what is called negative feedback because it leads to guilt or blame. In more tightly woven cultures it causes shame, dishonor, or loss of face. By creating a *neutral category* called "information," this gift opens a channel for giving critical information about what is missing or not working in a nonaccusatory fashion.

 OPINION: Openly and frankly share your opinions and preferences as your own. In this gift you share what you think, feel, suspect, surmise, read between the lines, intuit, would prefer, or advise about what someone has done, is doing, or plans to do.

Preface this gift by asking the individual if they would like to hear your personal opinions. In more loosely knit cultures, people don't usually take advice unless they are looking for it. Speak in such a way that the other can recognize what you say as your thoughts on the matter, rather than as facts, policies, or demands. When getting and giving feedback to people from more tightly woven cultures, especially if you are of higher rank, state specifically that your opinion is not a demand or expectation. Do this both at the beginning and at the end of your opinion giving. Preferences are to the heart what opinions are to the mind. Preferences are not wants or expectations. If you want to make them so, use Gift #7, Clear Expectations. Giving opinions or preferences implies that the recipient is free to follow your advice or go in another direction. Stress this if necessary. Disclaimers may be needed until the listener understands that opinions and preferences are just that, no more, no less.

Ways to State Your Opinion

State your opinion in the first person to make it clear to the listener that you are the source of what you say.

- Would you like my advice about this?
- I've been thinking that . . .
- Here are some opinions of my own on the subject . . .
- I'm not, but if I were in your shoes . . .

 POSSIBILITIES: Share ideas and suggestions you have for the other's work or performance. Tell them about suggestions, possibilities, alternatives—anything that would contribute to their performance, task, problem, or communication. In what other ways can it be done or said? What else could be done with what they have created? Offer the results of your own brainstorming and get the other person to brainstorm possibilities, opportunities, and alternatives with you. Point to new objectives that have shown up as a result of what the person has done.

Later you may want to negotiate clear expectations, (Gift #7) but this gift of possibilities opens the door to a set of alternatives that empower the individual to choose what he or she needs to best meet job and organizational objectives. As with opinions, label this feedback clearly so that the other person knows you are *offering* possibilities, not insisting on them.

Ways to Open Possibilities

- When I heard what you said/were doing, the idea struck me that . . .
- Here are possibilities that I see . . . What do you see?

- Have you thought of trying/saying it this way . . .?
- Would this be an alternative . . .? What do you see in it?
- That reminds me of . . . [range of possibilities]
- Would this work . . .?
- Here is something I/you/we could do with that . . .

EXPERIENCE: Tell about your experience with activities or work similar to the recipient's. This is a gift of storytelling. Tell what you (or others) did and what happened as a result of being in similar projects, activities, or circumstances.

This is a hard gift to give well, perhaps because we give it too readily. Most of us have drawn our own culturally conditioned conclusions from what has happened to us or around us. We tell our own stories to enforce our views or keep others from what we ourselves fear. Explicitly or implicitly we say, *"I would(n't) do . . . if I were you, because . . . [story].*

To avoid moralizing:

- Label what you say as simply your experiences. Tell it as factually as possible, separating specifics and details from your interpretation and judgment.
- Invite the recipient to construct their own interpretation and draw their own conclusions.
- Invite them to interview you and ask their own questions about your story.
- Tell third-party experiences only as an invitation to investigate for one's self. Anything else is gossip.

Ways to Introduce Telling Your Experience

- "Let me tell you what happened to me when I did/said THAT (or was in that situation), and see what you think . . ."
- "I have some insights/conclusions/assessments about . . . Would you like to hear how I came to them?"
- "This is what happened to Ho. . . . You could probably get more and better information from him/her."

There is a fringe benefit in retelling your story to someone else. Their questions or interpretation may offer you new insights, too.

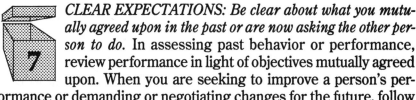 *CLEAR EXPECTATIONS: Be clear about what you mutually agreed upon in the past or are now asking the other person to do.* In assessing past behavior or performance, review performance in light of objectives mutually agreed upon. When you are seeking to improve a person's performance or demanding or negotiating changes for the future, follow these steps:

1. (Re)state specifically what it is you propose(d) to achieve.
2. Show how the past behavior did and did not contribute to it.
3. Agree on both the (new) objective and the means and measures for accomplishing it.
4. Make sure you both understand the same thing. The skills of active listening and "Ask and Tell" in Chapter 4 are critical here, though they are useful for all forms of giving and getting feedback found in this chapter.

With individuals from loosely knit cultural groups, clear expectations reduce stress by giving the individual specific goals to work for and precise standards so that she or he knows when they are being met or achieved. Put such agreements in writing and refer to them in the feedback session. This is *de rigueur* in some cultures, e.g., when working with Germans.

In more tightly woven cultures, contracts and agreements do not have the same finality. A person may agree with you without agreeing to what you ask. They will change agreements for what they think will please you or to satisfy other important relationships. If you want such a person to produce a specific outcome or use a specific approach, insist on a combination of benchmarks and spot checks. Break the objective into measurable stages with deadlines. Discuss breakdowns or potential breakdowns using Ask and Tell skills. Offer support by making clear to the other person what help, information, etc., they can count on from you. (See Gift #9, Support.)

Give feedback often enough for individuals to assess their progress against expectations. This keeps the expectations clear, and offers the chance to renegotiate them in the light of changing feelings, perceptions, or circumstances. Working through expectations is one of the most powerful ways of avoiding and bridging misunderstandings between individuals of differing contexts.

When mixing contexts, continually troubleshoot agreements. Days can be lost over seemingly insignificant differences. For example, an assembly project was stalled for a full day because a worker, told to get a "box" of screws, insisted that there were none—the supplier had started packaging the screws in plastic bags! This individual's desire to follow orders exactly brought work to a standstill.

Ways to State Expectations Clearly

- We agreed that . . .
- Here's what I expect(ed) . . . Do (Did) you agree to . . .?
- Specifically, I am requesting you to . . .
- I ask that we now decide on how/what . . .
- Here's what I asked . . . Here's what you promised . . .
- Can you tell me how you understand what we agreed on . . .?

The more loosely knit the work culture or situation, the more likely it is that expectations will be seen as legitimate only on the basis of an explicit previous agreement. A request must be made, a promise given, and the standards must be spelled out in clear detail. Otherwise, saying, "I expected you to . . ." seems both foolish and unfair. Working together is mindsharing, not mindreading.

Behavior in North American Business Culture

North American managers should make sure that newcomers (almost always from more tightly woven cultures) are aware of and thoroughly understand what is expected of them and the feedback processes used here. What makes perfectly good sense to a North American manager may have to be explained repeatedly for the first year or more to an international manager or immigrant working here.

- Feedback and criticism are normal techniques for managing and developing others. They are not intended to humiliate or offend, but to assist the receiver to enhance his or her professional skills and performance.

- Direct, open, and eye-to-eye talk is perceived as honest and professional behavior.
- Leveling with others and telling it like it is are seen as authentic and constructive behaviors. Confrontations that look aggressive to you may, in fact, be a commonly accepted form of assertive behavior. No *conflict* is intended or understood by the people engaging in it.
- Do not confuse directness with talking down to others. North Americans, even as subordinates, feel themselves as equals and will resent being bossed around or dealt with as inferiors.
- You may be judged on how well you compete with your peers, even with your collaborators. A certain competitiveness is seen as constructive and healthy. Learn what these limits are in your organization.
- There are strict laws and standards that govern what one may say or do to members of the other sex and other groups. These are meant to promote fairness and equality.
- Time is of utmost importance. Individuals who arrive consistently late, people who do not formally *plan* and *prepare* for a business presentation or who forget appointments will be accused of wasting others' time and judged as unprofessional.
- Tasks hold priority over personal considerations and family matters in many circumstances. Your personal concerns may be simply ignored or you may be told that they are irrelevant.
- A woman may, in fact, be your boss, with *all* the implications that this may have. She will expect you to receive directions and feedback from her as you would from a man.
- Superiors, ideally, are supposed to always be approachable. You can ask them for feedback, but you may not ask them to do your own work. This would run counter to another North American norm, individual responsibility—one should always be in charge of one's own shop.
- There will be consequences for not meeting your goals and keeping your commitments.
- North Americans can be quite territorial. Resources and places that look like they may be used by all may be considered private property by some.
- Interpersonal relationships with superiors, peers, and subordinates are on a professional basis. Friendliness and enthusiasm should

(continued)

(continued from previous page)

not be confused with deep personal friendship and intimacy. You may or may not be told directly when you have overstepped the bounds of propriety.

 CREATIVE QUESTIONING: Raise questions that clarify the content or direction of the recipient's performance. Though good questions are often more valuable than answers, humans are more prone to giving opinions and answers even when asking questions. In addition to what you learned in "Ask and Tell," here are more useful lines of questioning:

How to Question Creatively

1. Ask questions that continue to *unfold the story,* ideas, and possibilities in the recipient's performance.

   - *And then what . . .? And then what . . .?*
   - *Do you have other ideas about that?*

2. Ask questions that *reveal the logic,* time sequence, order, availability of resources, etc., in plans and projects.
   - *Which would you do first. . . . or next or . . .?*
   - *How do you think you can accomplish that . . .?*
   - *What resources/help can you identify/count on for that . . .*

3. Ask questions that *highlight the kind of commitment* that the recipient is making.

   - *Are you asserting . . .? (Declaring/proposing/promising/requesting, etc., restate what you believe they are saying.)*
   - How does that fit with what your commitment to . . . or, with what you said before about . . .?

You are not a lawyer goading a suspect to convict him or herself, but a Socratic friend and sometimes gadfly. Creative questions are not meant to be subtle expressions of your own beliefs or skepticism. You are not putting words in other's mouths or planting ideas in their heads, but looking for ways to stimulate them to perform and to encourage them to overcome obstacles.

 SUPPORT: Offer support, resources, and information, to enable the other person to fulfil their agreements and meet your expectations. Effective delegation and commitment to getting a job done while maintaining a good relationship means making sure that people have the wherewithal to perform successfully. In a loosely knit culture where independence and empowerment go hand in hand, support may take the form of loosening control or creating access to resources and information. With people from more tightly knit groups than your own, you may first have to clarify what their expectations of an authority figure are. They may expect you to actually do what you propose when you say something like, "Would it help if I . . .?" when all you intended to do was outline a possibility. When in doubt about the support people expect, ask, "What would a good manager in your culture do in such a situation?"

Ways to Offer Support

- How can I support you to do this?
- What resources can I provide you with?
- Are there obstacles I can help your get around?
- Here's what you can expect/look for from me?
- What do you see as my role in this?

 ACKNOWLEDGMENT: Recognize what each of you have contributed during and after the feedback. Acknowledging how we have been enriched or helped by someone else is a good way to conclude a feedback session. If the feedback session has been difficult, remember that even karate experts acknowledge their opponent with a gracious bow after a bout.

- Acknowledgment adds appreciation to the other gifts of feedback. It may be given both publicly and privately.
- Acknowledge the contribution or creativity of the person to whom we are giving feedback.

- Acknowledge those who have given us feedback.
- Acknowledge those who are the source of our ideas, or who have helped us develop them, or assisted in the creation of a project or product.

Acknowledgement boosts morale in a loosely knit environment. Because people from a loosely knit background are motivated by achievement and not linked together by family or other ties, they need to know that their contributions make a difference, and acknowledgement tells them this. With those from more tightly knit cultures, acknowledgement tells them that they are fitting well into their group and working well with their superiors. Some groups will be embarrassed by public acknowledgement or by being singled out from their group for praise, so carefully choose both the time and place, as well as your words. Whatever the background of your employees, appropriate acknowledgement is one of the principal ways of valuing differences and a powerful key to productivity.

How to Acknowledge Another

To acknowledge another well:

1. Take personal responsibility for what you say. Speak in the *first person* or show clearly that you are recognizing the other person or group.

2. Use the other person's *name* or address the group directly with "you." Here are some ways to start an acknowledgement:

   - I acknowledge you, [name(s)/group] for . . .
   - I recognize (applaud/commend/compliment/ congratulate/honor/pay tribute to/toast) you, [name(s)/group] for . . .
   - Thank you, [name(s)/group], for . . .
   - [name(s)/group], I appreciate/am grateful for your . . .
   - [name(s)/group], You have helped me/us by . . .

3. Be factual, and tell the *history* of what the group or individual has done. A man wants to know more than that he is a nice guy. Women get too many remarks about their figure, appearance, and temperament. Describe or summarize what the recipient has done or

achieved that is worthy of recognition. Brevity will be a virtue with those who are embarrassed by praise.

4. Be *specific*. Acknowledgment is only as effective as it is specific. *"I got some ideas from (you) Terry"* is not as effective as, *"I am particularly grateful to (you) Terry for the information on how to synchronize the visuals with the audio."*

Acknowledgments are not set-ups for requests or criticism. Avoid acknowledgments with a hidden agenda or a "yes . . ., but . . ." quality to them, e.g., *"I congratulate you on the concept, but you could have executed it better,"* is not an acknowledgment. Use other Gifts to express your opinions and set expectations.

Feedback and Coaching

Read each of the following cases, then:

1. Point out the differences of culture and context that might be at work in each case. (Refer to Appendix A as necessary.)
2. Decide on a tentative (based on the limited information here) plan for coaching or giving feedback to the individual. What gifts of feedback would you give?

A. Christine Skoldsvik has finished the first month of a five-month intensive training program at the Philadelphia headquarters of an international bank. While it has taken hard work on her part, it has not been as hard as she had expected before leaving her native Stockholm. She is receiving high scores on her exams, and feels she is doing really well. Today, as her on-site mentor, you asked her to stop by for a minute on the way to lunch. Christine was shocked when you told her about negative comments made about her performance both in and out of the classroom. Instructors had commented on her slowness to participate in discussions and classroom exercises and her unwillingness to work with others. Her peers and the administrative staff described her as indifferent, unfriendly, and even rude.

(continued)

(continued from previous page)

B. Danny Ramos is working as the night security supervisor at an industrial plant site. Danny is alert and hard working with a solid background of military experience and police work in his native Mindañao. His staff consists of two other Filipinos as well as one Anglo and three Latinos. Last week several teenagers entered at a remote point of the yard and vandalized one of the storage buildings. At the next staff meeting, you, as security chief, were very upset and berated Danny for allowing this to happen. Later you realized that you were a bit harsh and went to apologize. It seemed like Danny hardly noticed you were there and made no response to your apology. You thought you smelled beer on his breath, but couldn't be sure.

C. Al Cross, an African-American engineering manager in a high-tech firm, has been sent to a recently acquired affiliate in Switzerland. He is the only American in his department and directs a mixed group of European engineers working on component compatibility. Despite his matter-of-fact, businesslike style and hands-on approach to managing, Al feels he is failing to get his people to report problems to him and keep him advised on progress. Though you find no problems in Al's performance, he comes to you as his next in command to express his worries about the situation.

Coaching and Disciplining Across Contexts

In more tightly woven cultures, where harmony is critical to working relationships, a leader is expected to exercise restraint when a subordinate has misbehaved or performed badly. This doesn't always happen, however, and more tightly knit organizations are full of stories of having been treated badly by one's superior. Such cases are aggravated by the sensitivity to slight and shame, as well as the lack of simple redress in such cultures. In theory, all that should be necessary is an indirect message, often informal or carried by a third party, about the existence of the problem. The recipient is assumed to understand such a message and act on it as soon as it is possible without losing face. In this way the individual is empowered to act.

In more loosely knit cultures, expect problems to be dealt with directly. Involving third parties is looked on as cowardly and weak.

Explicit apologies and new agreements about performance are usually in order, and, ideally, the matter, once corrected, is closed. In more sensitive cases the session may be held behind closed doors; however, lesser corrections and directions can be given in public. The discomfort of being corrected in public is compensated for by objectivity and fairness and the understanding that the process is for everyone's benefit. Parents train children for this by saying, "I'm doing this for your own good." The more loosely knit the context, the more people are expected to be thick skinned about criticism. The distinction between being the problem and having a problem belongs to loosely knit groups.

When a manager with a more tightly woven background first begins to supervise more loosely knit groups, his or her messages may not be sharp and incisive enough to get through to subordinates. While subordinates can be trained to become more perceptive, success is much more likely if the manager can learn to communicate more directly and assertively. Whatever the dominant context, it is almost always more effective to train leaders and managers to change first, so that they can model new behaviors for their subordinates.

Paternalism vs. Playing Fair

In more tightly woven cultures, the manager has more discretion in dealing with a subordinate who is seriously out of line. More loosely knit environments often have set policies and procedures for dealing with specific infractions over which the manager has no control. Should the manager overlook a violation or not apply the sanction, he or she will be responsible for the consequences. These automatic sanctions can be misinterpreted by a worker from more tightly woven cultures, who, even when at fault, expect their manager to be able to lighten or excuse the penalty. North American managers could be seen as cold-blooded for not acting to help an individual save face. The shame of discipline can be so great that an individual or members of his or her family violently revenge their honor on the hapless manager who, from a loosely knit culture's point of view, was just doing his or her duty.

Conversely, employees from loosely knit backgrounds working for managers from another context may be indignant when a manager seems arbitrary in dealing with subordinates. They are quick to complain of favoritism, nepotism, special privileges for older workers, etc., and other behaviors that reflect the values of another culture.

The larger the mix of contexts in an organization, the more important it is to discuss and understand differences *before* a major breakdown poisons the working atmosphere. Formal programs where large numbers of employees are briefed about each others' values and allowed to practice how to behave in each others' cultures and mentoring individual managers who come from other cultures are two approaches. Such information needs to be repeated and reinforced. Our cultural values run deep and we lose sight of how they persist in our everyday reactions toward new groups of people. Empowerment will happen when we lead by using the best of everyone's values to shape a new context for everyone.

The "Sandwich" Approach

When dealing with employees from more tightly woven cultures, coaching and discipline are better received if one uses the Sandwich Approach (see Figure 7.1).

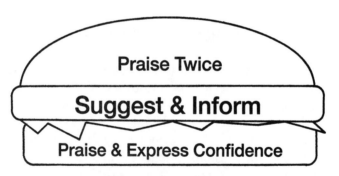

Figure 7-1. The sandwich approach.

Start the session by acknowledging and praising the employee for what she or he does well. Mention several things or say it in several ways. Then deal with the issue in the form of suggestion, to encourage the employee to discuss the issue and ask questions. The gifts of feedback work well in combination with this approach. Close the session with clear expectations and renewed praise and encouragement. Express confidence that the employee can make the changes needed to continue or improve his or her good work. Thank the employee for discussing this with you and for the efforts she or he is going to make.

If you give feedback and suggestions in this way it may not be necessary to get an employee to admit guilt or apologize. With some employees for whom face-saving is very important, it may be inadvisable or even impossible to do so. Being forced to apologize or admit guilt could intensify the shame and cause the individual to become totally nonresponsive and nonperforming, exactly the opposite of what you want to achieve as a leader. Trusting that a gentle reproof will get your message across may seem unproductive to some managers, but success may depend on precisely such behavior.

Dealing with cultures that use intermediaries to give feedback is not a simple matter. Before a manager from a more loosely knit context uses this system, he or she should be very well informed about how it works. Choose the wrong intermediary, and you may create even greater shame for the individual or start a round of gossip among peers that could cause more damage then the problem you are trying to correct.

Using Feedback to Manage Diversity

During 1989 and 1990, Frederick Hansen and Mark Kinnich designed a behavioral feedback tool for managers at Honeywell. Its purpose was two-fold: 1) to establish accountability and provide managers and supervisors with behavioral feedback about how well they manage individuals, and 2) to help division management understand, track, and improve diversity workforce practices.

Executives at Honeywell had two bottom-line concerns about managing in a diverse workplace, which this assessment tool was designed to address. They wanted 1) to reduce the perception of bias—the more employees perceive the corporation as biased against them, the more likely the organization is to lose valuable employees, be in violation of government standards, and be harmed by negative publicity and public protest, and 2) to enhance the employees' ability to contribute—if an employee is being managed ineffectively because she or he is different from the manager, that employee will be less productive. Honeywell wanted high performance—100% from 100% of its people.

The instrument gave managers feedback from their direct reports on four managerial practices that earlier interviews indicated workers from the dominant culture saw as critical to being managed well: building rapport, recognizing individuality, acknowledging value, and supporting development.

The results at Honeywell demonstrated that feedback and appraisal processes can make a healthy contribution to managing a diverse workforce. Sixty-six percent of the managers and supervisors felt that they better understood what managing diversity means, and 88% indicated that they would use the behavioral items on the instrument as targets for improvement. When the instrument was administered a second time, the percentage of managers who rated low the first time decreased, while the percentage of managers rated high increased. In addition, minorities and females had the perception that managers and supervisors held less bias against them. Both of top management's concerns for the project were met.

It makes sense to use the feedback and appraisal to improve how diversity is managed. Most managers want to be better managers of *all* their people. Given information about their performance, they are willing to learn to do things differently. Secondly, objective feedback is nonpolitical. The manager and his or her use of authority is not put on trial between right and wrong, fair and unfair. He or she simply knows what works and what does not, and sees which areas need improvement.

Because of cultural diversity, it is no longer easy to determine one specific set of objective leadership standards that "the good manager" can put into practice to be successful. Relativity and flexibility are the new norms. The manager must 1) use judgment relative to the time, circumstances, and person involved in a specific performance and 2) more than ever before, get feedback from peers and direct reports on what kind of supervision is helpful and not helpful for them. Non-normative evaluation tools are less culture bound and thus more valuable today. Non-normative, however, does not mean purely subjective. Such instruments can objectify feedback and prevent idiosyncratic and emotional evaluations.

A good example of a generic upward-influence assessment tool is PRIME (PRactices In Managerial Effectiveness), distributed by ODT Inc. PRIME enables the employee to tell a manager whether he or she is overemphasizing, underemphasizing, or paying the right amount of attention to what the report needs in fifty areas of management practice. Though anonymous, tabulating the results of the survey in a large organization can show how well the concerns of different groups are being met. Repeating the survey at intervals will indicate what progress both individual managers and the organization as a whole are making.

The primary value of collecting organizational information, analyzing it, and feeding it back to management and employees, is to let the data speak for itself. People can't blame a consultant or executive when objective data is presented representing their opinions, feelings, attitudes, or recommendations. Using objective data, one of the authors was able to report to an organization that about 3% of their workforce were bigoted and disrupting the work environment by inappropriate, un-American behavior. By documenting and quantifying the situation, the consultant was then able to confront employees with, "What are *you* going to do about it?

Drawing the Line

Where do I draw the line when it comes to the behavior or performance of another person that is at odds with the standards of the organization? This is the hard, practical question at the heart of managing diversity, the moment of truth. Many of us have discovered that we draw the line too soon or too late. We misjudge another's performance because we lack information or useful standards, and act out of the biases of our own culture. We are aware of how often we misunderstand, misinterpret, and misjudge, or we suspect we do so because others do it to us. Certain cultures look more easygoing than others, but push their hot buttons and they, too, will draw the line, though they may do it in less obvious ways. At a time when cultural difference is such a delicate topic, don't be surprised that a few people will use it to get away with things that even their own culture would not allow. Likewise, labeling others as culturally insensitive can be a way to take out one's frustrations on them.

A person immersed in an alien culture may feel that he or she must do things secretively or on the sly because the rules of the new culture are either unknown, seem too difficult or unfair, don't look like they will work, or run counter to strong feelings and values. This person and their culture may be seen as dishonest by the host culture. Songwriter Bob Dylan (1971) captured this host culture sentiment when he described the immigrant as "That man who with his fingers cheats, and who lies with every breath . . . who eats but is not satisfied, who hears but does not speak." We need to remember that the seemingly shifty immigrant or guest is a normal human being undergoing severe cultural stress.

Points to Remember From This Chapter

- Feedback can improve the performance of both managers and workers in a multicultural environment.
- There are ways of giving feedback that fit both more tightly woven and more loosely knit cultures.
- Though mixing cultures creates a loosely knit situation, feedback practices may have to be adjusted to meet the needs of the employee with a more tightly woven cultural background, e.g., using the "sandwich" approach to discipline.
- Objective, behavioral, non-normative instruments can be used successfully as diversity interventions in an organization.

CHAPTER 8

REWEAVING THE ORGANIZATIONAL FABRIC

*"The word 'culture' can be applied
to any size of social unit that has had
the opportunity to stabilize its view of
itself and the environment around it—
its basic assumptions."*

—Edgar H. Schein

Every organization that exists for more than a short period of time develops a culture. Deal and Kennedy, in their now classic treatise entitled *Corporate Cultures,* have defined the culture of organizations very simply as, "The way we do things around here." But what makes this "way" successful? As Leroy Malouf, a colleague of ours, insists on pointing out, *"Successful companies have values. They stand for something, i.e., they have an explicit philosophy about how to conduct business. The management spends time in two ways, tuning into (the) business environment, the marketplace, and communicating to (the) organization, with the result that these values are known and shared by all at all levels of enterprise."*

Organizations themselves can be macrocultures with a variety of microcultures coexisting within them. Even before the present surge of interest in diversity, Leonard Nadler, while discussing "The Organization as a Micro-Culture," observed this pluralism in large enterprises, where individuals hold a variety of membership cards in groups and organizations both inside the workplace and in the community. He also noted that people had the capability of changing their behavior according to the group in which they found themselves at the moment. This flexibility is an important part of the resiliency that we need in order to acculturate to each other's differences and learn the "language" we need to enter our common future. This is good news for our multicultural future.

Formal and Informal Systems

In addition, any culture has both formal and informal systems. A formal system, e.g., its stated mission, policies and procedures, structure, technology, and operations, tell its members and the larger society what it is about. Surrounding these formal systems is a vast network of informal systems, less obvious but nonetheless real, which consist of how people see the organization and feel about it, unwritten rules and information grapevines, and networks of relationships both within the organization and with others in its environment.

An organization may be what it says it is, or, there might be dissonance between its stated mission, goals, and modus operandi, and what it actually pursues and how it goes about it. This often happens when managers spend too much time with formal systems and too little with the informal ones. In a healthy organization, these two dimensions of culture are more or less in sync with each other. Changes in the environment as well as changes in the makeup of the workforce will put both informal and formal systems at odds with the real situation. Sometimes leaders will attempt to redirect the organization by simply modifying the formal systems, stating new goals and establishing new policies without managing the informal aspects of the culture itself. In the case of the advertising group we discussed in Chapter 2, the formal decision to hire senior women was a change that was not supported by either the formal or informal structures of the group.

Think of where you work or an organization to which you belong. What are some of the ways things are "done" there? Below is a short cultural assessment that uses some of the themes that Deal and Kennedy point out as significant in organizations. Answer these questions for yourself, and then discuss them with others.

- What are the goals and values of the organization, both stated and unstated?
- How do people show they are committed to them?
- Who are the heroes of the organization, the women and men, living or dead, to whom people point as "real" examples of the organization at its best? What stories are told about them?
- What symbols or images does the organization use to represent itself to the world around it? What are its rites, rituals, and ceremonies?

If the answers to these questions are not very clear cut, if the goals, individuals, and images are not apparent and driving forces in the organization, then the organization's culture is either not well developed, not well defined, or not well managed.

However, having even a strong culture does not guarantee success as a company, unless the corporate core values match the realities of the workforce and the marketplace. Go through the list of questions once more, this time asking yourself (and others, if you have the opportunity) about the organization's objectives, heroes, and symbols when it comes to valuing diversity. Do you come up with a set of answers? Are they adequate for the challenge that the organization faces in the now and future workplace? What is missing? What must the organization do to manage its own culture more effectively in this regard?

The Organizational Fabric

Let's take a look at how the fabric of an organization is woven so that we can understand how to reweave it to meet the needs of the present global economy with its diverse workforce. Figure 8.1 will help.

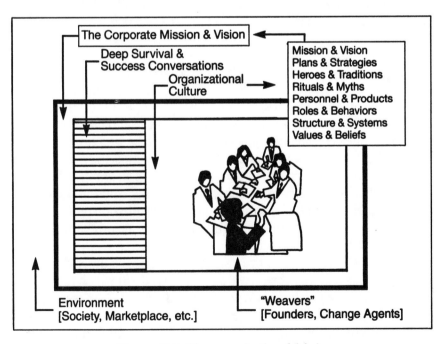

Figure 8.1 The organizational fabric.

First of all, like the tapestry in Figure 8.1, an organization is itself a cultural artifact of a larger society or environment. It comes into being because people need to survive and flourish in their environment. Business organizations are called into being by the opportunities and demands of the marketplace and the economy. The environment, like the air we breathe, is critical to organizations. When organizations no longer serve a purpose in their environment—when the environment changes (e.g., consumer needs, technology, workforce demographics, etc.) and the organization does not—they either adapt or die.

Today, many organizations start with a formal structure, often a business plan that turns into a mission and vision, stated goals, and procedures for carrying them out. Others simply emerge from the genius and success of their founders and acquire a structure as they go along. In either case, the success formulae, or what we like to call the deep conversations for survival and success of the organization's founders, form the basic threads upon which the rest of the organizational culture is woven. Inevitably, the image of the founders gets woven into the fabric of the organization. The enterprises reflects their beliefs, values, and behaviors. These get spelled out and carried out, as we have observed, both in formal and informal ways. The box at the upper right of Figure 8.1 summarizes the main features of a culture.

Reweaving the Culture

On a day-by-day and year-to-year basis, changes do occur in every organizational culture as a result of forces within and outside it. Often these changes are patches sewn onto the surface which we hope will cover the needs that prompted them. Sometimes they do. On the other hand, there are critical moments in the life of an organization when more radical change is necessary; for example, when an enterprise grows rapidly, goes public, acquires another organization or is acquired, or, as we have been discussing, when there are major changes in the markets, workforce, and technology.

In these circumstances, even small organizations must reexamine their assumptions about survival and success upon which the culture of the enterprise has been woven. They must see if their assumptions still fit reality, and, if not, change them and reweave the organization around them. In the box on pages 153–154, you will find a sample of an overall procedure for doing this. Because every organization is different, you will have to adapt and invent strategies for your own situation as you go along, but this example may suggest some broad directions in which to travel.

A Sample Procedure for Reweaving the Organizational Culture

A. Examine the Threads of the Existing Culture

1. Assess Personnel Diversity.

   - Who makes up the organization?
   - What forms of diversity do they represent?
   - What do they need to be productive and successful?

2. Assess the organization's deep culture.

   - What are the organization's survival and success rules?
   - How are they promulgated and enforced?

3. Evaluate the culture in the light of its present internal and external environment (workforce, technology, markets, etc.).

   - What results was it designed to produce and what results does it actually produce?
   - Who was the organization designed to work for and serve? How does the design function to do this?
   - Which survival and success formulae or conversations must be discarded, changed, or created to suit the present objectives, workforce, and business environment?
   - How must the design be changed to suit the present workforce and environment?

4. Identify the "weavers."

   - Who are the power wielders, influencers, the advocates and change agents, the people who can make a difference?

(continued)

(continued from previous page)

B. Weave in New Cultural Conversations, Both Formally and Informally

1. Involve the organization in creating and committing to a new vision (as described in Chapter 5).
2. Anoint or appoint the weavers to weave, display, and celebrate the new culture. Feed, support, and reward them for their labor.
3. Weave the vision into the everyday life of the organization. Communicate not only along established lines, but especially through informal means; e.g., tell stories, cite supporting traditions, hang fresh art, point out new folk heroes, and celebrate new rituals.
4. Set up safeguards to prevent both contamination and permanence.

C. WEAR IT! Apply the new pattern to all systems, decisions, policies, and functions of the organization.

Reweaving a corporate culture takes not days or months, but years. Occasionally a new, perceptive, and charismatic owner or CEO can bring about a major shift or turnaround in values and behavior in an organization. Just as often such would-be hot shots are quickly leveled by the sheer power and entropy found in a large organization's culture. Normally corporate change occurs in fits and starts and then somewhat steadily over a long period of time. Sometimes external consultants, such as Elsie Cross at Johnson and Johnson and Roosevelt Thomas at Avon Products, have been able to shepherd this process in organizations on a long-term basis and report their learnings. In his book *Beyond Race and Gender,* Thomas provides a much larger blueprint for cultural change focused on diversity than we are able to do in this short chapter. What we would like to do is highlight some of the processes that fit into the task of reweaving the organizational fabric vis-à-vis diversity, and then focus on one activity in particular, mentoring, which we feel can make a substantial difference in the transcultural leader's ability to manage in the new workforce.

Organizational Context Survey

Part of discovering your organizational culture involves making a contextual analysis and then asking whether the context of the organization matches the context of the individuals and groups that make it up. Here is a quick, face-value instrument taken from *Managing Cultural Differences,* which you might use to get a feel for where your organization stands. Where would you place your organization on the continua below?

	Mostly	Midway	Mostly	
Democratic	···|···|···|···|···|···|···|···|···			Authoritarian
Informal	···|···|···|···|···|···|···|···|···			Formal
Playful	···|···|···|···|···|···|···|···|···			Serious
Playful	···|···|···|···|···|···|···|···|···			Hard Driving
Laid Back	···|···|···|···|···|···|···|···|···			Competitive
Cooperative	···|···|···|···|···|···|···|···|···			Rational
Young	···|···|···|···|···|···|···|···|···			Old
Emotional	···|···|···|···|···|···|···|···|···			Rational
Open to new ideas	···|···|···|···|···|···|···|···|···			Traditional thinking
Lower context	···|···|···|···|···|···|···|···|···			Higher context

These items relate to many of the more tightly woven and more loosely knit behaviors presented in detail in Appendix A. Turn there to make a more detailed comparison of the dominant culture of your organization and the various groups that make it up. You might ask yourself:

- What are the more tightly woven and more loosely knit features of my organization, its leaders, its workforce? Are there groups with more tightly woven and more loosely knit features working together?
- How do these features either support or hamper creativity and productivity?
- What advantages can I take from this mix in my ideal organization?
- What do the outsider groups (clients, markets) of my organization have to contribute to creating this ideal organization?

- What kind of communication system does my organization now have?
- What kind of system would be necessary if it were to be more productive and work better for everyone?

Deal and Kennedy and subsequent students of organizational culture have pointed out the benefits and risks as well as some of the means of changing organizational cultures. In our experience we find much of this to be valuable for addressing the cultural changes required both by the arrival of a far more diverse workforce as well as by everyone's migration into the 21st century.

Benefits and Risks of Strong Culture

Dr. Mark Silber, in his paper "Corporate Culture: Strategy or Tragedy?," equates obsolete culture with weak culture, calling attention to the intangible power of culture:

> "A strong culture produces electricity in the atmosphere.... People give that 'extra effort' because they experience emotional attachment and a sense of commitment to top management's directions.

> "A weak culture can *prevent* those necessary adaptations to changing needs and community demands and can prevent opportunities for responsiveness to the community—obsolete cultures stress historical tradition and preservation."

Just as having a strong familial or ethnic culture can support an individual's clarity, energy, and sense of self, so, too, people in organizations with strong cultures know what the organization is about and what they need to do to be successful within it. They know what is valuable, do it, and feel good about it. Having a clear mission, goals, rewards, and acknowledgement for their efforts, they work harder and better.

There are, however, parallel risks in a strong culture. This focused energy blinds us to other alternatives. It goes more easily out of date and is harder to turn around when it must face up to changes in the environment. This is why we suggested safeguards against permanence as a part of reweaving the corporate culture. Many strong-culture organizations find themselves in this dilemma when it comes to dealing with diversity. The old values no longer achieve the unanimity they once did. The result is friction and inconsistency as individual managers and workers can no longer live with the old values. If the organization, particularly its leadership, does not take stock of this and begin to manage culture in line with new realities, it risks following the path of the dinosaurs.

Reweaving the organizational fabric is not easy, especially as changes must be made more frequently now than in the past, even when one has an excellent new frame in the form of a clearly articulated mission and vision. For example, after reshaping General Electric during his first ten years as CEO, Jack Welch has envisioned a new level of cultural change for his organization, a company without boundaries, in which inner divisions faded into teamwork that involved customers and suppliers, as well as employees. Such a company, he felt, could be "at home" anyplace in the world. (Reported in *The Economist.*)

Leaders like Welch get the reputation of both brilliance and ruthlessness for their attempts to restructure both organizationally and ideologically. Being a transcultural leader requires courage and endurance as well as savvy about what works when managing culture.

The Making and Unmaking of Corporate Heroes

An outside observer of the contemporary American scene would surely remark about the fleetingness of fame. Heroes come and go, are made and broken, month by month. Does this make having heroes inconsequential? Hardly. It impresses us with how significant a function heroes play in a more loosely knit society where fewer rules of culture are commonly understood. So, too, in organizations, the heroes we venerate can either support intransigence or model flexibility and responsiveness to new situations. Leadership can both provide such heroism by its own behavior, and create the heroes in its workforce by whom it chooses to acknowledge and reward. Such heroism is powerful because, as Deal and Kennedy observe, heroes make success both attainable and human. They are the role models who set performance standards, and by their very presence motivate other employees to reach for them. If an organization's vision and mission are clear, particularly in the area of diversity, then such heroes can emerge and be acclaimed by their coworkers and recognized and rewarded by management. Where they have the competence, it may be a very good move to make such heroes weavers by putting them in charge of important parts of the culture change toward which the company is moving.

Heroes are usually singled out because they are creative in moments of crisis. Consequently, this is the kind of behavior their presence inspires in others. In many organizations, this unifying force is needed to help workers focus on creativity and draw them away from both the helplessness of victims and from vicious intergroup competition.

Telling Stories

An organization's culture is powerfully affected by the stories that circulate within it. While proposals can be debated and rationalized, stories have a symbolic power that resists dilution. Sylvester Taylor and Luke Novelli, in a recent article entitled "Telling a Story About Innovation," help us understand that symbolic power:

"Think of a recent event in your organization, such as a project, task force, celebration, or the like. What meaning did people give the event? Was it seen as being a symbol of some quality of the organization, such as its effectiveness, its values, or its creativity? Did people say, "That project shows how quickly we can adapt to market changes" or something similar? If so, people were giving meaning to the event. It stood for something, either good or bad, about your organization."

The same authors also provide us, as communicators, with a quick formula for tapping into that power to create meaning and support innovation and productivity in an organization. They point out that: They point out the qualities that a good story should possess when one has the task of effectively getting a message across within an organization:

- *Disseminate it widely.* Simply put, the story has to make the rounds if it's going to influence the people it's intended for. Each listener has to know that other people are familiar with the story and believe it. When this is the case, the story will be repeated, talked about, and grow in importance.
- *Make it vivid.* A story will come alive in the minds of the listeners if it concerns real people and the time and place of occurrence are made

clear. Vividness makes the story credible and memorable. The more descriptive and colorful the language, the better.

- *Make it instructive.* The storyteller must provide enough detail to make the story complete, and suggest how how the listeners ought to behave in the light of the story. The listener is inspired when the story defines a context for her or his own behavior.
- *Make it special.* The listener should draw the conclusion that this organization is unique among workplaces and they, by virtue of working here, are very special people. In this way they make the concepts, attitudes, and values of the story their own.

Productivity and innovation in many organizations are thwarted by the fact that people reinforce debilitating stereotypes with horror stories about people who are different, or about diversity efforts themselves. Despite the authors' commitment to effective training in this field, we would be the first to acknowledge that a few good stories, well told, could eliminate the need for hundreds of hours of training in many organizations.

Choreographing Culture Change

Some leaders are masters at reweaving culture change. The tools of culture change, like most others, can be used for good or ill, so it is important to probe and test one's core values along the way. This is not easy in the heat of the day. The framers of the Declaration of Independence, though we see them as patriots today, risked death for treason and had to wrestle with their consciences in choosing the course of independence. The orchestration of the culture change that turned Germany from a divided and depression-ridden nation into the Third Reich through the efforts of Hitler, Goebbels, and artists such as Leni Reifenstahl was a masterpiece of change, but with a violently ethnocentric core. One can still look at their propaganda images and be thrilled by them despite knowing the historical consequences. Both freedom and fascism can be found in organizations as well as nations, especially today when, despite a more sophisticated public, the media are infinitely more powerful in creating images and reinforcing values than they were half a century ago.

Managing productivity through culture is a leader's job, and its tools must be handled with supreme probity. One of the authors of this book frequently works in the Republic of Singapore and is repeatedly struck with how successful that nation has been if one thinks of it primarily as a corporation. Guided by strong and extraordinarily incorruptible leadership, with productivity as a cultural priority, it has encouraged both intrapreneurship and entrepreneurship, as well as alliances and partnerships of mutual benefit. Critics cite lack of certain freedoms in that tiny nation state, and this is true if one compares it with American political standards, but certainly not if one compares it with many corporate structures.

Politicians are expert at manipulating their constituencies by alerting them to threats, especially threats from outsiders. Outside forces, or those who are different, such as migrant workers, infiltrators, gay people, immigrants, males, and so forth, often become politicians' targets. Today's manager must unite people against both outside threats and internal ones in ways that support the reality of diversity. Competition can be used as an excuse to heap abuse on the Japanese or some other group along racial or other cultural lines, or as a prod to look at how we can become more productive and competitive. Leaders must zoom in on prejudice, lack of education and skills, unfair practices, and poor management as the real threats. Take charge of change rather than being its victim. Empower your workforce and enhance its skills.

Images, Visions, and Continuity

Some changes can become symbolic as well as real transitions to the new culture. Acquiring a new subsidiary that reflects the new values, redecorating, or even moving the plant or offices tell people that transition is under way. We know of one CEO who decided to make sure that there was always scaffolding moving around the outside of the 100-year-old main office, to make sure that everyone knew that change was in progress, even though it wasn't always physical construction.

The more tightly woven the environment, the more the need for a sense of underlying continuity in order for the organization to transition smoothly from the old to the new organizational culture. In any culture, many workers look for some degree of security and continuity. While in the American workplace it has been easy to dismiss workers when an acquisition, downturn, or culture change effort takes place, this is not so in most places in the world. When layoffs must occur, culture change efforts might be postponed until such layoffs are completed. It is important to assure workers that their jobs are not at stake when trying to support them in making other major changes. In one organization attempting to introduce a new, more participative, flexible, and creative work culture, we heard a top-level manager announce to a plant-site meeting, "You have until the end of the year to get with the new culture, or you are out of here." Culture changes take time and persistence, and leaders who model what they preach are most successful. Culture can be changed by a vision, but not mandated. People who believe in the vision will still need to work out their own picture of what it will mean for them. The best managers keep the vision alive and talk about it daily, but not so rigidly that others cannot find their own ways of expressing its values and visioning its outcomes, especially when workforces are as diverse as they are today. As Deal and Kennedy pointed out, peer group consensus is the major influence for the acceptance of change. Mandated change does not increase trust and reliance on each other and makes this more, rather than less, difficult to come by.

Leading and managing cultural change means managing your own thinking and helping others to think in new ways. People need to be taught what to value, how to behave, and how to make new distinctions and talk intelligently about them if change is to succeed. They need modeling and heroes, stories and information, hands-on effort and good coaching. Both leaders and workforce may need the perspectives brought by outside help, consultants, speakers, and trainers in order to handle transitions well.

When undertaking cultural change in a diverse organization, as most organizations are today, it is essential that everyone be involved. Today, given the demographics of the new workforce a *minority* can be redefined as *a group of people who do not have a hand in shaping the culture in which they work.* Often the insights for new directions begin at the bottom of the organization where the "rubber meets the road." From there an idea for change begins a painful process of working its way up to the top where, in particularly entrenched organizations, the leadership may resist. It may also come from the stockholders or, in public organizations, the variety of stakeholders, who insist on a change of leadership. Changes of leadership are often designed to rid the organization of a recalcitrant leader, rather than converting them. For those interested in further information on this subject, consult the chapter and survey instrument on organizational culture in *Managing Cultural Differences* (Chapter 6/Appendix D).

Mentoring in a Multicultural Workforce

The culture of an organization is passed on primarily in the relationships of people to each other. Mentoring can be a powerful tool for culture change and culture transfer from one generation of management to another. In a diverse workforce it serves not only to acculturate the newcomer, but also to make the mentor aware of her or his values and those of the organization, with the result that the mentoring process, if properly structured and carried out, can be one of the most potent forces for reweaving the organizational culture, especially where rapid change in the new workforce makes generations of managers come and go in a matter of months rather than years.

Everyone in an organization can personally and professionally benefit from being mentored at different stages in their career. *Informal mentoring* begins when an experienced employee takes an active interest in a newcomer, or the newcomer approaches the more experienced one for information or help. If the chemistry is right, a productive relationship can begin. The active interest of the mentor and the person being mentored in each other continues until its purpose is exhausted and the relationship ends. In *formal mentoring,* the organization itself matches individuals, and sets expectations for what should be accomplished.

What to Expect From Mentoring in a Multicultural Environment

Mentoring should help make the transition from background, home, and education to work life, from outside to inside. It helps people acculturate. Two of this book's authors regularly teach visiting international professionals how to learn, work, and relate to others in a U.S. business environment, after which the international professionals are assigned to seasoned American managers who will mentor them through the rest of their stay.

American managers commonly assume that those individuals who have studied for a time in the U.S. will be familiar and comfortable with work life here. This is almost always not true. Going from education to work life is hard enough for native-born individuals, and almost always a major transition for those who are not. Students have a system to help them live and learn, but full-time workers may live alone with little, if any, support. As workers, they may be assigned to a part of the U.S. with different cultural values. They enter a work culture with unwritten rules about how things are done around here and need an organizational road map. Graduates must often overcome the disdain with which some academic cultures view the world of work. All of this is challenging enough for native-born white males, more difficult for women and other native-born groups, and even harder for the non-native. The newcomer must learn how to relate to the other sex, as well as to bosses and subordinates, under rules quite different from those they were familiar with at school or even at work in their place of origin.

In this project, we also prepare American coaches and mentors for international workers who will be mentored by them. This is a far more challenging task. The newcomers know they are on strange ground, expect pitfalls, and start the program with trepidation and curiosity as well as enthusiasm. The U.S. managers, on the other hand, come with a sense of confidence and mastery. They resist the suggestion that they might not know how to handle their protégés until repeated breakdowns, often costly ones, occur. The mentoring they expected to be a piece of cake can become a nightmare. Without international work experience, they have little sense of, and often less sympathy for, what the international managers need beyond technical know-how. They rarely imagine that the newcomers could contribute anything from their own cultures. For these mentors, failures are a first painful step in becoming aware of what it means to be a transcultural manager.

Gender Concerns

Many foreign-born protégés are not prepared to treat women in the more egalitarian way of the American workplace, and even treat their female mentor as a personal servant. Gender roles and expectations should be clarified at the outset. This is, however, not just a problem for international visitors.

When a man and a woman or two gay individuals of the same sex enter into a mentoring relationship, there are normally some sexual under-

Table 8.1
Positive and Negative Consequences of Workplace Romance

+Plus+	−Minus−
People can become more creative and productive, have higher morale, and become better team players. For people who have demanding careers and work long hours, affection and romance can make the difference between excitement and energy and loneliness or depression. The risks and frustrations of casual liaisons are reduced.	Organizations fear and often punish office romances because they threaten to disrupt lines of authority. Romance is seen to interfere with the productivity of the people involved and those around them. Some relationships carry with them the potential of adverse publicity, especially when they involve corporate higher-ups or people already in committed relationships with others.

tones. Managing this sexual electricity well can result in high energy and mutual appreciation. Failing to manage it can be a disaster for both parties and for the organization. As one of the authors and his partner observed in *Men and Women, Partners at Work,* there are positive and negative consequences of workplace romance (see Table 8.1).

Such mentoring relationships require a great deal of propriety on the part of the participants. Even in the best managed of them, jealousy or simply gossip on the part of others in the organization can cause problems for the couple or public-relations problems for the company. When a woman is the younger protégé, she almost inevitably pays a dearer price than her male mentor when a debacle occurs.

Margo Murray, author of *Beyond the Myths and Magic of Mentoring,* suggests these guidelines about personal attraction for orienting mentors and protégés*:

- Acknowledge the potential for sexual attraction, particularly in the closeness of a mentoring relationship.
- Discuss the organization's policy on sexual harassment, homosexuality, dating other employees, employment of related persons, and related concerns.

*Excerpted from Murray, M., and M. A. Owen. *Beyond the Myths and Magic of Mentoring.* San Francisco: Jossey-Bass, Inc., 1991. Used by permission.

- Identify the negative and destructive as well as the positive aspects of sexual tensions on the job.
- Specify the types of relationships that are absolutely taboo—for example, between co-workers reporting to the same supervisor, when one of the pair is reporting to the other, or when one or both are married.
- Describe the consequences of violations of policy and/or taboos.
- Establish the recourse available when either one has behaved inappropriately in the relationship.

Person-to-Person Strains

Like attracts like. We tend to be most comfortable with people like ourselves when it comes to mentoring. Background differences reduce the likelihood of an informal mentoring relationship springing up of its own accord. This is why companies with a multicultural workforce need more than an informal mentoring system.

In a formal cross-cultural mentoring program, arranged marriages inevitably take place. This is not bad in itself, particularly if matches are made with careful research into the background of the parties involved. Such relationships, however, should be carefully monitored from the outset. If the chemistry is not right, give the parties an opportunity for a no-fault divorce; i.e., a chance to dissolve the relationship without penalty or bad repute, and enter into different relationships.

Multicultural mentoring relationships take more work. At the outset, differences may be exciting, but ultimately hard-core conflicts of values and perspective will surface and persist. Both mentors and protégés need to accept this, without making each other wrong.

Protecting and Challenging a Protégé

As our colleague Diane LaMountain notes, mentors as well as bosses can, with the best of intentions, overprotect their protégés, particularly women or traditional minorities. Wanting their protégés to succeed, mentors may keep them from the exposure and risks required for becoming seasoned managers. A mentor who appreciates the difficulties a protégé will face may want to reduce the risks. This should be discussed with the protégé, not decided unilaterally by the mentor. A mentor fearing to be labeled insensitive, or even racist or sexist, may be reluctant to push a minority or (if one is a male) female protégé, or hesitate to give frank criticism.

Career Development

As a model, the mentor's own person embodies another step in career development. People who have mastered and become comfortable with their present post can look to their mentor when they begin to ask, "Is this all there is?" or "What's next for me?" In many organizations, the lack of role models for women and traditional minorities may be even greater than for international managers. Few willing guides who have navigated their group's obstacles to success are available for the great number who aspire to advancement. Those that do exist can be overworked and compromised, too often called on to represent and mentor their background group. Consequently, less experienced mentors from the insider culture must be pressed into service. Not only do they not know the problems their protégés face, but their own route to success may have been achieved by unconsciously following the insider culture's rules to success. Such insider mentors need effective training in diversity issues and transcultural communication skills.

The mentor as model and advisor shows the individual how to manage self in order to manage one's career. Few mentors see how culture-bound their own behaviors are, and accept alternative ways of behaving. If there is a large context difference between mentor and protégé, both are likely to have expectations and needs that go unrecognized and unmet. So it is important for protégés, too, to receive solid training in transcultural communication skills in their orientation.

If you mentor protégés from your own microculture you may be accused of favoritism. Tough it out and be consistent. Confront accusers with facts. Make them aware that mentoring has always been going on informally, and it always involved the advancement of individuals; it's just that when it only involved traditional workers, it was simply taken for granted and almost invisible.

Mentors from the insider culture whose protégés are from outside may also be told to go slow by other members of the insider culture, or may themselves unconsciously hold back their protégés for fear of competition (even for their own positions). Discuss these factors in the orientation or early in the relationship. Informal meetings, newsletters, etc., can monitor problems that arise, add to the corporate understanding of the mentoring process, and continue to improve the program.

Anyone who would start a mentoring program to globalize their organization, normalize a multicultural workforce, or simply meet the traditional goals of advancing women and other outsiders, has their work cut out for them. Preparing potential mentors is normally more taxing than training individuals to use a mentor effectively. Murray cites other difficulties. Choosing individuals for coaching and mentoring may be beset by jealousies and accusations of favoritism by individuals and by dominant and minority groups, unions, etc. Mentoring's payoffs are often long term, and the resources needed for a formal program may be contested by other corporate interests and developmental programs. Some fear cloning and the loss of individuality and cultural values in the mentoring process itself. Payoffs for the one mentored are usually plain to see, while the costs of mentoring for those who would do it well are more obvious than the rewards.

Mentoring women and newcomers is a greater challenge and liability. This is reflected in the answers given by a group of managers to a simple four-question survey about the selection of protégés for informal mentoring reported in an article that appeared in *The International Journal of Mentoring* entitled "Mentoring for Top Management" by Norma T. Mertz, Olga M. Welch, and Jan Henderson:

1. Between male and female protégés, who better fits the image of the company and its culture in the mind of the male mentor? *Answer:* MALE
2. Who do I see as a greater risk to me as the mentor? *Answer:* FEMALE
3. Who do I see as being more predictable? *Answer:* MALE
4. Who do I see as creating greatest payoff for me as mentor? *Answer:* MALE

Useful Suggestions

Here are a few more tips for multicultural mentoring:

1. Make mentoring a part of the company culture change. Establish mentoring programs at many levels in the organization, not

just for higher managerial posts. This will involve a greater diversity of people earlier in their career.

2. To address the shortage of mentors and role models from microcultures in the organization, consider *double mentoring*. Give the protégé a regular mentor from the macroculture but assign occasional mentoring to someone from their own microculture. Some more tightly woven cultures may prefer a group mentoring process. Where a program for a single protégé may fail, putting two or three in a group may succeed. The need for peer affiliation among Hispanics, for example, causes problems when individuals are promoted over their peers. Moving up as a group can be a solution. With a group or a buddy system, protégés have someone to talk to and share experiences with when the mentor is absent. If you mentor microcultures in groups, do not let it look as if you are economizing at their expense when you put them into groups.

3. When you identify and match mentors with protégés, pay attention to the protégé's concept of power distance. If you match them with executives, new hires may be intimidated, distrustful, and reluctant to ask questions. Protégés from more tightly woven cultures could find the power distance unworkable. Peer or close-to-peer mentors would be a better choice.

4. Coach mentors and protégés (and support staff if your program is a large one) in both tightly woven and loosely knit communication and management skills.

5. Assess the program regularly to see if you are getting the results you want. Evaluate both subjectively and objectively. How mentors, protégés, and the organization see the program is as important as how it performs if it is to fully benefit all concerned.

6. Modify the process and retrain participants whenever necessary. Multicultural mentoring deals with people's habits of thinking and feeling and touches their deepest values. These took a long time to acquire, and frequent repetition is needed to create new behaviors.

7. Create a process to end a mentoring relationship as well as to get it under way. Mentoring relationships often end in a power struggle and much bitterness, as the protégé begins to experience his or her own empowerment. The mentor may be reluctant to let go, either because he or she feels that the protégé is not ready, or because the mentor has become dependent on the protégé. In multicultural or

cross-gender mentoring, subtle prejudices about competence or paternalism may intensify this conflict.

8. Keep a broad perspective. Remember that not only the protégé, but the mentor and the enterprise itself, must benefit from mentoring if the program is to thrive.

Points to Remember From This Chapter

Reweaving Organizational Culture

- Examine the culture of your organization, both formal and informal, to see if it is in sync with the realities of the workforce and business environment.
- Make changes to the culture where needed, calling upon the informal (heroes, stories, images, etc.) as well as the formal (vision, policies, etc.) resources in the organization.

Mentoring

- Mentoring programs must benefit both the mentor and the person being mentored.
- Mentoring, to be a successful part of a culture change, must be seen as a long-term benefit to the organization and individual.
- Educate mentors and those being mentored, and support them along the way.

CHAPTER 9

CAUTION! WOMEN AND MEN AT WORK

*In the last thirty years, the rapid entrance of
women into the workforce, drawn by the banner
of equal opportunity, has presented complications
that force us to rethink and reshape Social Policy
relative to our children, elders, and our entire workforce. This is being felt in every sector—education,
federal and local, government, and industry.*

—Lavinia Weissman

Women Are in the Workforce to Stay

The transformation of the American workplace from predominantly male to half male and half female is almost complete, though a 50/50 split may not appear in most organizations. Were that so, we might more easily adjust to a male-female workplace. Nonetheless, knowing how to manage and work with each other will help us avoid alienating many good workers, thus avoiding the loss of their productivity and talent. Bad management of gender issues has resulted in divisive politics that has undermined the operation of many organizations and polarized workforces.

The entry of women into previously male occupations is a worldwide phenomenon. In Russia, women dominate the workplace. Even in Islamic countries women are leaving the hearth, often for workplaces run and managed entirely by women. In Japan, with its very tightly woven definition of gender roles, women account for 35.6% of the labor pool; 60% of the total working women are married. As more nations change from rural to industrial or meta-industrial economies and participate in the worldwide marketplace, an inevitable shift in gender roles will result in new kinds of female-male collaboration. This collaboration will force us to rethink our workplace values, redefine corporate loyalty, lead us to innovative forms of compensation and productivity measurement, and challenge our current design for corporate culture.

Where the number of females in a workforce approaches and exceeds the number of males, collaboration between women and men of all cultures is fast becoming the new work culture norm. In practice, this collaboration does not come about easily because, of all the cultural differences, gender is the most deeply rooted; it is also usually complicated by age, race, ethnicity, and other differences. Old breakdowns recur, just when we think we are beginning to manage them well. This is the reason we began this book on diversity with a case about gender differences. Another case, can be found in the following box, describing the frustration of many women in corporate settings.

Shattered by the Glass Ceiling

I started out as an administrative assistant in the early '70s for one of the country's largest banks. For ten years I pushed my way to the senior level, through management training programs and competent work. I solved business challenges that saved thousands of dollars, and attacked human resource problems, creating positive morale and increased productivity. Finally, I was invited to develop a corporatewide program and present it to the most senior operating committee (all men). I exhausted myself, ignored my family, and packed 60 hours of preparation into one week. I entered the meeting room quite nervous, but very confident in my work.

Over the past ten years, four men in this group had contributed to my career success as mentors and bosses. I began my presentation. Before I was three sentences into it, the senior chief operating officer explained that they had had a change of mind about the program. Although my work was appreciated, this program was not going to be given priority. While this announcement was being made, the other men in the room ruminated on last Sunday's football game.

(continued)

(continued from previous page)

I went back to my office and threw a fit. For ten years I had aspired to become a vice president. The organization had pretended to support me by opening doors for me, and by giving me promotions and management training. I felt the pain of this broken promise and thought about my other costs, taking my infant daughter to day care each day, and keeping a full work schedule while running a home. This day was pivotal. I stopped aspiring to a particular position and decided to choose my work in a way that would take care of me and my family. Within 45 days I was freelancing, controlling my own schedule, earning the same amount of money, and working fewer hours. Climbing to the top was not for me.

Recently more practitioners have begun to see gender differences as cultural and have started applying cross-cultural techniques to solving gender problems. We suggest another, more radical, mindshift, which says that gender is not only one of many cultural differences, but *the* cultural difference *par excellence,* the root paradigm of difference:

Women's culture is a subculture within ethnic, racial, and other forms of culture.	→	Women and men are the most basic cultural groups; in fact, the prototypical cultural distinctions after which all others are modeled.

Our experience as corporate behavioral experts leads us to believe that when gender difference can be accepted and dealt with, other cultural differences can be handled, not without effort, but in due course. On the other hand, a great deal of diversity work remains superficial when gender issues are not first recognized and managed. Because gender tells us in the most fundamental ways how to be with others and make choices in life, it influences our attitudes, feelings, and decisions at every moment. All of us inevitably grow up with and continue to maintain a set of culturally conditioned mental conversations, conscious and unconscious, about how men and women should be. Old habits continually reassert themselves as shown in the accompanying boxed example.

Sweet and Sour Names

I work for the president of a small family-run printing firm. He is in his 50s, smart, hard working, and a genuinely nice guy, but he used to punctuate all his sentences, when speaking with women, with "Hon," e.g., "Well, Sandra, Hon, I'm wondering if, Hon, could you schedule the program by March, Hon?" He used "Hon" like some people unconsciously use "umm" or "like," but only with women. I am sure he meant no harm and had no lascivious designs. When I knew him well enough, I asked him if he realized he used "Hon" so much and if he knew it offended some people. (I had heard complaints from other employees.) He was flabbergasted! He not only immediately stopped saying "Hon" to me—tough to do with a habit like that—but told me he felt it was a term of endearment and had no idea it could be offensive. "Help me understand, Sandra, why people take offense?" (No "Hon!") We discussed it and he thanked me for my feedback. For months, I never heard another "Hon" from him. Then, after 3-4 months away from the office on maternity leave, I had occasion to call him. He was back to his "So Sandra, Hon, how's it going with the baby, Hon?" So much for behavior change! I believe he meant no harm, and as I've grown to like, trust, and respect him, I have learned to not get irritated. But I know other employees are silently angry about this.

Gender roles are complicated by socioeconomic issues that cannot be addressed at the workplace alone. The demands these roles make are a source of conflict, whether one looks at the male senior manager who supports a suburban lifestyle, a wife working only in the home, and three children, or, in contrast, at the single head of a household who (in a recession economy) must provide housing for her two to three children and pay for essentials (laundry, shopping, cooking, day care) from a salary that barely supports one middle-class individual. Life is very different today from what baby boomers were raised to expect. Gender affects our workforce differently in each age group by individual social welfare and health concerns, family, and economics. The evidence, moreover, is mounting to show that misunderstanding, resentment, and violence between men and women are of the deepest, most frequent, and widespread kind. The boxed example shows how we need constant reminders of what does and doesn't work.

I had been working as a consultant for 30 days for a branch of a Fortune 500 chemicals company. A major turnover had resulted in a vice president's resignation. I helped to stabilize branch operations, assure customers of the best service possible during the transition, and produced market research that set a strategic direction for local efforts severely affected by a statewide recession. Two regional vice presidents flew up from different cities to interview me as a result of this productivity. Without formal introduction, the vice president of sales walked into my office, sat down and remarked "Well, who do we have here!" His body language and words reminded me of a man womanizing at a bar. I stood up at my desk, made a formal introduction, and put my hand out for a firm handshake. I mapped out an agenda and shared my background. Highlighting my sales and marketing history, I told him, tongue in cheek, how I worked in a financial firm of sixty men in the heyday of miniskirts, and how once guys stopped staring, my productivity increased. After my humorous anecdote, the bar-hopping tone and posture immediately ceased and we got down to business.

A New Tactical Position

Today, *socially speaking,* most men would prefer women to be their equals and partners rather than their caregivers. *Professionally,* however, because corporations are work dominated and not socially driven, their traditional male culture forces both men and women back into old patterns. As a result, many of us continue to have a traditional system of family values as well, unless divorce or another powerful interruption causes that system to crash. *Socially* women want more help from men at home, particularly with care giving, while *professionally* they want to balance professional life with a social home life, one that does not just include children. This conflict of values is what some women call "male domination." The true target is not men per se, but the established dominant system, which in most cases happens to be a white male system.

Accepting gender as a cultural difference is a tactical step that helps us address gender issues in the workplace. It fits this changing social paradigm. We encourage managers to experiment with this new tactical position and researchers to explore it. This will be an uphill battle where gender relations are highly politicized or when the "politically correct" insist that *men dominate and women are victims.* Even where it has been admitted that white males may also be targeted, this is never seen as of the same order, nor has it had any practical impact on the pursuit of cultural politics.

To demonstrate that they can work as effectively as men and deserve equal treatment and rewards, women, for many years, have minimized their differences and stressed equality, while the men who supported them tried not to notice this most noticeable of differences. Admitting ones differences in the American workplace has traditionally meant accepting inferiority. Our minds jump too easily to the conclusion that differences are either good or bad, or functional or dysfunctional, rather than a source of interesting possibilities. Those who are different are commonly relegated to the edge of a work group. They may be devalued personally and their contributions ignored. Focusing on difference was taboo because it generally led to subordination in the distribution of labor and, as Ann Morrison has observed, effectively kept women from advancing in wages and enterprises as many men do. This is the trend that the valuing differences movement sought to counteract.

As a result, the situation is now changing. It is becoming clear that many women in the workplace must be treated differently, e.g., provided care for their children, flex-time, and so forth, if they are to contribute fully and be recognized fully in the enterprises they serve. Just as working men have traditionally had wives who supported them in many ways, women who are expected to perform well in the new work culture require equivalent forms of support.

As Rick Beinecke, a Brandeis University Heller School Associate recently pointed out at an ODNET presentation on work and family, "My colleagues continue to be upset with me because as an expert researcher, I am unable to provide research on the cost benefit of these programs. Managers want this information to persuade themselves to implement these programs." Countries such as Sweden have realized that such programs are investments both in today's productivity and in the education and nurturance of a future workforce. As Weissman notes, American management's well-documented failure to recognize the consequences of ignoring the needs of women in the workforce to families, children, and workers should be argument enough. Solid bottom-line evidence is also beginning to appear in companies like Stride Rite Corporation, where programs they have implemented show a return on investment in the form of high employee morale and work satisfaction, as well as in increased revenue. In their book, *Managing Workforce 2000,* Jamison and O'Mara have clearly shown what can be done to make fairness and productivity go hand in hand if one is willing to manage for differences. Once properly understood, special treatment for differences, even among women, creates fair workplaces rather than workplaces in which rhetoric of equality and an accent on sameness oppress almost everyone.

Women as a More Tightly Woven Culture

In her publication *How to Work with Men,* Attorney Rita Risser adapted a checklist from one of the authors that you might use to explore how women's and men's cultural values differ in respect to work and success. Assign 5 points to each pair of statements in the list. Divide the points according to your opinion between each statement on the left and its partner on the right. Total your results at the bottom of each column.

What Do You Think?

☐ 1. Hard work alone will lead to success.

☐ Hard work is not the only key to success. Luck, wisdom, and time are also required.

☐ 2. People can change and improve their environment.

☐ People should adjust themselves to the environment.

☐ 3. People should be realistic.

☐ People should be idealistic.

☐ 4. Deadlines must be met even if quality suffers.

☐ Deadlines are important but only in relation to other priorities.

☐ 5. The primary obligation of an individual is to the company.

☐ The primary obligation of an individual is to family and friends.

☐ 6. Objective qualifications alone should determine employment practices.

☐ Family considerations & friendships should affect employment practices.

☐ 7. Employees should be removed if they do not perform well.

☐ Employees should not be removed unless there is no other alternative.

☐ 8. People should express opinions freely even if they do not agree with the boss.

☐ People should not express opinions contrary to the boss.

☐ 9. Employees should promote themselves to improve their position in the company.

☐ Personal ambition and power plays are frowned upon.

☐ 10. Competition stimulates high performance.

☐ Competition is counterproductive to high performance.

☐ 11. A person must do whatever is necessary to get the job done.

☐ Some work is below one's dignity and it is an insult to be asked to do it.

☐ 12. People should be evaluated objectively.

☐ People should be evaluated on subjective and objective criteria; everyone has some good in them.

☐ Total Column 1

☐ Total Column 2

Interpreting Your Results

Did you score higher in Column 1 or 2? Men tend to value the items in Column 1 more, while women tend to choose those in Column 2. When this list first appeared in *Managing Cultural Differences,* it compared loosely knit U.S. cultural values with values held by other, more tightly woven cultures. Since Risser first used this approach for gender differences in 1984, the gap between women and men has been closing, particularly among professionals, but women still tend to prefer more tightly woven values. As Risser observes, "though American women are raised in the U.S., their beliefs and values are not the same as those of the dominant culture."

Gender in Culture

In more tightly woven cultures, roles women and men play, husband and wife, mother and father, superior and subordinate, are presented as predetermined and unalterable, and women are almost always subordinate to men and restricted in their public behavior. Painful illustrations of this abound. A Vietnamese woman working in the U.S. started coming to work bruised and battered shortly after she was appointed to head a work team. The woman refused to speak about what was happening. Finally one of her co-workers reported that the woman's husband was on the same team and that he was upset at losing face whenever she contradicted him or opposed him in the course of team planning. He would punish her at home for this violation of the traditional male-female roles. Once this was discovered, placing him on a different work team solved the problem.

In more loosely knit cultures like our own, which have long valued the freedom, individuality, and personal responsibility of each man, the same values, with a time lag, are being applied to women and other traditional minorities. In the workplace, merit or competency becomes the norm of success, or at least the ideal to be sought. This norm insists that individuals, male or female, be hired, promoted, rewarded, and respected for how successfully they do the job, not because of who they are, where they come from, or who they know. In theory, females are as free as males to develop their human potential and serve in a variety of roles, including CEO and head of state. Many women hear this as a fading promise as their opportunities are curtailed by the uncertain economy and the resulting reductions in middle management positions. Social welfare issues that previously concerned the poor are now beginning to affect the middle class. Many women now live in a permanent state of stress as a result of working at home and taking care of parents and children, while simultaneously acting as full-time breadwinners. Women see it as imperative to forward their education and focus at least on some modicum of their own personal interests. Men, though less frequently, may bear the same burden, but they are more accustomed to giving up personal needs when facing pressures at work.

For the foreseeable future, gender will remain our most volatile diversity factor. The remainder of this chapter will focus on the insights and skills that a transcultural leader needs to deal with the issue of gender.

The Male Managerial Model

The largely male workforce that emerged from the industrial revolution not surprisingly developed a male model of the worker to which women and even children were required to conform. Women in the workforce, as Henning and Jardim reported in *Forum,* are still being judged by standards created for men. Managers need to redefine what they think of as normal if they are to incorporate the full range of possibilities that women bring to the workforce. For example, while women tend to see work teams as composed of equal relationships, men see different places of differing importance on the team. Women aim at getting individual satisfaction from the teamwork itself, often focusing on appreciation of skills, expertise, and training, while men focus on winning the game. It seems obvious, then, that work teams that utilize gender differences can bring more and different energies to the task at hand. In *Men and Women, Partners at Work,* co-authors Simons and Weissman addressed these differences in their model for partnership in productivity. Men and women must take separate responsibility for their own issues under the umbrella of an organization that manages gender diversity at the level of policy and personnel management.

Even today, many women masculinize their appearance and behavior to play on the men's team. They defeminize themselves to avoid being trapped by old stereotypes that hamstring them in the workplace. Paradoxically, lectures and training courses are offered today on how to flirt and use sexual energy to create a positive working relationship between the sexes. Women need to adapt traditional female skills, not abandon them.

As men and women work to develop a new relationship on the job, the typical corporate culture pushes back, making it more difficult, rather than easier, for them to succeed. According to Deal and Kennedy, "When the newcomer is different—a woman in a man's world, or a black in a white managerial echelon—no rituals exist to socialize this individual. In the place of comfortable rituals are taboos . . ." Stereotypes get reinforced, collaborative relationships between men and women are viewed with suspicion ("I wonder what is really going on between those two . . ."), and barriers and sanctions are created that appear benign but undermine attempts to create nontraditional working relationships. Organizations, like people, resist change, sometimes with violence, sometimes with passivity. Changing roles cause organizational dilemmas, for example:

- As more and more women and men travel together on business should an organization set rules and policies relative to behavior, accommodations, etc.?
- When creating a new project team or task force, should gender diversity be sought—the group might take longer to become productive—or should the more traditional composition be maintained?
- When rewarding the efforts of a mixed gender pair or group, how do we properly and equitably apportion the feedback, both financial and otherwise?

Instead of ignoring such dilemmas, postponing them, or treating them lightly, the transcultural manager learns to *address gender issues with the same urgency as any other basic business decisions.*

Capitalizing on New Strengths

What would a work culture look like that truly recognized the values that women bring to it as well as those traditionally fostered by men? Envisioning this in your workplace is a necessary exercise, if you are to arrive there someday—and that someday should not be in the too distant future.

Look at what the newcomers bring with them to the workplace. While many of their skills overlap, men and women, driven by culture, have come to specialize in separate strengths that each can learn from the other. As Frances K. Conley, a distinguished surgeon who resigned her post at Stanford after years of sexual harrassment from a colleague, pointed out in her rationale for departing Stanford, women surgeons manage operating rooms with a team approach while males tend to be captains of the ship. While both approaches work, perhaps a blend would be even more successful.

Swedish Management Consultant Gunilla Masreliez-Steen cites another example of cross-gender learning that occurred in an industrial plant. Polluting spills were occurring when mechanical shut-downs occurred. These spills started diminishing when a group largely consisting of women began working in the problem section. Investigation revealed that because these women handled the machinery more gently, less mechanical shutdowns resulted and less polluting spills resulted. As a result of this discovery, the men began handling the machinery differently as well.

Today's organizations, and those of the future, need a different mix of values, not only because women are present in larger numbers, but because of how work itself is changing in the age of the smart machine. Jobs require less muscle and motor skills and more information and person-to-person skills. While women continue to acquire many traditional male business and workplace skills, men must also now mas-

---

The New Women's Touch

Dr. Sigmund Ginsburg, in an article in *The President,* suggests that there are "Lessons for American Management from Female Dominated Organizations." They seem to offer a "focus on the individual and personal fulfillment which results in greater organizational effectiveness and better bottom-line results." Ginsburg found that in female-dominated organizations there was some emphasis on the factors below. Check those that you believe your organization or you personally might benefit from if they were increased:

☐ More emphasis on collaborative decision making.
☐ Less concern with titles and formal authority, more concern with responsibility and responsiveness.
☐ Less concern for empire building, power, domination, and consciousness about one's turf.
☐ A greater concern with process and fairness.
☐ More decentralization.
☐ More democratic, participative, consultative management; less autocratic, domineering, ego-involved management.
☐ More concern with the quality of outcomes.
☐ A greater responsiveness and concern for individual feelings, ideas, opinions, ambitions, and on- and off-the-job satisfactions.
☐ High value placed on loyalty, longevity, and interpersonal skills.
☐ More emphasis on skills as a listener and conversationalist.

ter things women have been taught to do well. What these are becomes clearer when we look at organizations run largely by women.

Women and Men as Teams

Today's female-male collaboration should provide powerful models for the future. Studies in negotiation and mediation done by Weingarten and Douvan, researchers at the University of Michigan, for example, suggest that men seem to be good at figuring out what needs to be done and women are good at collaborating and getting others to collaborate in doing it. Men tend to take neutral, logical, and objective stands on problems while women become involved in how the problems affect people. Each brings a separate perspective to resolving conflict, which can help them function more effectively as a team. As they become more common, teams of men and women will give us a closer look at the new synergy this can bring to productivity and creativity.

Gender and Subordination

What is typically female or male today, because it is a cultural construct, may cease to be so in a couple of generations. For example, our culture is full of stories about women's sensitivity and intuition. This may prove a rather shallow reality, a result of women's traditional subordination rather than something innately female. Gary Powell, in *Men and Women in Management,* cites research that suggests that women have no particular advantage in sensitivity over men, but that subordinates of either sex tend to be more sensitive to those in positions of authority. Though this might statistically occur more frequently in women, it must be seen as an individual endowment, not a stereotypical gender trait. Still, when it exists, this sensitivity, which is still more likely in women, like any other ability can be used to the advantage of the individual and the work team.

The Not-So-Vanishing White Male

While the demographic projections of *Workforce 2000* certainly indicate radical change in workforce composition, we can expect the power structure of organizations to be strongly held by white males well into the twenty-first century. Very much with us, the white male is not always the person we think him to be. John McPherson, who has been very supportive of our work on gender, has also provided important insights about the predicament of men, which are reflected in the following pages.

Though men have a substantially different emotional makeup than women, a generation of sensitization has left them raw, with their proverbially hidden feelings much closer to the surface. What is happening in the new workplace and its culture is causing them pain. Many are leaving a secure, clearly defined role as head of family, father, wise man, and problem solver who builds things or makes things happen, for an ambiguous, constantly changing, collaborative role where power and authority are shared, and the consequences of the collaborative process are not always predictable. This pain can and often does express itself in anger, resentment, stress, illness, and withdrawal. The boxed example illustrates this.

An Old Boy's Lament

When I joined this outfit twenty-five years ago and looked around at my competition, we all looked pretty much alike; white, male, Ivy League education, bright, and ambitious. And when we looked at those in charge they looked like older, more experienced versions of us. The message was clear; do your job, keep your nose clean, emulate your superiors, and you will be rewarded by promotion to the level of your ability. We didn't concern ourselves about women in the business; they were secretaries, not managers. Now look. I just lost a promotion to a woman, and at my age, this may have been my last chance. In my resentment I find myself thinking all kinds of nasty things about women, even though I know for a fact that they aren't true.

It is important to acknowledge that *both* the man and the woman potentially bring anger and pain as well as special skills from their acculturation to the business relationship. Women bring emotions resulting from being cast in a one-down role with men. Even where overt sexism is absent, a woman has been exposed to cultural conditioning that subtly and sometimes blatantly portrays her as inferior. Her anger, however, may be masked or suppressed, appearing only in socially acceptable ways. Like "Black Rage," which sees color-based prejudice as all pervasive, many women develop a "Women's Rage," which prevents productive collaboration with men. Though women have used this rage, along with their networking and collaborative skills, to begin their own flourishing businesses, the real sources of women's and men's rage has not been addressed. Women's rage is also focused on the demands of work and blind corporate loyalty that conflicts with other valuable parts of their lives. Any organization that wants women's full participation must look at this seriously. The core issues, both social and professional, can only be addressed when women and men explore and create a partnership where professional and social relationships are managed out of respect for individual talents and needs, and aligned with a common vision that includes more than profit making. Such partnership balances caretaking and breadwinning, and views social and spiritual needs on a par with economic responsibility.

Gender Preferences

Being gay, lesbian, bisexual, or even celibate in one's private life can lead to unfair treatment at work. Historically less protected by law, such people have been subject to both vicious and subtle discrimination on the job. Although there is a vast developing literature about these lifestyles, a few simple points can guide the your managerial practice and help you to inform others.

1. Such people are not broken. Don't fix them. While homosexuals are granted a special place in some cultures, those who have opted for nonheterosexual lifestyles in Western society have been subjected to constant religious and social persecution. Like anyone else, gay, bisexual, and celibate people can be intelligent and emotionally well-rounded or in pain and psychologically distorted. The rejection they experience would take its toll on anyone. Not surprisingly, many prefer to keep their lifestyle secret, which also has its emotional costs. Such people should be provided advice and counseling in the same measure as any other employee.

2. Assume that gay people are already a part of your organization and that you and others are already dealing with them successfully. Your organization if it is of any size, will have people of differing sexual preferences working in it. Heterosexual workers can be victimized by their own fears when they suspect or discover that a co-worker is different. Such people may need considerable help to become comfortable again even with someone with whom they have long collaborated. While many gay people have made outstanding contributions to the history of invention, design, music, and art and continue to do so, this should not be made a stereotype for them, either. People of different sexual preferences can be found in all walks of life and at all skill levels.

3. AIDS and indiscreet liaisons are everybody's problem. You must make it common and accepted knowledge that AIDS, despite its decimation of the gay community, is not a peculiarly homosexual problem. It is one of many social crises we face, which include child poverty, the deterioration of public education, hunger, and homelessness. The organization that values its people will disinform them of myths and educate them about high-risk behavior. Continued employment of those who suffer from whatever noncontagious malady, as long as their work can be mutually beneficial for the individual and the organization, should be part of the organization's mission.

4. Value the unique perspectives that many people have gained by being gay, lesbian, bisexual, or celibate. You cannot dismiss the probability that these perspectives can benefit your business and help you penetrate your markets.

Points to Remember From This Chapter

- Gender creates some of the hardest-to-manage cultural differences because it lives at the deepest level of the psychological and social context.
- Applying cross-cultural knowledge and skills to gender issues in the workplace is a better alternative to politicization.
- Be aware of context differences (Appendix A) when addressing gender issues.
- In the changing workplace, the traditional male management and teamwork models need to be enriched from the practices of women and other microcultures.
- White males have frustrations and needs in the changing work culture. Viewing them as the source of all or most workplace problems is simplistic. It will cause more problems than it will solve.
- Dealing with the small daily misunderstandings and irritants that arise from gender differences is as important as dealing with overt sexual harassment.
- Manage your own and help others manager their fears about people with different sexual preferences.

CHAPTER 10

ALL ROADS LEAD TO EMPOWERMENT

*"Man, I need to be who I am
if you want me to become
who I can be!"*

—Overheard in a company cafeteria

Empowerment has become such a buzz word in corporate America today that for some it has become a turnoff! Not so for us. We began by enumerating the forces changing the workplace, and will close by looking at empowerment and the worldwide efforts to renew organizational culture for productivity and service in response to the challenges of diversity and the global economy. When fewer workers must do more with limited resources and in less time, it is clear that they are the key to organizational success. The transcultural leader manages diversity by enabling individuals and teams to take responsibility for productive work in the context of a clearly defined vision. This leads to competence and empowers people to contribute at their highest skill levels.

Some leaders are positioned to be organizational visionaries with ultimate responsibility for both personnel and for the bottom line. Leaders at every level, however, can become enablers. Empowerment provides a leadership role for today's thinning ranks of middle managers whose task it is to enable workers to collaborate, make their best contribution, and understand the role that each plays in producing a major project: service. Such leadership gives the organization of the future the greatest possibility of balanced budgets, profit, high morale, and a satisfied workforce.

Obstacles to Empowerment

Why is empowerment both such a hot topic and a resisted one? Because organizations must change their structure and management style and then train people to use these changes to the greatest advantage. It would be a Herculean task, even without diversity. Now leaders must deal with an evolving, ever more varied workforce, with different perceptions of authority and communication styles, and, for many, the need to process information in a second language or multiple languages. Many managers are reluctant to let subordinates make their own decisions for fear things will get out of control. "Cover your backside" is the unwritten rule in many workplaces. Managers fear both that a subordinate will fail and that she or he will succeed the manager. Theory "X" beliefs that workers produce only under surveillance and tight control can be coupled with bias when dealing with a diverse workforce. The manager's mind may be mired in, "They're too dumb to get it right," or, "They're too lazy to do it on their own." Deep insecurity rattles the North American and European workplace when immigrants and non-Westerners prove that they are willing to work hard and can do the job as well as or even better than traditional workers.

Much Hierarchical Thinking Must Go

Hierarchical thinking and communication styles get in the way of shaping an agile and competitive workforce. As one consultant, Erika Penzer, writing in *Incentive,* puts it, "Bureaucracy is high, hierarchies are complex, workers are told what to do and then hammered to improve. Most managers think that the way to run a company is for the executives to make the decisions and the employees to execute them. Workers are asked to check their brains at the door when they come in." Despite the loosely knit nature of North American organizations, such habits do not die easily. In many tightly woven cultures they are even more entrenched. Still, a new kind of leader is appearing on the scene around the world.

Traditionally, organizations used titles and clearly defined roles to create and support the boundaries of authority. This made it easy for employees to respond to the hierarchy with clear-cut patterns. In a diverse workforce, perceptions of titles, authority, roles, work ethics, what is acceptable work, and subordinate behavior differs from culture to culture and generation to generation. We may have a corporate culture in flux, transitioning from a linear management style to a circular one. Some, usually outsiders, never had a chance to learn the linear style in the first place! Now everyone is culture shocked and stressed. Titles may remain in organizations with an empowered culture, but the roles and behaviors belonging to those titles are largely delegated. Many employees are empowered to act in areas that were traditionally reserved for management. Not surprisingly, both old-timers (from the organization's more tightly woven past) and newcomers (from more tightly woven cultures) hesitate to make decisions, or they become paralyzed in the face of blurred boundaries. "What if I make a mistake?" "How can I handle all this?" Having to think about what is being done, not being able to say, "That's not my job," and having to collaborate with individuals of different backgrounds, adds to the stress of empowering an organization.

The rules have changed. All workers, not just newcomers, need time to develop a new mental framework and acculturate to today's work culture. Most organizations can expect an initial slowdown in productivity before they begin to realize the benefits of diversity and empowerment. Managers need to be aware of their reactive behaviors toward the transition as well as those of their subordinates. Self-empowerment requires understanding why and how we fear and resist change.

Managing Fear

Fear and empowerment are opposites. As Ryan and Oesterreicher show in their book, *Driving Fear Out of the Workplace,* fear enables us to meet some short-term emergencies and threats well, but in the long run it is excessively wearing on individuals and their relationships. Fear tends to paralyze thinking and prevent action.

Diversity raises fears, both real and imagined: fear of those who are different, fear of tribalism and favoritism, fear of misunderstanding, fear of an unfamiliar culture, fear of the unknown. Though newcomers are motivated, they often are not given the tools and the trust. Old-timers have strong values, but because they are not shown how to apply them to meet new challenges, they are afraid of losing them.

Managing Adversarial Relationships

American management still has much to learn about handling employees well, even if diversity were not the factor it is becoming. A recent article in the *Los Angeles Times* quoted Floyd Wood of the Federal Mediation and Conciliation Service as saying, "In the majority of our workplaces we have never come to grips with management and control versus freedom and power sharing." His comment continues, "In many companies, the relationship between workers and managers will likely resemble a shaky marriage, in which the partners go through a series of divorces and reconciliations until, after years, they finally overcome their bitterness and distrust." Another mindshift is required:

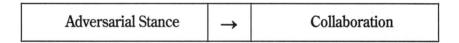

Adversarial Stance	$\rightarrow$	Collaboration

American management and labor have been adversaries not only in the positions they have taken, but in principle. Opposition has been a great part of American workplace culture, as is pulling together when a common threat appears. When, on the eve of Independence, Ben Franklin said, "Either we shall all hang together or we shall all hang separately," he was trying to bridge the individualism that was already rampant in the American character. In the same vein, a UAW member at General Motors, cited in *Work in America,* declared, "We're working together or we're going under" when his facility was threatened with closure. Union and management collaborated to not only save the plant but to make it competitive and growing.

The adversarial stance of management and labor reflects our lower context individualism. It cannot be counted on to serve us well now. The changing, diverse workforce is a buyers' market, and leaders must learn to sell to it. Diversity reminds us once again of the need for better human relations and improved human resource practices. Though there is an urgency to invest in newer technology to upgrade America's aging industrial infrastructure, high-tech machinery is not a guaranteed fix for productivity. A recent comparison of automotive plants, reported by auto industry researchers Krafcik and MacDuffie, showed that, "High technology strategies in the absence of significant changes produces no significant productivity or quality improvements.

It took 34 hours to produce a car with an average of 1.16 defects per car in the traditional low-tech plant. After an expenditure of $650 million on high technology, it still took almost 34 hours to produce a car with an average of 1.37 defects." On the other hand, self management in the work process as MacDuffie has shown, contributes substantially to making an organization productive and innovative. Self management cannot flourish where mental energy is overly consumed by adversarial thinking.

Empowered and Empowering Leaders

In essence, in an empowered organization, transcultural leaders are:

- *Visionaries* with broad perspectives. They have a clear and powerful vision and a long-term outlook.
- *Communicators* of organizational and personal expectations, visions and responsibilities who include *all* in their information list.
- *Role models,* who are empowered high performers themselves.
- *Realists,* who realize that the person on the front line is closest to the problem and usually has the best view.
- *Delegators,* who they believe in people and their potential, and assign individuals and teams their own goal setting.
- *Mentors,* who are accessible to *all.*
- *Service oriented,* who see employees as their customers and allow them to select the kinds of support and tools they need to get the job done, so they are:
  —Able to recognize and reward performance.
  —Ready to lead others into empowerment by example and support not by fiat and coercion.

Driving Decisions Downward

Lower level decision making is another feature of empowerment. Organizations have shown outstanding success when they have experimentally allowed employees and employee teams, who are knowledgeable of and aligned with the organization's mission, to make the decisions necessary to reach their goals. While "Cover Your Backside" management frustrates and angers clients and customers, those who encounter the empowered organization, where people "just do it" (the motto of the San Francisco Ramada Inn's empowerment and customer service program), are reluctant to do business elsewhere. Penzer cites these examples of empowered employees in action:

"Without checking with the supervisor, a team of loading dock workers reject a shipment of defective parts. A retail salesperson, hoping to establish a long-term relationship with a customer, drives to the customer's house on the weekend to see how the items he sold are holding up. A disgruntled hotel guest receives a free night's stay—from the housekeeper who cleaned her room."

What is outstanding about these examples is not that employees are doing things they never would have done in the past, but that they are empowered by understanding the mission of the organization and the goals of their work unit and encouraged to take whatever steps are needed to carry it out.

Managing vs. Empowering

What are the leader's responsibilities in an organization that fosters empowerment? There is no pat answer to this question; however, one simple way of expressing the difference between much of old management behavior and empowering is represented in this mindshift:

Old Managing Mindset	→	Empowering Mindset
Planning, controlling, checking on employee performance		Letting go, creating a learning organization, and setting high standards for employees' performance.

The old management mindset focused on a hierarchy and control, with an almost paternalistic flavor—father knows best. Employees were told what to do, how to do it, and when to do it, with the decision making, planning, and necessary organizational information resting solely at the top. Typical management models in the '60s and '70s stressed conformity in employee behavior and uniformity in management practices. Many of the more tightly woven groups and organizations, even in the loosely knit North American culture, are deeply invested in this approach and are finding it difficult to improve the performance of workers while maintaining continuity of cultural values.

The new mindshift of empowerment challenges power hoarding, and hands down power by means of intensive training, allowing employees to share in the creation and expression of the corporate and/or departmental vision, acknowledging and recognizing the employee's creative contributions, and opening the decision making process. In a nutshell, for management the challenge of empowerment concerns control, and with employees it is about responsibility and accountability and, as author Peter Koestenbaum observes, about self esteem: "The quality [of one's work] is its own reward. . . . Pride in quality makes sense because pride in oneself makes sense."

Successful leaders are students of human commitment and loyalty. They balance technical components of work with social ones and value and meaning with efficiency. They also establish flexible boundaries and expect high performance, requiring continuous learning. Each organization develops its own road map to empowerment; however, here are three fundamental questions that all organizations must somehow ask:

- How do we inspire commitment to high performance?
- How can we value the uniqueness and creativity of our employees, giving meaning and pride of ownership to what they do, and still be able to establish boundaries?
- How do we build intelligence, continuous learning, foster synergy from conflicting ideas and differences, and incorporate creative ideas without neglecting others?

Few yardsticks can be found for doing this, but we can learn from the examples of those who have tried and succeeded.

Working in Tandem—An Example

Smilor and Kuhn, authors of *Corporate Creativity,* point to Tandem Computers, Inc., as a classic example of the benefits reaped from implementing the new leadership mindshift. James Treybig, president and principal founder of Tandem Computers, Inc., describes its work culture as follows*:

*Reprinted by permission of Greenwood Publishing Group, Inc., Westport, CT, from *Corporate Creativity* by R. Smilor and R. Kuhn, Copyright © 1984 by Praeger Publishers.

Fast Growth By High Performers. A little more than a decade old, Tandem was listed in the Fortune 500; in that time it grew from zero to half a billion dollars in sales, and from 4 to 5,000 employees.

High Productivity and Creativity. These traits come from competent people who continue to learn, especially about customer satisfaction. *Datamation* magazine rated Tandem first in customer satisfaction because of outstanding, motivated, dedicated personnel.

Open-door Policy Toward Workers, Visitors, and Customers. Leaders are responsive to their employees and treat them as equals. These attitudes are demonstrated in the weekly "Friday Popcorn," where employees from all levels meet and mix for two hours of unstructured communication. Throughout the rest of the week, each morning's electronic mail is used for similar exchanges.

Self Management and Peer Management. Tandem employees are expected to take on responsibility and are held accountable; as a result, they are involved in the computer business, with a feeling of personal ownership and belonging to the corporation—they *enjoy* working.

Information and Technology. Tandem prides itself on being a paperless factory; personnel not only build computers, they use them exclusively to conduct their business. The computer is every worker's tool—each has a terminal for setting personal quality standards and reviewing personal quality production. Everyone controls quality, not just members of a separate department. Electronic mail connects personnel from California to Switzerland, and Tandem encourages all employees to use the system to help one another, especially in global problem-solving. The company has also used its electronic network to produce a daily, real-time internal newspaper that combines print, graphics, and media; employees from all over the world submit news. Other innovations include a journal that discusses corporate strategy, a TV network consisting of 43 locations to promote organizational communications and trust as well as marketing, and a program of training through computer business simulations.

Participation—Everyone Is Part of the Management Process. Everyone shares supervisory responsibility through membership in various manufacturing committees concerned about everything from quality to asset management. Worker democracy extends to voting on corporate policy. As workers contribute to the success of the enterprise, they earn rewards in the form of bonuses, stock, sabbaticals, or other forms of recognition. All concerned, including worker families, know where the company is going; the five-year corporate plan is shared, even with spouses of the employees.

Organizational relations at Tandem are such that contributors have the ability to influence the decision process through systematic representation.

Following is a demonstration of management that actually *leads* in the creation of an empowered high-performance work environment. Jim Treybig, as quoted by Smilor and Kuhn, shares with us his management philosophy:

> "The key to productivity in our business, and in fact in 90 percent of the jobs in our company, comes from its emphasis on people. We develop people concepts; we involve people in what we do.... The bottom line for business is that the major change facing companies in the United States today is the shifting roles of managers and individuals. Managers must integrate several functions—caring about people, working on strategy, expanding communication, generating creativity and innovation, raising productivity, improving quality, and strengthening the organization."

Self-Empowerment and Diversity

Empowerment goes in two directions. It must be understood and accepted by its recipients as well as practiced by leadership. Here lies an added challenge: fostering self-empowerment.

Self-empowerment is the ability to feel capable and motivated in pursuing a goal. It is having the self-assurance needed to fulfill any endeavor, knowing that we have the authority to act and that our idea or initiative will be acknowledged and valued.

Culture plays a major role in how we perceive empowerment and self-empowerment behaviors. All of us view reality our own way. We certainly cannot see or understand any concept that is not within the framework of our experience. It is one more way of saying, "We don't know what we don't know!" Our value system and, as a result, behavioral framework, derives from a hodgepodge of traditions, beliefs, experiences, and knowledge. We grow up learning how to behave and communicate, and by the time we reach adulthood, we have made decisions about what is expected, appropriate, or inappropriate. In other words, we have created a frame of reference that works, but only within the context of the culture in which we grew up, or with the people with whom we have been working, and—*as long as that culture doesn't change.*

As we saw earlier, we all have a mental picture or screen that helps us decide what is right and wrong, acceptable and unacceptable. All information is filtered through this screen. It is no wonder that we are frustrated in our daily communications at work when we are faced with multiple mental frameworks. Sending my mental message through your mental framework may result in a distorted or totally different message than was intended. This could throw us into despair, but take heart: this same reality can bring synergy, positive energy, and enthusiasm to the surface. A wealth of alternatives, creativity, and energy can be created as we negotiate our different frameworks, learning from each other. That gives us information on how to enhance our products, reduce costs, do what turns us on, and, last but not least, tells us how our clients think and what they want. After all, our clientele comes from the same world our own corporate community comes from.

Managing By Values Leads to Empowerment

Empowerment behaviors on the part of management will inevitably begin from the cultural framework that management knows. Therefore, putting what we said in Chapter 6 about managing by values into effect is extremely important for empowerment.

A major financial services organization in the Northeast, concerned with the lack of initiative and poor time management on the part of some international professionals, provided assertiveness and time-management training for those employees. Many of the international professionals had to juggle a heavy work schedule and visits from relatives who would come to see them in the U.S. The first group to go through time-management training was composed of Saudi men. After sitting in the training room for almost half a day, one of the men closed his manual and exclaimed, "How can we plan for tomorrow or next afternoon when everything is in the hands of Allah?!"

This participant had no context for managing time, a value that underlies anything and everything we do in this country. Through his cultural filters, not one of the skills could cross this barrier. Time management violated not only an ingrained habit but a sacred belief.

Flustered for a moment, the trainer mulled over the statement, looked at the participant and said, "What a wonderful contribution to our concept of time! Even more wonderful, Allah willed that you come to this seminar to give you skills to succeed in this country." This simple statement changed the perspective of the Saudi professional, and he tried once more to digest the skills and put them into practice. The trainer had managed the situation by making the participant right rather than wrong, stronger rather than weaker. The trainer and participants created a new cross-cultural synergy.

Managing by values requires the ability to think beyond one's own framework, to value other frameworks, and to integrate them into the achievement of work goals and objectives. Empowerment does not come from cloning the effective models we already have. In a culturally diverse work environment, management needs to understand that synergy only surfaces from differences. The power of an empowered workplace comes from the merging and mixing of various ways of dealing with the same work issues and business concerns. *Self-empowerment happens in diverse ways.*

A Culturally Different Empowered Leader

Read the case below then answer and if possible compare and discuss your answers with others.

Ming Lee is a mid-level manager for a computer company in Vancouver. Employed for about a year, she has already occupied her first management position for six months. She is an extremely committed professional, with outstanding skills and a good performance record. She perceives herself as an efficient and caring leader and demonstrates this by working very long hours and completing work to very high standards. She takes care of her team, always providing hints to improve their work. She never insults them by pointing out their errors directly, or interferes when they may have difficulty with a task. Sometimes she will complete a task herself when, after repeated suggestions, her team members are unable to understand what needs to get done. She gives her superiors complete and thorough reports, always careful not to speak off the top of her head. She always accepts suggestions quietly and never speaks out of turn. Ming Lee makes sure that she arrives at work before her superiors and leaves only after they have left the premises.

Ming Lee's lower context superiors, team members, and subordinates are completely baffled by her behavior. They perceive her as aloof, into her own perfectionism, and unwilling to share her knowledge and expertise. Everyone wonders what her real expectations and agenda are.

- How would you transform this situation from conflict into synergy?
- Can you identify any behaviors that demonstrate empowerment?
- How can all the parties involved share their discomforts without violating personal and corporate values?

We acknowledge that culture shock is chaotic. Answers to questions like those in the time-management story and the case of Ming Lee are always sticky, but, unless dealt with effectively, they become toxic.

The Five C's

Each organization will find its own way to empowerment. Existing corporate culture can be used to shift from existing monocentric, linear mindsets to circular, polycentric, and culturally diverse ones. Identify and use the values of the existing culture. Assess where you are, what your needs are, where you want to be, and what impact the changes will have in organizational survival and the bottom line. Then, whatever your industry or history as an organization may be, pay attention to these five C's. They will give management a compass to plot their journey to a transculturally empowered workplace.

1. Continuous Learning
2. Consistent Leadership
3. Centeredness in one's own culture
4. Commitment to a Vision
5. Ceaseless Communication

Let's look at each in detail.

1. Continuous Learning. The empowered worker is the educated worker, one who knows not only his or her specialty but the company, its culture, and its environment. To become intelligent resources, capable of taking initiative, workers require an understanding of the business, its finances, and its market. This means continuous learning, focused on a) knowing the customer and the product, b) familiarity with the work system and the hows and whys of the processes used, and c) understanding their own tools and technology and having a say in what best suits their needs and the organization's.

Most of all, workers need to learn about people. Lead them to understand how others think, behave, and communicate. Train and encourage them to express their differences so that they can trust their ability to reach agreements and perform together. Fear of conflict keeps an organization's diversity from reaching its potential. Because a continuously learning environment values the unknown, it has the key to turn conflict into synergy and healthy competitiveness. When continuous learning becomes part of an organizational culture, it reverses old values, e.g., secrecy is replaced by sharing information and knowledge. Everyone is capable of learning, perhaps at their own pace and in a different way but definitely capable. Continuous training in human communication skills, as well as making technical programs and opportunities accessible to all, fosters whole-system thinking. Employees see themselves as an integral part of the entire organizational system. Such inclusion and belonging reap loyalty, trust, and self-empowerment.

There is always tension between learning and producing. After a period of study, people reach a saturation point where learning plateaus. Focusing on application and discovering new problems and challenges gets people ready to learn again. The payoff for an organization committed to learning and self improvement can be enormous. When intelligence permeates the system, fears disappear and decision making and creative initiative take over. If we are able to educate, the other four C's fall into place.

2. Consistent Leadership. Empowering leaders can teach, train, mentor, and coach because they know how to let us use their power to free rather than confine. They have a full picture of the organization, its mission, vision, strategies, goals, and, most of all, its people. They are able to draw this full picture for the staff, and provide them with the information and moral support to perform according to standards and expectations. They learn from their staff, peers, and superiors and personally model high performance through their knowledge, expertise, camaraderie—and *vulnerability*. They know that empowered people learn from the mistakes they make. They reward and value ideas that surface from differences even if they don't always agree with them. They understand the value of recognition and acknowledgment. They are accessible, reachable, and willing to broaden their perspectives by listening to and implementing insights that come from other values.

Managing problems that involve culture—corporate, ethnic, gender, or any other kind—is like peeling onions. It takes patience and persistence, and there can be a lot of tears along the way. When you remove one layer, the next often looks exactly the same. Only when you have attacked quite a few layers do the problems start to look really smaller, even though their flavor may persist.

3. Centeredness in One's Own Culture. Power comes from being in touch with one's own cultural roots, as well as from the experience of managing challenges and being acknowledged by others. A transcultural manager is not a chameleon taking on other's characteristics, values, and opinions to avoid trouble. Effective transcultural leaders and workers know who they are culturally and are proud of it. They express themselves, value and empower others, and continually learn how to do both better. They are also aware of their own culturally biased reactions to change and to people and values that conflict with their own norms. They don't allow these to interfere with fair treatment. They know what competencies their organization needs to succeed, have a good solid definition of each, and are able to itemize the behavioral indicators that support it. They focus on behavior, always ready to negotiate agreements that work and foster the initiative of others. They share their expectations and listen attentively to others' responses. They know and teach others that there is more than one way of succeeding and achieving the same goal.

"Keep an open mind. An open mind is a very good thing. But while you are keeping an open mind, just make sure your brains don't fall out." These words by Maharani of Jaipur remind us that while it is important for leaders who foster empowerment across cultures to be flexible, they must not jeopardize their personal values. When we begin to feel "our brains are falling out," it's time to acknowledge our own values and share our perspectives. This fosters the centripetal force that holds an organization together when the centrifugal forces of a changing workforce and diverse work values would tear it apart. Comfortable with our own truth with all its limitations, other perspectives become opportunities to speak another language and "experiment with a different program."

4. Commitment to a Vision. As Pascarella and Frohman point out in *The Purpose Driven Organization,* only purpose and commitment will provide the framework for decision making in the new work environment. Purpose and commitment in more loosely knit culture are not easily inherited. Chosen directions must be articulated in a vision. Without a vision, organizations are ships lost at sea. An empowered, committed workforce needs a vision like a fleet needs a flagship. Don't be afraid to reach high. Think about how many visions have been fulfilled in our own lifetime! Many of us never expected to see a moon landing, but someone visualized it and implemented an action plan. *Life* recently published an article about efforts to resuscitate the planet Mars and make it livable. Another dream . . .? There's already an action plan. Committed and empowered leaders constantly share the dream and invite others to build on it as well as to build it.

5. Ceaseless Communication. In the diverse organization, communication is at the heart of empowerment, the most important tool for getting things done, and the basis for understanding, cooperation, and action. Communication is a two-edged sword that cuts but also heals. It distorts messages, hinders empowerment, causes frustrations and makes people and organizations ineffective, and yet we must use it to contain its damage. Effective transcultural organizations acknowledge that:

- Everyone is a versatile communicator. People use both verbal and nonverbal communication, and also express themselves in what they do and create.
- Everyone operates within his or her own private world. Perceptions are, in fact, reality.
- Everyone projects him or herself into communication. Human beings are comfortable with other human beings that are similar to them. Differences cause natural rejection.
- Every generation sees life differently. As we evolve into a more sophisticated world from one generation to the next, our experiences vary and our cultural framework changes.

Effective transcultural organizations create a framework where people learn about each other and from each other. They foster an open communication where employees surface their sensitivities and negotiate cross-cultural agreements that work professionally and personally. Leaders include others by mingling and sharing information both socially and professionally. The external image of such an organization is consistent with its internal image. In other words, what you communicate to your community and your clients is consistent with the message that your employees get about who you are and what you do. Effective transcultural leaders are accessible for informal and formal training. They facilitate communication exchanges and help resolve conflict. Effective transcultural leaders empower their employees by listening to different perspectives, probing for clarity, and implementing and acknowledging new ideas. Effective transcultural leaders commit to action and follow up with their employees. They clearly communicate the "what fors" and "why yous" of assignments. Effective transcultural leaders effectively and openly value employees who are different, and celebrate individual successes and group synergy.

Empowerment, to sum up, comes from commitment to vision, being at peace with one's own culture and flexible with others, and from having the information, alternatives, and resources that come from regular and timely communication.

Resentment in the Workforce

Empowerment means being honest with people, both old-timers and newcomers, insiders and outsiders, about what they are up against in the changing culture, especially when resentments such as these appear:

1. *Jobs and life-styles in jeopardy.* Given the lack of preparedness in the native-born North American workforce, even with an unforeseen economic boom, many people from the present generation of workers will be surpassed and supplanted by newcomers and immigrants. Resentment will run high, particularly among traditionally targeted groups who feel that they have been previously passed over and, just as they are making some progress, are being passed over again. Commitments to our targeted minorities must con-

(continued)

(continued from previous page)

tinue to be fulfilled. Newcomers need to be advised about the risks that such resentments pose for them and be given the tools to both protect themselves and integrate themselves into their new situation. This is an important part of acculturation training.

2. *Education and training.* Educational reform is more than a public social issue, it is a bottom-line corporate concern. We cannot look for the American education system to train and educate our workers adequately for the foreseeable future. Companies will have to do it themselves. It will be a key part of empowerment. Many employers and managers will resent this. They had not planned to spend their time and resources this way. Older, better educated workers will resent the demands from and advantages given to younger workers whom they see as lazy and incompetent and both getting and costing the enterprise far more than they deserve.

3. *Personal privacy.* Newcomers to the American work scene may indeed be shocked to find that while government surveillance of individual citizens in the "Land of the Free" is kept well in check, business is far less restricted in collecting and disseminating information about employees. Their American bosses can be far less respectful of their rights to privacy than are the bosses in many other parts of the world. They may be subjected to electronic surveillance systems as well as unauthorized inspections of briefcases, desks, automobiles, and personnel and medical files. Companies doing this claim they are protecting themselves against expensive medical claims, inadequate and unreliable letters of reference in the hiring process, and the general climate of a litigious society that uses any lack of information as a basis for lawsuit. The numbers of people who may have access to personal information about one may cause resentment in people coming from more private cultures.

American Cultural Solutions

We live in a world in which the majority of people are barely surviving. We must meet that challenge, with a vision of a world in which all can thrive, not just compete. That vision of plenty is a traditional part of

American mythology. Variations of it drive the ideals of the best of our organizations. The transcultural manager must be committed to making it a reality.

It is an American value to judge others by what they do, not by who they are or where they come from. This cultural peculiarity affects our identity. Americans are not born into who they are, they have to make themselves into who they are. This has its shadow side as well. Failure in America means failure as a person. This explains why religious and other affiliations in America are so prevalent as a source of identity. In Darwinian terms, the fittest here are now the ablest. This works well when one is among the ablest, but when the ablest turn out more and more to be immigrants, or of a different race or gender, the fragile identity of many Americans is threatened.

How to be productive and care for all of the human resources of society is a challenge that American egalitarianism and belief in progress is clearly far from meeting, though it may be the best we have and can contribute to a solution. The failure and disarray of Marxist and Socialist experiments in recent years is a double tragedy. One is obvious—the human economic misery we read about daily in the newspapers. The other is less obvious, but perhaps even greater—the spiritual depression that occurs when the powerful hope for human egalitarianism has been betrayed, perverted, and turned into cynicism. Billions of dollars in aid to Eastern Europe will not address this deep malaise of the spirit.

We must look to not only the preservation but the *improvements* of the free enterprise system. As with individuals, so with systems—our greatest strengths overused become our greatest weaknesses. Capitalism for all its virtues requires alternative points of view and strong competitors to remain robust. Ecological concern will assume this role more fully in the future. In the meantime, as Barbara Ehrenreich warns in a *Time* editorial, before multiculturalism fills the vacuum left by the demise of Communism in the American vocabulary of fear, workforce empowerment can serve as one transforming force that can protect us from our singlemindedness.

Empowerment in a diverse workforce must draw from both more tightly woven and more loosely knit cultural strengths. There should be no mistake that the empowerment involves acculturating our people to the highest and best values developed by Western culture and by the American experiment. Barry Lopez, author of *Crow and Weasel,* offers perhaps the finest definition of culture we have seen, from the mouth of one of his storybook characters:

> "The stories people tell have a way of taking care of them. If stories come to you, care for them. And learn to give them away where they are needed. Sometimes a person needs a story more than food to stay alive. That is why we put these stories in each other's memory. This is how people care for themselves."*

Stories of empowerment are still perhaps the best contribution America can make to a world that both needs so much and has given it so much.

* Excerpted from Crow and Weasel, copyright © 1990 by Barry Holstun Lopez. Published by North Point Press and reprinted by permission.

Points To Remember From This Chapter

- Empowerment requires new patterns of nonhierarchical, nonadversarial thinking and behavior.
- Driving decisions downward requires less planning and controlling and more efforts to create a learning organization with high aspirations and standards.
- Successful empowerment efforts and managing by values result in habits of self-empowerment.
- Use the 5 C's to reach your empowerment goals.
  1. Continuous learning
  2. Consistent leadership
  3. Centeredness in one's own culture
  4. Commitment to a vision
  5. Ceaseless communication
- Stories of empowerment lead to empowerment.

EPILOGUE

By now it must be clear that we have not provided you with a blueprint of the transcultural leader, because such simply does not exist. In the course of our writing this book, the context of diversity has changed substantially, as it no doubt will again between our finishing these last lines of the Epilogue, and when this book reaches your hand.

We have seen the Gulf War, the dissolution of the Communist bloc, ethnic "cleansing" in former Yugoslavia, a global economic recession that reinvents itself month after month, and the Thomas-Hill Congressional hearings. We have watched the explosion of rage in Los Angeles, the neo-Nazi brutalization of asylum seekers and foreign guests, the Tailhook scandal, the opening of Ku Klux Klan offices in Europe, and South Africa turning upon itself. Each of these has added to the price, the pain, and the challenge of living and doing business together. We have survived another U.S. election campaign in which virtually no one had anything substantial to say about these issues.

While each turn of events caused us to rethink and rewrite details, the book's theme emerged ever more strongly. Our discussion has been less than thorough. In addition to the flood of current events, we could have touched on the generational differences and the aging of the North American population, focused on resurgent sexual harassment, and explored corporate and national immigration policies. We chose to focus on a few basic managerial functions and a handful of test models. The reason is simple—more than ever, we need women and men who can listen carefully to the world around them, envision something better, influence, mentor, and empower others, and take steps themselves to carry out their hopes and dreams in flexible and inventive ways. To those eager and fit for the task, we offer not unassailable truths about diversity, but a few currently usable tools and insights, hoping to nourish the souls of those who must, as immigrants to the future, lead this ragtag world of organizations, politics, and education to its new home in the twenty-first century.

Shortly after drafting the "Culture's Continuum Model" found in Appendix A, a combined business and holiday trip took one us to Vienna. There, in a tiny bookshop, he encountered a wall chart dating from about the year 1734, a matrix that attempted to describe "The Peoples of Europe and their Characteristics." It listed, in the then most scientific way, their virtues and vices, their life- and death-styles, their religious habits, and even the diseases to which they were prone. Though many items caused a smile, it is sad to say that not a few of these eighteenth-century biases are alive and well today. Perhpas someone in a future generation, who picks up a used copy of this title in a bookstall, will chuckle knowingly in recognition of how far humanity has come in understanding, acceptance, and collaboration since this writing. This is our fondest hope.

CULTURE'S CONTINUUM: A MODEL OF HOW PEOPLE THINK, WORK, AND RELATE TO EACH OTHER

This model classifies cultures, subcultures, groups, and individuals along a continuum from "more tightly woven" to "more loosely knit," and tells about the kinds of thinking and behavior that are characteristic of where they fall on the continuum. Besides collecting and summarizing much of what has been explained in this book, this appendix serves as a tool for managers to compare their own culturally preferred values and forms of behavior with those of the diverse people with whom they work. It provides a rough hypothesis about how they and others are likely to behave, to the degree that they as individuals are consistent with these cultural tendencies.

How to Use this Model Effectively

1. Remember, *each individual is unique,* though he or she may share many characteristics common to the group(s) and culture(s) to which he or she belongs. While we have divided the continuum into three separate bands or segments (Alpha, Beta, and Gamma cultures), specific groups may bridge or fall between or participate in several of these categories; for instance, African-Americans and Hispanics, long in the North American workforce, share characteristics from more tightly woven cultures while borrowing much today from the more loosely knit environment in which they live and work. Some of the people we work with are also bicultural, sometimes blending their cultures in how they behave, sometimes switching back and forth from one cultural pattern to another, depending on the context in which they find themselves.

Many women today, for example, regularly do this when they move between the workplace and home. Consultant and author Liang Ho, who uses a similar model, calls this process "cross-cultural swinging," and sees it as both inevitable and necessary for our ability to acculturate and collaborate with each other.

2. The numbered items indicate preferred forms of behavior, or the way people in a group might normally respond if they are true to their cultural formulae. However, most people are capable of a far wider range of behaviors than they regularly use, and, given certain circumstances, may behave in ways that are less common or atypical to their own culture.

3. Each numbered item is a range of behaviors. Some items are actually expressed as polarities with dotted underlining to indicate this. At other times we have broken the behavior differences into two or three more distinct classifications because they seem more or less characteristic of certain groups of cultures; such classification gives us more useful insights when dealing with them in the workplace. Even where three choices are given, this is a relative positioning and not a rigid classification. In many cases we lack the data to do this.

4. When working with an individual or a group from another culture, observe their behavior, then, using the model, ask yourself, "Am I from a more tightly woven or a more loosely knit group than the person or group with whom I am working or communicating?" Then check the model again to see where you might suspect differences of behavior or value conflicts to appear.

5. This model cannot tell you what specific people or groups in your workforce are like, or enable you to predict how they will behave in any given situation. Its purpose is to help you think, analyze, and ask the right questions when, as a leader or coworker, you try to resolve or head off breakdowns. No specific group we know of will embody all of the characteristics of A, B, or Γ cultures. Still this summary helps you explore your own or another group's values and behavior more sensibly and sensitively than you would if you relied on common stereotypes or your limited individual experience. If you determine that a person or group comes from a more tightly woven or more loosely knit segment on the continuum

than yourself, you can suspect that they may also differ in various other ways found in the same column or range on the list. Thus while the model does not directly give you absolutely certain information about a person or group, it helps you know which things to look for as potentially different in their work behavior. You will be able to recognize differences as cultural when they occur, and be clearer about what questions to ask and what further information you need.

6. Not all cultures or individuals develop equally on all items listed in the model. Besides, many cultures and individuals are in transition today—in both directions. So this model provides you with a series of working *hypotheses to be tested,* which should function better than the stereotypes that most of us have been brought up to use when looking at and evaluating others.

7. Use the model as a checklist of differences when you are deciding how to apply the 80/20 rule to a breakdown with someone different from you. Assume that at least 80% of what you react to in others is cultural and that 20% or less is personal. Look for what the model tells you about the 80% of the situation that is cultural. Referring to the model in times of friction may help you reduce negative feelings, blame, and other destructive behaviors that may accompany cross-cultural conflict.

   Remember that when you look at your own culture it is as an insider. You tend to see many differences in people of your own cultural groups and be somewhat tolerant of them. Your characteristics as a group and what you have in common is less visible from inside. On the other hand, when you are an outsider you tend to see the general characteristics and similarities of a group while overlooking the range of differences that actually exists in that culture. This outsider/insider phenomenon of perception is not unlike what happens when it seems to us that all blacks, or all whites, or all Asians "look alike." Not only do we tend to flatten out the diversity of others by outsider judgments, but we also tend to misinterpret or be offended by others because we use our insider values to judge groups to whom we are outsiders.

8. Use items in the model to find alternative ways to see and resolve problems. Peek around your cultural blinders by becoming open

to people with other points of view. Trying on others perspectives yourself may help you consider a problem or make a decision in a new light.

9. The model will also help you recognize the different layers of context in yourself. What are your more tightly woven and more loosely knit sides? Are they in harmony or conflict? What would your more tightly woven side have to say to your more loosely knit side and vice versa, if you listen to them talk to each other in your mind? How can you use other sides of yourself to enhance your understanding and empathy and better your leadership and communication abilities when dealing with people whose cultures resemble these sides of yourself?

10. When you read this model the first time, skim through the alphabetized headings. These are in the form of questions that a group might ask about itself. Then, read through slowly in more detail, focusing on how each cultural group (A, B, or Γ) tends to answer each question. Then personalize the process by positioning yourself in each numbered item, e.g., asking yourself "Am I more to the right or the left (on polarity items)?" and "Am I more like A, B, or Γ (on 2 or 3 category items)?" Once you have a fix on your own cultural preferences, you can see how others you work with might compare to you, given what you know about them. Ask yourself and others how specific items in the model might be playing themselves out in workplace situations you are actually facing. Finally, use this information to experiment with and change how you communicate or manage by values.

Modeling Culture

Here are some of the assumptions which we have used in assembling this model. More technical information follows the model itself on pages 237–238.

- All cultures and subcultures and features of cultures fall somewhere on a continuum, i.e., they are more or less tightly woven or loosely knit. Unless interrupted, most cultures tend to become more tightly woven over time. While efficient and economical on one hand, it nonetheless makes them less capable of coping with changes in the environment. Cultures that have change as a value respond quickly to changes in the environment, but can easily lack sufficient infrastructure and follow-through to take full advantage of the changes and new developments

- Deep culture is like the warp of a weaving, the long strands attached to the frame of the loom over which the rest is woven. It lies beneath and holds the more varied and sometimes changing design together. Deep culture is how the human mind maintains consistency as it connects new things with the old. Surface culture is more like the woof, the yarn or filling that provides the design we see. It appears to change more readily and rapidly. It looks new and different but is usually aligned in some fashion with deeper thinking patterns and values. It's made of the same stuff. Under stress we tend to revert to earlier, deeper, and more traditional values and forms of behavior.

- When dealing with diversity, we are always thrust into a more loosely knit situation. We all have to either learn about the tightly woven aspects of the other person's culture and behave their way, or teach them ours, or fail to function effectively with them. Certain cultures have, because of their constant diet of change and diversity, actually committed themselves to being loosely knit, i.e., have made it a value. They may embrace change, while more tightly woven cultures keep it at arm's length.

- Almost all cultures are a mixture of these elements. Since we all deal with stability and change, we all need to master some of the behaviors in both sets.

- In this model, we're always talking about culture as it exists, first and foremost, as a function of the human mind (primary culture), which is revealed in what people do and produce (secondary culture).

(Appendix A continued on next page)

The Model

More Tightly Woven		More Loosely Knit
A Cultures	B Cultures	Γ Cultures
An image or metaphor for this kind of culture might be:	An image or metaphor for this kind of culture might be:	An image or metaphor for this kind of culture might be:
A Woven Basket	**A Silk Brocade Tapestry**	**An Electronic Network**
a design that takes advantage of its materials for function and beauty or meaning simultaneously. Reflects mythology, nature, and the understanding of how life is lived in both materials and its decoration.	with highly stylized motifs and, in some cases, a life-style or even a historical scene. The design is tight, highly detailed, stylized—even abstract motifs are familiar because they have been handed down.	or a modern macrame wall hanging, loose like a net, with objects woven into it, e.g., driftwood. The design is abstract. You have to imagine the details.
These cultures have an integrated closely woven design in which style and function are one.	These cultures have a tightly woven fabric in which variety is constrained by style. There are many close, irreplaceable connections.	These cultures have many loose, distant connections with interchangeable and replaceable elements. Style is usually secondary to function.
As an insider you know how to read the message. It is obvious.		Even as an insider you may need to determine or agree on the meaning with others if it is to have one.

More Tightly Woven		More Loosely Knit
A Cultures	B Cultures	Γ Cultures
What's tightly woven often produces a more tailor-made fit and more elegance, but is less flexible and all purpose.		Multipurpose, "unisex." Unfinished. Elegance lies in flexibility.
These cultures tend to be complete. Little gets in once they have been woven. When the basket is broken, its function is lost. These cultures are fragile, easily disrupted and destroyed. They change very slowly on their own.	The fabric of these cultures has great tensile strength, but when actually torn or cut, they are extremely hard to repair. Such brocades are rarely rewoven, but rather patched with a similar fabric when necessary. Similarly, such cultures assimilate foreign elements and make them their own. They can incorporate much without need to change quickly.	These cultures are more unfinished. New things can get in without ruining the design. Individuals, like the fibers of a macramé, often have great strength. The whole is more easily repaired if torn. Could be rewoven or easily become something else without being destroyed. Change and newness are norms.
Woven as needed. Carries only what is necessary.	Woven slowly. Little gets in, but little gets through. The individuals in such cultures, like strands of the tapestry, are close together, each in its place. One moves, the whole fabric moves. The weave holds it together.	Knit together quickly. Things easily fall through. Individual strands and objects will move around unless they are deliberately tied to each other with a special knot. (Explicit commitments, agreements.)
Aesthetic and economic values are not separated from nature and function.	Values are clearly established and become classic.	Values are either unknown, to be negotiated, or fluctuate greatly with the market.

(continued)

More Tightly Woven		More Loosely Knit
A Cultures	B Cultures	Γ Cultures

A. *Who are we?*

1. Native American, Pacific Islander, Africans, Latins, Arabs, etc.	Chinese, Japanese, Indochinese, Korean, East Indian, Thai, etc.	White Western European, North American, and places settled or colonized by such groups.
2. More female .... More male		
3. More rural .... More urban		
4. More stable environment .... More rapidly changing environment		
5. Longer standing groups .... More freshly formed groups		
6. More developed industries .... Newer technology businesses		
7. Old-timers .... Newcomers		
8. More indigenous groups .... More transient groups		
9. More people of color .... More white people		

B. *How do we value each other and ourselves as members of a society and of a work group?*

1. Belonging to the blood group, having a role, creates my social worth. I do what is needed for our survival as a group.	Membership in the family, class, and caste determines my social worth. I do what I do because of who I am in the group.	Contractual arrangements say what and who I am and establish my social worth. I am what I do. This determines my value to the group.
2. I am respected and allowed to lead because of my age, important role, or status in the group and because I behave correctly and honorably according to my role in my group.		I am respected or given status and become a leader because of my personal accomplishments, competence, and contribution to the group, as well as having the right kind of personality.

More Tightly Woven		More Loosely Knit
A Cultures	B Cultures	Γ Cultures
3. Men, women, and children are valuable because of their role in the survival or continuation of the group or family. Children become adults by being initiated.	Women and children are valuable because of their role in the continuation and status of the family. Children participate in the work of the family when they are able. They are little adults.	Men, women, and children should be valued as individuals possessing equal rights and claims on the group or society. Children live in a special category called childhood and are a protected class in the world of work.
4. Sex determines my role in the group. Males are usually given more status.	Sex determines my role and status in the group. Males are almost invariably given more status.	Sex may determine my role and status in the group. Though equality is an ideal, males are often given preference.
5. My success results in visible riches and my earning power is demonstrated by my ability to care for others in my group and by conspicuous spending.	My success, my earning power, belongs to the family or group and enhances its respect and status.	Success brings me inner wealth. My material wages and rewards are symbols of my achievement.
6. My status in the group will increase as I become older and acquire seniority.		I maintain status by remaining youthful, vigorous, and able. Beauty and good looks enhance my status. Seniority is secondary to performance.

(continued)

More Tightly Woven		More Loosely Knit
A Cultures	B Cultures	Γ Cultures
7. I am initiated into my role in the group and shown by example how to carry it out. This involves fear of shame and reverence for others. I should be able to do what my status requires.	I am brought up to understand and carry out my role in the group and understand the roles of others. I may perform many roles to meet the needs of the group before I arrive at my own. This involves learning respect for the members of the group and fear of shaming it.	I am brought up to be a group-independent, self-sufficient individual. This involves an emphasis on equality, much discussion and interpretation, learning to accept risk and fear guilt, especially in the form of failing to perform well. I am trained to do specific tasks.
8. We can be punished by being excluded from the survival system. This may mean not only social but physical death.	More corporal punishment is likely. Punishment fits the crime. Disowning and excommunication are social death. The authority exercises much personal discretion over rewards and punishments.	Punishments can frequently be negotiated. Disinheritance and firing from a job can be severe punishments but one can move on. The authority has less personal discretion over rewards and punishments.
9. There is a clearer separation of men's and women's worlds and tasks.		Men and women may perform the same tasks according to their individual abilities.
10. Strong insider-outsider distinctions .... boundaries		More permeable group
11. Outsiders remain strangers unless assimilated into our group. We are friendly but wary with outsiders until we come to trust them.	We prefer long-term working relationships built on strong ties. Our business partners become like family. Assimilation is the rare exception.	I do not need to like or be like someone to work with her or him, though I might prefer it. Assimilation to the group is expected but ideally not required.

More Tightly Woven		More Loosely Knit
A Cultures	B Cultures	Γ Cultures
C. How do we think of, manage, and use time?		
1. We are one with the flow or vagaries of nature. Everything is present in some form or other. We must be aware, listen. Time is indefinite, incidental to things, when noticed at all.	Time is cyclical. What goes around comes around. We must be patient, observe, wait. The present is driven by the past.	Time is linear and historical. You never stand in the same stream twice. Days, hours, seconds, etc. are measured. Sense of urgency. The present is driven by the future.
2. "Once upon a time..."	"History repeats itself."	"What time is it?"
3. I can deal with time in a flexible, intuitive way. For us time is immediate, here and now. We do what the situation demands without thinking of time.	We think in the long term, generations. Our good work may be invisible now, but it will show up powerfully later.	We maximize the short term, make it happen. We work by setting and meeting deadlines, and by performing on schedule.
4. We will act when we sense the time is right.	We will act when all is ready.	I will act at nine o'clock, or, when I'm good and ready.
5. Everything is here and now.	We remember or yearn for the return of a golden age, the good old days.	Time is a measurable substance, often "money." We use it to buy the future and pay for the past.

(continued)

More Tightly Woven		More Loosely Knit
A Cultures	B Cultures	Γ Cultures
6. Many things can happen at once. It is okay for simultaneous conversations or events to occur.(Polychronicity can be widespread.) Get the big picture before going on to details. Polish things as you go along.		We should pay attention to one thing at a time, e.g., people should take turns speaking. We attend to the details in a linear and orderly fashion. We break our jobs into component parts. (Monochronicity is usually preferred)
7. We take as much time as we need for the task. Accomplishing work, a task in harmonious relationships with others, is what gives it value and completeness.		Our activities and efforts will be expanded or condensed to fit a certain period of time. Time measures the value of the event or task.
8. Our timetables when they exist and our meetings are flexible to accommodate the interaction with people which is how we produce the best results.		I will be valued and promoted because of my ability to manage tasks and people in time.

D. *How do we feel, think and make decisions?*
1. Yin .... Yang
2. "Both ... and ... " .... "Either ... , or ... "
3. We take decisions more slowly. .... We decide more quickly.
4. We find unanimity before acting .... I act individually, create unanimity as necessary.
5. We defer to authority. ....We defer (if necessary) to power.

More Tightly Woven		More Loosely Knit
A Cultures	B Cultures	Γ Cultures
6. Truth is based on nature. Because it's so.	Truth is based on authority. Because you, I, or they say so.	Truth is based on what I see as objective data. I say so, because . . .
7. Nature, the situation, people speak. We listen and speak with it.	We search for wisdom, authority, and respect sages and gurus.	We do what works. Be pragmatic, practical. We respect inventors, scientists. We even deconstruct reality to explore chaos.
8. We value personal experience, testimony, more highly as processes for making decisions.	We prefer commentary, discussion, consulting authority as processes for making decisions.	Experiment, analysis, research more highly valued as processes for making decisions.
9. Metaphors and stories are valid forms of evidence and are often preferred.	Tradition, precedent, are the best evidence and are usually preferred.	Research findings, statistical data, examples, are preferred as evidence.
10. We come to consensus in the group by reading the signs.	We should be in agreement with those who are in authority.	I can argue it out, negotiate to reach consensus, or agreement with others.
11. We walk with the elders, interpret the signs, consult with the shaman, leader, manager.	We consult and obey parents, leaders, managers and other authorities in order to avoid mistakes.	Learn to do science, create and test hypotheses. We learn from our mistakes.

(continued)

More Tightly Woven		More Loosely Knit
A Cultures	B Cultures	Γ Cultures
12. We tell stories (myths), perform the rites.	We listen to the priests, theologians, and philosophers who comment on traditions, (sacred) writings and rites.	We measure all by personal experience and reason.
13. Be in harmony with nature and the group.	What is wisest most harmonious choice for our group? What does God or the lawgiver (parent, boss, etc.) want? (Voluntarism).	What does my conscience tell me? What do I want? What must I do? (Voluntarism).
14. We act in concert with the gods, the world, and each other so as not to bring wrath or shame on our group.	We honor our family or group's members and values. We seek to preserve its good name and cause no shame.	Be an ethical person. I alone am responsible for what I do and say, for doing the right thing.
15. Misbehaving results in disorder, threat to the group's survival. We talk about it among ourselves and take care of it.	Misbehaving results in shame to myself and others, a threat to the group's honor and good name. We keep it quiet from outsiders.	Misbehavior results in guilt, personal and organizational liability. I should own up to it and deal with it before the consequences get worse.
16. Take risks only with the consent of the group, because they are involved in the risk.	I can be brave and sacrifice myself in carrying out my role and responsibilities. But I should not take unknown risks lest I fail and embarrass my group.	Risk taking is part of the game. I am responsible for my own behavior. Nothing ventured, nothing gained.
17. I do not want to stand out as an individual. I am reluctant to contradict others, urge changes, challenge the system.		It's okay to stand out from the group. I can bring up new ideas, urge changes in procedures and policies.

More Tightly Woven		More Loosely Knit
A Cultures	B Cultures	Γ Cultures
E. *What must we do to survive and succeed as individuals and as a group? What are our critical questions today?*		
1. I must remain a part of the group to survive.	I must remain connected to the family to succeed.	I must be able to go it alone if necessary to survive and succeed.
2. We participate with others. We dig a well together.	We serve others. We draw water from the family well for each other.	We become empowered and empower others. I learn to dig my own well and teach others to dig theirs.
3. How can we survive as a people?	How can we survive without despotism?	How can we survive on the earth? How can we preserve human and ecological diversity?
4. Do we want power? How can we get power?	How should we distribute and exercise power?	Are there limits to the exercise of power? What are they?

F. *How do our values motivate us and guide how we behave?*
1. Maintain honor in the eyes of others. .... Righteousness in my own eyes is what counts.
2. Keep interpersonal ....Surface interpersonal conflicts inside. .... conflicts and resolve them.
3. Competition tends to demotivate us .... Competition motivates us.

(continued)

More Tightly Woven		More Loosely Knit
A Cultures	B Cultures	Γ Cultures
4. We feel strong when in harmony with the gods and spirits of nature.	We feel strong when we show respect, duty, honor to those to whom it is due and perform our duty.	We feel strong when we take charge, gain ownership, freedom, commitment, and take responsibility.
5. We care for and enjoy each other. Open competition with each other would be embarrassing.	We seek wealth, success, social mobility, security for our family. Competition with outsiders may motivate.	We seek personal fulfillment, self esteem. I can compete even within my group to win. Competition improves everyone's performance.
6. I look for rewards for my group by succeeding and performing to expectations. I would not want to be praised in public or in a way that set me above or against my group.		I look for personal credit, and enhance my self esteem through personal excellence. Praising me or promoting me in front of others enhances my self esteem.
7. We work for the good of the tribe.	We strive for the good of the family. The city, the state is a family of families.	We pursue individual interests while respecting the rights of others. The state is the sum of individuals.
8. Initiate others.	Serve others and be served by them.	Empower others and collaborate with them.
9. How will what I do shame me in the eyes of others?	Have I lost status or face in the eyes of someone else?	Have I done something wrong? How will it diminish me?

More Tightly Woven		More Loosely Knit
A Cultures	B Cultures	Γ Cultures

G. *How do we govern, manage, and relate to authority?*

1. We should not question parents, teachers, bosses, etc.		Authority improves by being questioned. It is my responsibility to question.
2. Authority should foresee and know best how to provide what is needed and faithfully do so.		Authority must be informed by its constituents requests. Ideally, it enables individuals to act and provide for themselves.
3. Authority discerns what is right and wrong.	Authority decides what is right and wrong.	My conscience decides what is right and wrong.
4. Authority determines responsibility.	Authority defines responsibility. Law and order	Responsibility is inherent in authority. Authority and responsibility go hand in hand.
5. My role in the nature of things determines how I behave toward others.	I am responsible to higher authority for my behavior toward my constituents.	I am responsible directly to my constituents for my stewardship.
6. The will of nature determines good decisions.	The will of the lawgiver determines good decisions.	The reasonableness and utility of the law is predominant.
7. The authority expresses the wisdom of the group.	I am judged by a wiser authority.	I am judged by my peers.

(continued)

More Tightly Woven		More Loosely Knit
A Cultures	B Cultures	Γ Cultures
H. How should we behave towards others?		
1. I should behave towards others according to my and their role or status in the group.		I relate to others according to my and their personality and the agreements we have made with each other.
2. I should be polite, respect convention, boundaries.		I should be open, personal.
3. We value the relationship highly and strive to keep it harmonious. We don't let the content of the relationship damage the relationship itself.		Value the content of the exchange. Keep it true, honest. This is the best way to value the relationship.
4. I am by birth related to those within my group. Serious outside relationships are a rarity.	Entering a relationship takes more time and effort, but acceptance, once given, tends to be total.	I can enter new relationships easily, but relationships are usually limited or compartmentalized to a specific area of my work or life.
5. Suspect strangers until they prove themselves.	My family is more important than friendships. Blood is thicker than water. Good friends become family.	I suspend my judgment about strangers. It depends on experience.
6. Hospitality and friendship are the business of my group as well as myself. Private friendship is uncommon and divisive.		My friends do not have to relate to my family or group to be my friends. I can entertain them in private.

More Tightly Woven		More Loosely Knit
A Cultures	B Cultures	Γ Cultures
7. Hospitality for us is a great responsibility, even when reciprocity is sometimes lacking.		I can choose whether to be hospitable or not. Reciprocity may be a factor.
8. More of our property is held in common. "What's mine is yours. What is yours is mine."		More property is private "What is mine is mine. What is yours is yours."
9. We can be quite emotional, even if our emotions are hidden.		We are more functional when rational. Emotions can and should be restricted.

I. *How are our workplaces, our organizations, and our community structured?*		
1. Less vertical social mobility. Sometimes more horizontal mobility		Greater vertical social mobility. Sometimes more .... compartmentalization.
2. My position in the community, family, society, depends on my birth.		My position in the community depends on my accomplishments. What I become by acting on my own behalf and for others.
3. Our rules are rarely articulated, but roles are modeled according to our age and status.	Different rules and behaviors may be in effect depending on the person and the situation.	We want similar rules to exist for every level and have them applied impartially.

(continued)

More Tightly Woven		More Loosely Knit
A Cultures	B Cultures	Γ Cultures
4. Honor and status are mostly external. Dress reflects the order of nature.	Honor and status are mostly external. Dress represents ranks and roles.	Honor and status are mostly internal. Costume reflects success.
5. Nature is good, harmony with it is good.	Sharp dividing lines are drawn between what is good and bad.	Very little is absolute, good or bad. Many shades and gray areas exist.
6. Emphasis on community. Elders and leaders emerge or are chosen according to age and natural bent.	Emphasis on hierarchy. There is an order in nature (inequality).	All are created equal. Differences are the result of individual choices and behaviors. Leadership emerges and is recognized.
7. My contacts and relationships with others are more important than specific agreements we make with each other.		Agreements stand on their own and are less dependent upon the relationship of the contracting parties.
8. I must plan flexibly because people's minds, the situation, the universe may change.		I can do fixed-term planning, using scientific analysis, depending on a reliable universe.
9. I can rely on others in my group to take the initiative to help me and support me.	I can rely on others in my in-group to help me. I can ask them for advice, financial help, etc., but I should keep my problems quiet and at home.	I should be self-supporting and independent, but I can look for third–party assistance from agencies, service professionals, etc. I am responsible for getting the resources for solving my own problems and getting my own needs met.

More Tightly Woven		More Loosely Knit
A Cultures	B Cultures	Γ Cultures
10. Service and reciprocity from members of my group are required.		Strangers may provide service to me and I to them. Volunteer work is more common and respected.

J. *How do we communicate with each other?*	
1. Establish, build, maintain the relationship.	Focus on information, facts, issues, and programs.
2. Almost everything seen and taken as personal.	Distinctions made between personal and factual.
3. Give more socially desirable responses. .... Give more uniform responses.	
4. Prefer implicit speech. .... Speak more explicitly.	
5. We prefer standardized responses to situations. .... We improvise for each situation.	
6. We prefer metaphor, stories, analogies. .... We employ abstractions.	
7. We emphasize form, how things are said. .... We emphasize content, what is said.	
8. The whole context communicates (including status, social situation)	Communication occurs when messages are sent and received.
9. We rely on many nonverbal signals (body language, tone, etc.).	We use fewer gestures, rely more on words.
10. We value politeness, indirection.	We value directness, assertiveness.
11. Use intermediaries more often. .... Prefer face-to-face contact.	
12. I hesitate to call attention to myself, my skills, and achievements, which would set me off from my group.	It is okay and often beneficial to call attention to myself, my abilities, and accomplishments.
	(continued)

More Tightly Woven		More Loosely Knit
A Cultures	B Cultures	Γ Cultures

K. *How do we prefer to give and get feedback?*

	More Loosely Knit
1. We lighten, perhaps withhold, the negative side, bad news, complaints so as not to bring disharmony into relationships.	We deliver both positive and negative assessments, good and bad news, in order to improve oneself, and one's performance.
2. We often give criticism, raise problems through a third party so that feelings or "face" are protected.	We give criticism directly. Third-party feedback is usually seen as cowardly.
3. We wait for appropriate time and place, make it private and casual. Don't embarrass the individual or the group by a public display.	The sooner the better, often publicly.
4. We should always measure our words, think before we speak.	We think out loud, give "gut" feelings. "Let it all hang out."
5. Feedback when given directly is often given to the group without singling out individuals.	We focus our feedback on individual responsibility and performance.

L. *How do we use space?*
1. More sacred spaces. .... More profane space.
2. Clear boundaries. .... Permeable boundaries.

More Tightly Woven		More Loosely Knit
A Cultures	B Cultures	Γ Cultures
3. Many of our boundaries result from class differences or group identity. They are often invisible though very real.		Physical separation creates differences for us, e.g., open, or closed offices, being in the middle, or up front etc. Visible boundaries may not be real limits.

M. *How do we handle conflicts?*	
1. Open confrontation would be destructive for us. It should be discouraged or forbidden.	Confronting another directly and openly can be productive for us.
2. We find respect more important than facts when there is a disagreement.	We believe facts are more important than preserving appearances.
3. We want conflicts to be avoided.	We want conflicts to be quickly resolved and terminated.
4. Our emotions can be strongly expressed if conflict actually occurs.	We prefer our emotions to be suppressed as much as possible in conflict.
5. Personal or familial retribution, feuds, are possible means to righting a wrong.	We should use legal recourse to seek justice.
6. Interpersonal and intergroup aggression may on rare occasions be required (vengeance).	Aggression is uncivilized and should be unnecessary, but force may be met by force.

(continued)

More Tightly Woven		More Loosely Knit
A Cultures	B Cultures	Γ Cultures
7. Some quarrels can be functional.		Quarrels are usually destructive.
8. Maintain harmony.		Find a solution.

N. *How do we see and handle nature?*		
1. We are a part of what is. Magic and ritual can effect and affect things.	Accept what is, what occurs. The world rarely appears manageable and changeable (fatalism).	Strive for mastery and control. The world appears manageable and changeable (pragmatism).
2. The sun is god.	There is nothing new under the sun.	I can invent solar energy panels, etc.
3. Change is slow, normal (evolutionary).	Change results from unfolding of what already is (devolutionary).	We believe in progress and create change (revolutionary).
4. Cause and result are not necessarily connected.	From results we are able to see causes but change is frequently not in our power.	We rely heavily on cause and result.

O. *How do we relate to the divine, the supernatural, the ultimate(s)?*		
1. We live in a sacred world.	Various schools or religions can be part of our life.	Religion is only one force in an essentially secular world. Religious pluralism is our norm.

More Tightly Woven		More Loosely Knit
A Cultures	B Cultures	Γ Cultures
2. Religion and magic are an integral part of our everyday life.	Religion and philosophy can provide us with answers to the important questions of life. Ritual can be marginalized.	Every one of us has the right to choose what she or he will believe. (Confessional religion.)
3. Devotional, emotional religion.	Piety, theological, intellectual religion.	Social gospel, religious activism.
4. The gods are everywhere.	Everything is god, One.	Relationship to a god, when we have one, is usually personal.
5. Our ultimate purpose is to be a part of nature as were our ancestors.	Our ultimate purpose is to come to an end to earthly existence through enlightenment, or union, with the one. We should honor our ancestors.	My ultimate purpose is to fulfill myself, reach my potential (individuation). I should surpass my forbears.
6. Today is part of the mythological story.	We remember, study and apply tradition.	We create, collect, store, recall, apply, and discard information.
7. Nature, the gods are familiars; we learn by speaking and listening to them.	We deduce the unknown from what is known, existing premises.	We gather information to learn from what is unknown. Inductive reasoning from experience.

(continued)

More Tightly Woven		More Loosely Knit
A Cultures	B Cultures	Γ Cultures

P. *What is not to be communicated?*		
1. It is not okay for us to discuss sexual matters in mixed groups.		We avoid public expression of emotion, especially anger (except in certain circumstances by men).
2. We can be reluctant to discuss politics.		Often money is an embarrassing personal subject.
3. We will avoid past humiliations and attempt to respond to other touchy subjects with evasive answers.		We believe that everything can be compartmentalized and spoken about.

Q. *What are our commitments and how do we become involved with others?*

1. To the relationship..	To the action, content of the relationship.
2. Talking together.	Doing together.
3. Caring for others. .... Enabling others to care for themselves.	
4. Expressing concern, sympathy for problems.	Encouraging others to overcome problems.
5. Broad, less-defined involvement.	Compartmentalized, limited, more highly defined involvement.
6. Focus on commitment to the group.	Focus on commitment to the individual.
7. Highly defined, specific rules.	Abstract definitions to be applied.

More Tightly Woven		More Loosely Knit
A Cultures	B Cultures	Γ Cultures
8. Religion integrated, often dominating, sharia.	Judge, guru, Napoleonic law. Religion influential.	Jury of peers, Common Law. Separation of "church" and state.
9. Emotional. Direction should be felt.		Visual. Direction should be clearly seen.
10. Our direction is driven by how we read and interpret nature.	Our ruling, direction, is driven by how we interpret tradition, authority.	Our direction is driven by individual and common visions.

R. *How do we communicate our commitments and do business with each other?*		
1. We value politeness in making requests.		We value directness in making requests.
2. Third-party intervention can be useful; sometimes necessary for us to bridge power, distance, age, and class distinctions to avoid embarrassment or loss of face.		We deal face-to-face. Using a third party, arbitrators, and mediators can be seen as an admission of failure.
3. Promises made orally are valid and usually all that we need to do business.		We prefer written contracts. Oral agreements may not be honored.
4. We expect continuing reciprocity. Our commitment to the relationship is long term.		Our transactions compartmentalized. Our commitment to the relationship is short term. We may do business with someone else the next time.

(continued)

More Tightly Woven		More Loosely Knit
A Cultures	B Cultures	Γ Cultures
5. Our commitment to terms may be short term due to changing conditions and changing needs of the parties.		Long-term (length of contract) commitment to terms.
6. Informal agreement suffices for us to take action.		We usually require a formal contract to begin implementation.
7. General and vague content are okay, we can work it out as we go along.		Detailed and specific content are essential. We prefer to spell it out now and avoid surprises later.
8. Our agreements can be open and incomplete. Agreement is an ongoing process with someone.		We prefer closed and complete agreements and sales. Agreement for us is a single act in time.

S. *How do we negotiate with each other?*	
1. The authority of our negotiators may be limited.	Our negotiators may have fuller authority.
2. We negotiate as a team.	We negotiate as individuals on a team.
3. Preliminaries (relationship issues) are critical, often formal, and long-lasting concerns for us.	We engage in fewer, sometimes no, preliminaries.
4. We see negotiation as part of a larger relationship.	Our relationship may exist only for this deal.

More Tightly Woven		More Loosely Knit
A Cultures	B Cultures	Γ Cultures
5. The positions we take tend to be focused on the mutual interest of the parties.		Our negotiation is often based on the position we take as individuals.
6. We are concerned with status, who is on the team.		Our players are more replaceable.
7. Our positions may be conveyed implicitly.		Our positions are usually conveyed openly, laid on the table.
8. We may ask third parties to broker information or positions as part of the normal course of things.		We usually prefer direct exchange. Intermediaries are a rare recourse.
9. We use more metaphorical language.		We prefer more quantitative language.
10. "Right-brained," circular reasoning.		"Left brained," linear reasoning.
11. Our agreements based on personal commitment to the relationship.		Our agreements, once made, exist outside of parties—the contract is an entity.
12. We are more likely to reopen, reinterpret negotiation.		We are more likely to stick to the terms or to default.
13. We use more bargaining, haggling.		We set more fixed prices.

(continued)

More Tightly Woven		More Loosely Knit
A Cultures	B Cultures	Γ Cultures

T. *How do we prefer to learn and work?*

A Cultures	B Cultures	Γ Cultures
1. We observe the model in whom form and performance are one.	We study and imitate the masters, pay attention to and imitate their form and style, in order to avoid mistakes.	We like hands-on practice and coaching in order to learn from mistakes and develop an individual style.
2. We listen to the lore, perform the rituals.	We learn from authoritative lecture, wisdom being handed down.	We prefer discussion, individual exploration, and discovery.
3. We are instructed and initiated by the elder(s).	We respect, listen to, obey, and imitate the teacher.	We contest and challenge the teacher or trainer.
4. We ask few but simple questions, and expect the authority to answer or not as wisdom dictates.	We avoid asking too many questions—might show our ignorance and embarrass our group, or might imply that the teacher or leader has not done a good job.	I ask lots of questions, form my own opinions, and test my own hypotheses. I will be a maverick if necessary and will be rewarded for it if successful.
5. We work as a group or team to solve problems or address challenges.		I prefer to go it alone, and ask for help, advice, information only when absolutely necessary.

More Tightly Woven		More Loosely Knit
A Cultures	B Cultures	Γ Cultures
6. We prefer traditional, tried and true, well-thought-out procedures.		I prefer to combine planning and innovation and make on-the-spot decisions.
7. We value leaders and managers who are solid, consistent, and present to give us good directions and supervise our work.		I value aggressive managers who can show flexibility, agility, and motivate and support me to do the job but leave me to do it.

Technical Notes About This Model

This model has its roots in the study and practice of many researchers, writers, and practitioners. Those who informed our own efforts include among others: Edward Hall, Jim Kennedy and Anna Everest, Liang Ho, M. Maruyama, Raymond Cohen, D. Pinto, and Sondra Thiederman.

Our classification of cultures from "more tightly woven" to "more loosely knit" attempt to improve on the more traditional ones of "high" and "low" context cultures by 1) eliminating the evaluative overtones of the words "high" and "low"; 2) using the metaphor of "weaving" and "fabric," which for us give an image and a feel to the more abstract term "context," which in its Latin root actually has the more vivid meaning of "interwoven"; and, 3) making the categories relative to each other and less absolute by speaking of "more" tightly woven or loosely knit. This takes into account the fact that one can speak of "white American men" as belonging to a slightly more loosely knit group than "white American women," who would belong to a more tightly woven group, although both might be seen as belonging to a far more loosely knit group if one compared them, for example, with Malaysian women and men.

Each case is subject to verification, of course, but using the model helps us make educated guesses and reduces our confusion when encountering differences. It lessens the time it takes to get a useful profile of the culture and the individual with whom we are working. While we have tried to use the best information and informants in creating this model, it will ever be a work in progress. Almost daily we receive new and different information. As cultures that are living, changing dimensions of living, changing human beings themselves develop and shift, so must this mental. We are also aware that many of the behaviors of more loosely knit cultures approach those of more tightly woven cultures, and see that the model could be viewed as a cylinder in which each culture touches the other two in some ways. We have experimented with three-dimensional versions of the model that reflect this, but find it at the moment impractical, to portray this fine point in the two-dimensional format of this book.

Most of the numbered behaviors in this model are written in such a way as to reflect the inner conversations of the people involved, i.e., how they talk to themselves about survival and success. Besides being in line with out definition of culture, this gives the analysis a sense of everyday reality and makes it more useful when one is trying to understand and communicate with others.

The authors welcome feedback, refinements, and reports on the use of the model by readers.

GLOSSARY OF KEY TERMS AND DEFINITIONS

Here defined are some key terms used in this book and in the field of diversity.

Acculturation. The process of becoming familiar and comfortable with and able to function within a different culture or environment, while retaining one's own cultural identity.

Affirmative action. Legally mandated programs whose aim is to increase the employment opportunities of groups who have been disadvantaged in the past.

Anti-Semitism. Latent or overt hostility toward Jewish people, often expressed through social, economic, institutional, religious, cultural, or political discrimination as well as through acts of individual or group violence.

Assimilation. The full adoption by an individual or group of the culture, values, and patterns of a different group, to the extent that attitudinal and behavioral affiliations with the original group are eradicated or no longer significant.

Assumption. Taking things for granted about others. Something accepted or supposed true without proof or demonstration.

Attitude. A way of thinking that inclines one to feel and behave in certain ways.

Attribution. The act of assigning one's own cultural interpretations or meanings to the behavior or words of someone from another culture.

Awareness. Bringing to one's conscious mind that which is only unconsciously perceived; for example, becoming conscious of the real differences among people and a sense that these may have to do with how people are or should be treated by others.

Behavioral or Value orientation. "A generalized and organized conception influencing behavior of time, of nature, of man's [sic] place in it, of man's relation to man and of the desirable and undesirable aspects of man-environment and inter-human transactions." (Kluckhohn, 1951)

Bias. Preference or an inclination to make certain choices, which may be positive (bias toward excellence) or negative (bias against people), often with a resultant unfairness to someone.

Bicultural. Quality of a person who (by birth and/or upbringing) lives and functions as a native of two different cultures.

Bigot. A person who steadfastly holds to bias and prejudice, convinced of the truth of her or his own opinion and intolerant of the opinions of others.

Confirmation bias. Resisting new information about others by trying to "fit" new information into old categories; to make or force what we learn, agree with what we "think" we already know.

Cross cultural. Involving or mediating between two cultures, one's own and that of another. (*See also* Intercultural and Transcultural.)

Culture. A way of life. It is developed and communicated by a group of people, consciously or unconsciously, to subsequent generations. It consists of ideas, habits, attitudes, customs, and traditions that help to create standards for a group of people to coexist. It makes a group of people unique. In its most basic sense, culture is a set of mental formulae for survival and success that a particular group of people has developed.

Cosmopolitan. Literally, "a citizen of the world." A person capable of operating comfortably in a global or pluralistic environment.

Culture shock. The reactions within an individual to drastic change in his or her cultural environment. Just as a person may be psychologically disoriented by a way radically different from one's own, so too an institution or system may experience *organizational shock* when subject to a rapid change in its culture. Similarly, humankind is undergoing *future shock,* as the traditional way of living and working is quickly altered in this postindustrial Information Age. Both of the latter are manifestations of mass culture shock.

Cultural values. An integrated system of rules, regulations, behaviors, and ways of communicating for a specific group of people. A set of norms that define a feeling of differentiating "us" from "them."

Differently Abled. Refers to individuals with physical and/or mental endowments or impairments whose ability to participate in work requires special aids or assistance. Used to replace the term, "handicapped," which has taken on a pejorative connotation.

Discrimination. The denial of equal treatment to groups because of their racial, ethnic, gender, religious, or other form of cultural identity.

Diversity. The current term used to describe a vast range of cultural differences that have become factors needing attention in living and working together. Often applied to the organizational and training interventions in an organization that seek to deal with the interface of people who are different from each other.

Dominant culture. Refers to the value system that characterizes a particular group of people that predominates over the value systems of other groups or cultures. (*See also* Macroculture.)

Emigré (E). An individual forced usually by political circumstances to move from his or her native country and who deliberately resides as a foreigner in the host country.

Equal employment or Equal opportunity. Legally mandated guidelines whose objective is to guarantee that all people, whatever their background, are treated equally and fairly in such matters as pay, promotion, dismissal, etc.

Employment equity. The Canadian term for legally mandated efforts similar to affirmative action and equal employment in the United States.

Empowerment. The ability to feel capable and motivated in pursuing a goal. It is having the self-assurance needed to carry out and fulfill any endeavor. Empowerment can be self-initiated or the result of the proper kind of attention and support on the part of others.

Ethnicity. Refers to belonging to a group with unique language, ancestral, often religious, and physical characteristics. Broadly characterizes a religious, racial, national, or cultural group.

Ethnic group. Group of people who conceive themselves, and who are regarded by others, as alike because of their common ancestry, language, and physical characteristics.

Ethnocentrism. Using the culture of one's own group as a standard for the judgment of others, or thinking of it as superior to other cultures that are merely different.

Expatriate. Describes an individual who works abroad in a culture different from his or her own.

Flex time. A workplace policy that allows full-time workers to determine their own schedule of working hours.

First Nations. Canadian term for "Native Americans."

Foreign-born. Any person born and raised in a country different from the one that he/she has chosen to live in as an adult.

Glass ceiling. An invisible and often perceived barrier that prevents some gender or ethnic groups (who are different from the dominant group) to become promoted or hired.

Gender. The cultural dimension and consequences of being masculine or feminine.

Genocide. Deliberate extermination of an entire group on the basis of their racial, ethnic, or cultural peculiarity.

Globalization. The internationalizing of a country, group, business, or social structure through the mixture of peoples or technology. The "shrinking" of the globe.

Global connectedness. The sense of or commitment of kinship with all peoples of the world. The human family, the world, or planetary culture.

Global manager. The culturally sensitive manager capable of operating in a world market with an understanding of contemporary technology and media.

Hate literature. Media used to perpetuate or intensify antagonism or stimulate violence against a specific group.

Homophobia. A strong emotional bias against homosexuals, usually expressed as fear or anger.

Immigrant. Any individual who moves from one country, place, or locality to another.

Intercultural. Describes the situation when several cultures are in the process of exchange with each other.

Macroculture, Majority, or Dominant group. The group within a society that is the largest and/or most powerful. This power usually extends to setting cultural norms for the society as a whole. The term "majority" (also "minority" below) is falling into disuse because its connotations of group size may be inaccurate.

Mediation. The use of an impartial third party to intervene as a facilitator in a difficult conflict or dispute. The mediator helps the parties to listen, to come up with alternatives, and to arrive at a workable agreement but does not have decision-making or coercive power.

Mental map. A mindset insofar as it can be applied to a specific set of activities or problems.

Microculture or Minority. Any group or person who differs from the dominant culture. Any group or individual, including 2nd- and 3rd-generation foreigners, who is born in a country different from their origin and has not adopted or embraced the values and culture of the dominant culture.

Mindset. An interlinked set of cultural values, judgments, and ways of seeing things.

Mindshift. Moving from an existing mindset, or part of one, to another in order to see things differently.

Monochronic. Describes a culture or cultural group that tends to focus on one activity or behavior at a time in a linear and sequential fashion, e.g., carrying on conversation with one person at a time and completing or closing it before moving on to the next. Also see "Polychronic."

Multiculturalism. The existence within one society of diverse groups who maintain their unique cultural identity while accepting and participating in the larger society's legal and political system. Also a popular term of opprobrium for the threat posed by excessive deconstruction of Western culture.

Native Americans. Popularly called American "Indians." People whose origins can be found in Asia and subsequently in those groups who first migrated to North America whose descendants became the indigenous or aboriginal peoples of America.

Paradigm shift. What occurs when an entire cultural group begins to experience a change that involves the acceptance of new conceptual models or ways of thinking and results in major societal transitions, e.g., the shift from agricultural to industrial society.

Perception. What exists in the mind as a representation (as of something comprehended) or as a formulation (as of a plan). Each person operates within a perceptual field or life space.

Polychronic. Describes a culture or cultural group that tends to focus on more than one activity or behavior at a time, often in a random, circular, or interrupted fashion, e.g., carrying on conversation or meeting with several people at a time and moving from one topic to another. (*See also* Monochronic.)

Prejudice. The inclination to take a stand for one side (as in a conflict) or to cast a group of people in a favorable or unfavorable light, usually without just grounds or sufficient information.

Psychological construct. The system that each of us creates to make sense out of our experiences and endow them with meaning. Originally inherited from our parents and our culture, it changes as we grow up and become more distinct through the events and turning points that individualize us. Essentially, one constructs a unique way of reading meaning into our private world or perceptual field, but life experience and learning should then cause us to alter and expand this psychological construct.

Quota. A numeric limit or objective used for the admission of immigrants or the hiring of a specific cultural group.

Race. A group of persons of, or regarded as of, common ancestry. Physical characteristics are often used to identify people of different races. These definitions should not be used to identify ethnic groups.

Racist. One with a closed mind toward accepting one or more groups different than one's own origin in race or color.

Racism. Total rejection of others by reason of race, color, or, sometimes more broadly, culture.

Refugee. A person who flees for safety and seeks asylum in another country. In addition to those persecuted for political, religious, and racial reasons, we also speak of "economic refugees" who flee conditions of poverty for better opportunities elsewhere.

Repatriation. The process of returning an expatriate to her or his country of origin; includes efforts to prepare the individual before the actual return, and to socialize her or him afterwards.

Stereotyping. Believing or feeling that people, groups, events, or issues typify or conform to a pattern or manner, and lack any individuality. Thus a person may categorize behavior of a total group on the basis of limited experience with one or a few representatives of that group. Negative stereotyping classifies people in a group by slurs, innuendos, names, or slang expressions, which depreciate the group as a whole and the individuals in it.

Subculture. A group with distinct, discernable, and consistent cultural traits existing within and participating in a larger cultural grouping. (*See also* Macroculture and Microculture.)

Synergy. The benefit produced by the collaboration of two or more systems in excess of their individual contributions. Cultural synergy occurs when cultural differences are taken into account and used by a multicultural group.

Systemic. Refers to values, orientations, and habits that are institutionalized in an organization, and which are (usually unconsciously) prejudicial to different cultural groups in the organization.

Telecommuting. Working at home or in a remote location with work being transmitted by phone, fax, computer modem, etc.

Third Age. Refers to people who are 55 years of age and older. Popularly, but less appropriately, "Senior Citizens." This term has also been used to describe our present stage of development—the First Age having been the hunting and rural way of life, the Second Age the industrial stage, and the Third Age the postindustrial or information age.

Transcultural. Grounded in one's own culture but having the culture-general and culture-specific skills to be able to live, interact, and work effectively in a multicultural environment.

Values. Sets of internal instructions based in culture and personal experience, which determine acceptable behavior for a group or individual. Such cultural priorities can be expressed in terms of moral, family organizational, or even national values—namely, what a group considers important or desired behaviors for its members.

Variable time. Allows full-time workers to put in a lesser or greater number of hours per week depending on demands from family and workplace. (*See also* Flex time.)

Visible minorities. Groups of people whose identity can be seen because of distinctive biological or physical characteristics. Replaces the less adequate term, "people of color."

Authors' Note: The above terms and definitions are culturally relative; that is, their use, meaning, and spelling are dynamic and subject to change in the context of a specific culture, time, and circumstance.

BIBLIOGRAPHY

Abramms, R., as interviewed by Beth Brophy, "Perceptions Can Trip You Up At Work." *USA Today,* Dec. 1984.

Adler, N. *Intercultural Dimensions of Organizational Behavior.* Boston: PWS-Kent Publishing Co., 1991.

Allen, R., as interviewed in *Training & Culture Newsletter,* 3:3, Jan. 1991.

Anderson, S., and T. Brinkman. *Intent vs. Impact: A Sexual Harassment Prevention Training Program.* Rockville, MD: BNA Communications, Inc., 1988.

Anderson, W. *Reality Isn't What It Used To Be.* New York: Harper & Row, 1990.

Andres, T. *Management by Filipino Values.* Quezon City, Philippines: New Day Publishers, 1981.

Andres, T. *Understanding Filipino Values: A Management Approach.* Quezon City, Philippines: New Day Publishers, 1981.

Armour, M., and C. Friere. *Human Resource Development Programs for Multicultural Multiracial Contexts.* Toronto: Transcultural Consultant Services, 1989.

Barker, J. *Discovering the Future: The Business of Paradigms.* Lake Elmo, MN: ILI Press, 1988.

Beinecke, R. "Work and Family," ODNet Conference, Boston, May 1991.

Berlew, D., and R. Harrison. *The Positive Power and Influence Program.* Hanover, MD: Situation Management Systems, 1987.

Block, P., *The Empowered Manager.* San Francisco: Jossey-Bass, Inc., 1988.

Brooks, M., *Instant Rapport.* New York: Warner Books, 1989.

Byham W., and J. Cox. *Zapp! The Lightening of Empowerment.* New York: Harmony Books, 1989.

Casse, P. "Global Trends of the 1990's: The Cultural Challenge," Keynote Address at the 1990 SIETAR International Conference, Kilkenny, Ireland, 1990.

Chesler, P. *Women and Madness.* New York: Harcourt Brace Jovanovich, 1989.

Coates, J., J. Jarratt, and J. Mahaffie. *Future Work: Seven Critical Forces Reshaping Work and the Work Force in North America.* San Francisco: Jossey Bass, Inc., 1990.

Cohen, R. *Negotiating Across Cultures.* Washington, D.C.: United States Institute of Peace Press, 1991.

Cohen-Emerique, M. "Le Modele Individualiste du Sujet Ecran á la Compréhension des Personnes Issues de Sociétés non Occidentales." *Les Cahiers de Sociologie Économique et Culturelle,* Paris, June 1990.

"A Company Recasts Itself To Erase Decades of Bias." *The New York Times,* Oct. 1990.

Conley, F. "Why I'm Leaving Stanford: I Wanted My Dignity Back." *Los Angeles Times,* June 9, 1991.

Cross Culture, 1:1. Hampshire, UK, 1990.

Davidson, F. *Macro.* New York: William Morrow, 1983.

Deal, T. and A. Kennedy. *Corporate Cultures: The Rites and Rituals of Corporate Life.* Reading, MA: Addison Wesley, 1982.

Dee, T. D. *Managing the Workforce of the 90's: What Needs to Change and Why,* Executive Briefing Videotape #3605JF. Stanford, CA: Stanford Alumni Association, 1992.

Denison, D. *Corporate Culture and Organizational Effectiveness.* Somerset, NJ: John Wiley & Sons, Inc., 1989.

"Don't Pry." *The Economist,* Oct. 6, 1990.

Dreyfuss, J. "Get Ready for the New Work Force." *Fortune,* April 23, 1990.

Dylan, B., "I Pity the Poor Immigrant." *John Wesley Harding* (Columbia Records album), 1971.

Ehrenreich, B. "Teach Diversity—with a Smile." *Time,* April 8, 1991.

Elashmawi, F. and P. R. Harris. *Multicultural Management.* Houston, TX: Gulf Publishing Co., 1993.

Emery, F. E., "Some Hypotheses About the Ways in Which Tasks May Be More Effectively Put Together to Make Jobs," Doc. No. T813. London: Tavistock Institute, 1963.

Esty, K., and M. Wheatly "Managing Diversity—It's Not Just EEO Anymore." Unpublished paper of the Ibis Consulting Group, Inc., Cambridge, MA, 1988.

Flores, F. *Management and Communication in the Office of the Future.* Unpublished monograph, 1982.

Flores, F., and T. Winograd. *Understanding Computers and Cognition.* Reading, MA: Addison Wesley, 1987.

Furnham, A., and S. Bockner. *Culture Shock—Psychological Reactions to Unfamiliar Environments.* New York: Methuen, Inc., 1987.

Geile, J. "Challenges, Visions, and Policies for the Changing American Family." Presentation at the Heller School of Social Welfare, Brandeis University Conference, April 23, 1991.

Ginsburg, S. "Lessons for American Management from Female-Dominated Organizations." *The President,* New York: AMACOM Books, May 1989.

Golden, C. *Understanding the Gender Gap: An Economic History of American Women.* New York: Oxford University Press, 1990.

Hall, E. *The Basic Works of Edward T. Hall. Vol. 1: The Silent Language; Vol. 2: The Hidden Dimension; Vol. 3: Beyond Culture; Vol. 4: The Dance of Life,* New York: Bantam/Doubleday, 1989.

Hall, E., and M. Hall. *Hidden Differences: Doing Business with the Japanese.* Garden City, NY: Anchor/Doubleday, 1987.

Hansen, F., and M. Kinnich. "Changing Diverse Workforce Practices with Behavioral Feedback: A Longitudinal Study." Presentation at the National ASTD Conference, 1990.

Harris, P. R., as quoted in "Colloquium." *Issues & Observations,* Center for Creative Leadership, Winter 1988.

Harris, P. R. *High Performance Leadership,* Glenview, IL: Scott, Foresman/Harper Collins Publishers, 1989.

Harris, P. R. *Living and Working in Space: Human Behavior, Culture, and Organization.* Chichester, UK: Ellis Horwood/Simon & Shuster, 1992. Distributed in the U.S. by Prentice Hall.

Harris, P. R. *Management in Transition.* San Francisco: Jossey-Bass, Inc., 1985.

Harris, P. R. "The New World of Creative Work," in Kunn, R., ed. *Handbook for Creative Managers.* New York: McGraw-Hill, 1988.

Harris, P. R., and R. Moran. *Managing Cultural Differences, Third Edition.* Houston, TX: Gulf Publishing Co., 1991.

Heller, R. *Culture Shock: The Office Revolution.* London: Hodder & Stoughton, 1990.

Henning, M. *The Managerial Women.* New York: Pocket Books, 1988..

Henning, M., and A. Jardim, as reported in *Forum,* Issue 11, 1990.

Hepworth, J. *Intercultural Communication: Preparing to Function Successfully in the International Environment.* Denver, CO: University Centers, Inc., 1990.

Hepworth, J. *Things to Know About Americans: An Orientation for International Visitors.* Denver, CO: University Centers, Inc., 1991.

Hepworth, J. "When the Melting Stops: Diversity in the Nineties." Unpublished paper, University Centers, Inc., Denver, CO, 1991.

Hofstede, G. *Culture's Consequences: International Differences in Work-Related Values.* Beverly Hills, CA: Sage Publishing, 1984.

Hudson Institute, The, and Towers Perrin. "Workforce 2000—Competing in a Sellers Market: Is Corporate America Prepared?" Quoted by McConville, Daniel J., in "That's a Big 10-4." *North American International Business,* Sept. 1990.

"Jack Welch reinvents General Electric—Again." *The Economist,* March 30, 1991.

Jamison, D., and J. O'Mara. *Managing Workforce 2000.* San Francisco: Jossey-Bass, Inc., 1991.

Johnston, W., and A. Packer. *Workforce 2000: Work and Workers for the Twenty-First Century.* Indianapolis, IN: The Hudson Institute, 1987.

Kano, (initial unknown). "Voice of the Customer." *Innovata,* 1:3, 1990.

Kanter, R. *Men and Women of the Corporation.* New York: Basic Books, 1979.

Kennedy, J., and A. Everest. "Interviewing Candidates from Diverse Backgrounds." *Training and Culture Newsletter,* 3:3, 1991.

Kinsman, F., *The Telecommuters.* New York: John Wiley & Sons, 1987.

Krafcik, J., and J. P. MacDuffie. "Explaining High Performance Manufacturing: The International Automotive Assembly Plant Study." Paper presented at Third Policy Forum, International Motor Vehicle Program, MIT, May, 1989.

LaMountain, D. "Subtle Discrimination." Audiotape produced by ODT, Inc., Amherst, MA, 1991.

Le Borde, G. *Influencing with Integrity.* Ithaca, NY: Syntony, 1987.

Le Clere, W. *Chaos, Organizations and the Future.* Milford, NH: LMA, Inc., 1989.

Leo, J. "The Politics of Feelings." *U.S. News and World Report,* March 23, 1992.

Lewis, B., and F. Pucelk. *Magic Demystified.* Boston: Shambala Books, 1984.

Lopez, B. *Crow and Weasel.* San Francisco: North Point Press, 1990.

Maruyama, M. *Asia Pacific Journal of Management,* 100, January 1984.

McClenney, H. "Recruiting Diversity Means 'Sharing Power.' " *Training and Culture Newsletter,* 3:3, Jan. 1991.

McLuhan, M. *Understanding Media: The Extensions of Man.* New York: McGraw-Hill, 1964.

Mertz, N. T., O. M. Welch, and J. Henderson. "Mentoring for Top Management." *International Journal of Mentoring,* 2:1, 1988.

Miller, S. *Painted in Blood: Understanding Europeans.* New York: Macmillan, 1987.

Moran, R., P. R. Harris, and W. Stripp. *Developing Global Organizations: Strategies for Human Resource Development Through Cross-Cultural Learning.* Houston, TX: Gulf Publishing Co., 1993.

Moran, R., and W. Stripp. *Dynamics of Successful International Business Negotiations.* Houston, TX: Gulf Publishing Co., 1991.

Morris, D. *Manwatching: A Fieldguide to Human Behavior.* London: Jonathan Cope, 1978.

Morrison, A. M., et. al. *Breaking the Glass Ceiling.* Reading, MA: Addison Wesley, 1992.

Morrison, A. M., et. al. *The New Leaders: Guidelines on Leadership Diversity in America.* San Francisco: Jossey-Bass, Inc., 1992.

Morrison, A. M., and M. Von Glinow. "Women and Minorities in Management." *The American Psychologist,* Feb. 1990.

Murray, M., with M. Owen. *Beyond the Myths and Magic of Mentoring: How to Facilitate an Effective Mentoring Program.* San Francisco: Jossey-Bass, Inc., 1991.

Nadler, L. "The Organization as a Micro-Culture." *Personnel Journal,* Dec. 1969.

Naisbitt, J., and P. Aburdene. *Megatrends 2000: 10 New Directions for the 1990's.* New York: William Morrow, 1990.

Oomkes, F., and R. Thomas. *Cross Cultural Communication: A Trainer's Manual.* Brookfield, VT: Ashgate Publishing Co., 1992.

Ordiorne, G. "Beating the 1990's Labor Shortage." *Training,* July 1990.

Pascarella, P., and M. Frohman. *The Purpose-Driven Organization.* San Francisco: Jossey Bass, Inc., 1989.

Penzer, E. "The Power of Empowerment." *Incentive,* May 1991.

Pinto, D. *Interculturele Commuinicatie.* Houten/Antwerp: Bohn Stafleu Van Loghum, 1990.

Powell, G. N. *Women and Men In Management.* Newbury Park, CA: Sage Publications, 1988.

Practices in Managerial Effectiveness (PRIME). Amherst, MA: ODT, Inc., 1989.

Risser, R. *How to Work With Men.* Santa Cruz, CA: Self-published, 1984.

Ryan, K., and D. Oestreich. *Driving Fear Out of the Workplace.* San Francisco: Jossey-Bass Inc., 1991.

Shea, G. F. *Mentoring: A Practical Guide.* Los Altos, CA: Crisp Publications, 1992.

Silber, M. "Corporate Culture: Strategy or Tragedy?" Reprint from Mark Silber Associates, Inc., 1990.

Simons, G., et al. *The Questions of Diversity, Fourth Edition.* Amherst, MA: ODT, Inc., 1992.

Simons, G. *Working Together: How to Become More Effective in a Multicultural Organization.* Los Altos, CA: Crisp Publications, Inc., 1989.

Simons, G., et. al. *Diversophy: Understanding the Human Race.* San Mateo, CA: Multus Inc. & George Simons International, 1992.

Simons, G., and W. Hopkins. "The Gifts of Feedback." London: Castle Consultants and Toledo, OH: International Partners Press, 1979, 1989.

Simons, G., and P. McCrillis. *For Men Only: How to Live and Work with Women.* Toledo, OH: International Partners Press, 1981.

Simons, G., and L. Weissman. *Men and Women: Partners at Work.* Los Altos, CA: Crisp Publications, 1990.

Smilor, R., and R. Kuhn. *Corporate Creativity: Robust Companies and the Entrepreneurial Spirit.* New York: Simon and Schuster, 1986.

Strober, M. *Women in the Workplace,* Executive Briefing Videotape #3605MS. Stanford, CA: Stanford Alumni Association, 1992.

Tannen, D. *You Just Don't Understand Me.* New York: William Morrow, 1990.

Thiederman, S. *Bridging Cultural Barriers for Corporate Success.* New York: Lexington Books, 1990.

Thiederman, S. *Profiting in America's Multicultural Workplace.* New York: Lexington Books, 1992.

Thomas, R., Jr. *Beyond Race and Gender: Unleashing the Power of Your Total Work Force by Managing Diversity.* New York: Amacom, 1991.

Tulin, D. "Multicultural Communication Skills, Diversity Action Steps." *Training and Culture Newsletter,* 2:6, 1990.

Van Velsor, E., and M. W. Huges. *Gender Differences in the Development of Managers—How Women Can Learn from Experience.* Greenboro, NC: Center for Creative Leadership, 1990.

Wanning, E. *Culture Shock: USA.* Singapore: Times Books International, 1991.

Weingarten, H., and E. Douvan. "Male and Female Visions of Mediation." *Negotiation Journal,* Oct. 1985.

Weissman, L. Keynote Address, Federal Women's Program, Hanscom Airforce Base, March 1991.

Wood, F., as quoted in the *Los Angeles Times,* Jan 7, 1990

Further information on the subject matter of this book is available in the other volumes of the *Managing Cultural Differences Series,* listed on page ii. For details, write Gulf Publishing Company, Book Division, P.O. Box 2608, Houston, TX 77252-2608, USA.

Among the principal resources on the themes of this book are:

At Work—Stories of Tomorrow's Workplace, AV Communications, 68 Sunrise Mt. Rd., Cazadero, CA 95421, USA.

Anthropological Perspectives, P.O. Box 1721, Richland, VA 99352, USA.

BNA Communications, 9439 Key West Ave., Rockville, MD 20850, USA. Request the report entitled *The Challenge of Diversity.*

Copeland Griggs Productions, 302 23rd Ave., San Francisco, CA 94121, USA.

Cultural Diversity at Work, GilDeane Group, 1371 Lake City Way, NE, Seattle, WA 98125, USA.

Equal Opportunities International, MCB University Press/Bismark Publications, Enholmes Hall, Patrington, Hull, North Humberside, England HU12 OPR, UK.

Intercultural News Network, PACIA, 16331 Underhill Lane, Huntington Beach, CA 92647, USA.

Intercultural Press, P.O. Box 700, Yarmouth, ME 04096, USA.

Managing Diversity, P.O. Box 819, Jamestown, NY 14702, USA.

SIETAR International (Society for Intercultural Education, Training and Research), 8000 Westpark Dr., Suite 130, McLean , VA 22102, USA.

World Future Society, 7910 Woodmont Ave., Suite 450, Bethesda, MD 20814, USA.

INDEX

ABOUT THE AUTHORS

George F. Simons is principal of George Simons International, a consulting group specializing in gender and cultural diversity issues. His role is to direct research, design, testing, and delivery of products and services that create more productive partnerships and teams in the workplace. Prior to forming his own organization, Dr. Simons was most recently vice president and diversity product champion at LMA, Inc., a Milford, New Hampshire, consulting and training firm.

Dr. Simons received his master's degree from the University of Notre Dame and his doctorate from the Claremont Graduate School, in addition to special studies at John Carroll University and the University of Minnesota.

He has published extensively in the field of diversity, and is chief contributor and editor of *The Questions of Diversity,* a series of diversity assessment tools now in its fourth edition. Together with Multus, Inc., he has developed the training game *Diversophy: Understanding the Human Race.*

Speaking English, German, Spanish, and French, he has recently served such clients as: The Bank of Montreal, Digital Equipment (USA and Switzerland), Pepsico, P. T. Arun and Mobil of Indonesia, Procter & Gamble (USA, Switzerland, and the Philippines), Shell (Canada), Stolt-Neilson, Taco Bell, and Whirlpool Corporation.

Carmen L. Vázquez is an organizational development expert with 15 years' experience in creating, planning, designing, and implementing training programs. She specializes in total quality, team building, and cultural diversity. Her other areas of expertise include the training of trainers, time management, leadership, motivation, management skills, outplacement, career counseling, consumer service, and sales and marketing.

She holds a B.A. in psychology from the University of Puerto Rico, and a B.S. in applied behavioral sciences from Charter Oak College. Her graduate studies are in systems therapy at Fairfield University, Connecticut.

Ms. Vázquez has written a management tipsheet for relating and communicating effectively in a multicultural setting, entitled "Working with People and Diverse Backgrounds." She was featured in *Creative Management Newsletter,* and has been quoted in both *Newsweek* and *The Wall Street Journal.*

Fully bilingual in English and Spanish, her recent clients include: Sky Chefs, the American Management Association, B.P. Chemicals, Chase Manhattan Bank, Kaiser Permanente, and Ortho Pharmaceutical (a division of Johnson & Johnson).

Philip R. Harris received his M.S. and Ph.D. in psychology from Fordham University. Dr. Harris is a licensed management and organizational psychologist, and is president of Harris International in La Jolla, California, and senior scientist for NETROLOGIC, Inc., in San Diego.

As an international consultant in management and executive development, he has assisted more than 185 multinational corporations and associations, government and military agencies, and educational institutions. His clients have included Westinghouse, IBM, Diebold Europe, NASA, and the Department of Labor and the Department of the Navy of the United States.

A former college and corporate vice president, Dr. Harris was a Fulbright Professor to India and a visiting professor to many prestigious universities.

In addition to being the co-author of *Managing Cultural Differences* and co-editor of the series based on that classic book, he has written or edited more than 35 other volumes and 200 journal articles. He is currently a research project consultant with California's Law Enforcement Command College, as well as an editorial advisory board member for *The European Business Review,* a U.K. journal.